ABOUT THE AUTHOR

HELENA SHEEHAN is Professor Emerita at Dublin City University, where she taught philosophy of science, history of ideas, and media studies. She is author of many publications on philosophy, politics, and culture, including *Marxism and the Philosophy of Science*, *The Syriza Wave*, and *Navigating the Zeitgeist*. She has been active on the left for many decades.

Until We Fall

Long Distance Life on the Left

HELENA SHEEHAN

MONTHLY REVIEW PRESS

New York

Library of Congress Cataloging-in-Publication Data
available from the publisher:

ISBN (paper) 978-168590-027-4
ISBN (cloth) 978-168590-028-1

Typeset in Minion Pro and Brown

MONTHLY REVIEW PRESS, NEW YORK
monthlyreview.org

5 4 3 2 1

Contents

For those who will follow
After we have fallen
In the hope that you will carry on
Meeting, marching, organizing, striking,
*   speaking, writing, editing*
To bring into being
The better world we envisaged
And occasionally approximated
But failed to bring to fruition.
May you grow from the soil of our struggles
As we did from those who came before us.
We were part of the torrent
Of those who told the truth of the world
And built a mighty movement,
Of those who marched many miles,
Of those who mounted barricades and were
*   incarcerated in prisons,*
Of those who were shot down in the streets,
Of those who proclaimed from platforms
*   and wrote books,*
Of those who worked away quietly unnamed
*   and unnoticed*
In the back offices of revolution.
Forgive us our failures.
May they seed your successes.
We leave you with such a heavy burden,
Wishing you the wisdom and strength to carry it,
Even in the face of the most formidable forces
*   ranged against you,*
For you are the hope of the world.

Introduction

AS I PROCEEDED TO WRITE my story, I arrived at a book-length text and was only halfway through my life. I did not anticipate needing two books to do it, but I have lived through times of massive historical transformation and participated in many transformational movements. There was much to say about how I processed the world through all this turmoil.

In *Navigating the Zeitgeist* I wrote of growing up as a little Catholic cold-warrior in the United States in the 1950s, of entering the convent after I graduated from high school, of emerging from it into the vibrant turbulence of the 1960s New Left. In the 1970s, I moved from America to Europe, from New Left to Old Left, and became involved in various social movements and left parties. Within Europe, I traveled often from West to East, becoming quite caught up in the dynamics of socialist experiments, in what turned out to be the last decades of their existence.

I have taken up the story here in the late 1980s, when our hopes were raised by glasnost and perestroika only to be swept away in the bitter and brutal counterrevolutions that followed. I saw much of it up close and sought to see that history from below, from the point of view of the vanquished in a world where the triumphalist narrative of the victors held sway. The first two chapters of this book are centered on that experience of feeling the world turn upside down, but it is a thread running through the whole book. Many of the events I have written about here, such as the dramatic elections of 1989 and 1990 in Eastern Europe, have long been known and written into history, but I have striven to bring a "you-are-there" dimension to these pages. These events may seem long ago already, but the fallout from them continues in ways insufficiently understood, even for those who lived through them, as well as those who did not. Many of those born later, who know little of this history, are nevertheless buffeted by it. The Ukraine war is part of this fallout.

As well as this focus on Eastern Europe, I have traveled to many places where I interacted as meaningfully as circumstances allowed. In South Africa and Greece, I did so with particular intensity and built networks allowing me access to many perspectives and participation in crucial events. Indeed, I interrupted the writing of this book to write a whole book on Greece, titled *The Syriza Wave*. In this book, there is a whole chapter on South Africa.

Through it all, there is the unfolding reality of Ireland, which has been my base, indeed my home, during these years. I also gather the threads of my analysis of what has become of universities during the decades I have participated in them, eventually as a professor, with two chapters devoted particularly to that, but it is also a theme in other chapters. My final chapter, the hardest to end, because my story is still unfolding, tells of my "retirement," in which I have been far from retiring. Indeed, this phase of my life has turned out to be a period of vigorous activity and productivity.

The central storyline of the whole drama has been my political activism on the left and the turbulent transformations of our times as they bore down upon us. During every decade of my life, history has surged forward in so many mighty waves that constantly challenged my comprehension and commitment. History has rushed onward with a speed and scale unimaginable to our ancestors, making me feel as if I have lived epochs in decades.

Time has brought some victories but many defeats for the cause to which I devoted my life. In my early years on the left, I was buoyed up by a rising tide. When that tide receded, I was more truly tested. Many fell by the wayside, but those who persisted made it possible for this great, complex (and sometimes crazy) movement to continue, even in the hardest times, even when we could not prevail. We stood against such formidable forces. We had truth and justice on our side, yet we lost so many battles to those aligned with deceit and oppression.

The capitalist system is decadent yet still dominant. Gramsci's prescient characterization of his own times is even truer of ours. The old is dying and the new cannot be born. In the interregnum, a great variety of morbid symptoms appear. It is truly a time of monsters. The morbid symptoms and monsters multiply, yet we fail to enact the transition from capitalism to socialism that the world so desperately needs. It is hard for us not to despair at times, but despair would leave the terrain uncontested, and we cannot do that. Besides, there is no other way to live that is worth living.

My story has converged with the stories of others, so I have aspired to capture something of the truth of their lives, too, especially those who have gone from the world now and have not left their own accounts of these times. So much of human experience evaporates with so little trace unless it is written. I hope I have done justice to the history through which I have lived, and to those who have lived through these times with me.

I have continued what I did in my previous book in naming my chapters with the titles of songs resonating with their themes. I have taken the title of this book from a line in the great anthem of the left "The Red Flag," written by Jim Connell in 1889 and sung by so many here and abroad for more than a century:

> *With heads uncovered swear we all*
> *To bare it onward 'til we fall.*
> *Come dungeons dark or gallows grim*
> *This song shall be our parting hymn.*

I have chosen a red flag image for the book's cover too. I was always inspired by Geliy Korzhev's great painting of 1960, *Picking Up the Banner*, which captures the same incitement to us as the song. We may not have had to face dungeons or gallows and we may not be shot in the streets, but we need to take up the struggle of those who did and confront the challenges of our own times in the same spirit. The meetings, marches, occupations, lectures, articles, books, songs, and visual arts all contribute to a cause. The best of my generation of the left saw our efforts in continuity with those of the past, and I run my final stretch of the road in the hope that future generations will do so too.

CHAPTER 1

The World Turned Upside Down

IT WAS 1988 AND I was forty-four, perhaps at the midpoint of my life. I reflected on the waves of historical change that had swept over the world in my life until then and wondered what was yet to come. I did not feel that the world was stabilizing. On the contrary, the rate of historical change seemed to be accelerating. I could sense the next wave rising without yet seeing how steep would be its surge and how brutal would be its crash.

At first, it was all good. From 1985, many leftists, but especially critical communists, focused anew on the news from the USSR. We felt our hopes raised by the prospects of glasnost and perestroika. Mikhail Gorbachev was unlike any general secretary of the Communist Party of the Soviet Union (CPSU) we had ever seen or imagined. He spoke of socialism as we wanted it to be and with all the weight of the great CPSU. Socialism with a human face. Socialism with an honest voice. Socialism with an outstretched hand. Socialism with economic efficiency. When Gennady Gerasimov, witty and articulate foreign affairs spokesman, was asked in 1987 what was the difference between the Prague Spring and Soviet glasnost-perestroika, he replied: "Nineteen years." We grasped here at every detail of the news from there. We zapped from channel to channel to be sure we weren't missing anything. The *Irish Times* decided it was time to have a Moscow correspondent and we savored Conor O'Clery's every article, because he was not content with press conferences and wrote fascinating everyday life stories. We quizzed everyone who was there in those years. We talked about it constantly. There was a sense that history was open-ended. A tired tale transmuted into a thriller.

I found mixing with Soviet diplomats to be far more interesting now. They spoke more freely, at least to those who wanted to engage seriously with what was happening. The normal discourse at Soviet embassy functions on both sides had performed the ritual of circulating clichés with sad predictability. I wondered what Soviet diplomats really thought when listening to delegations recounting their trips: about visits to museums and factories, about much vodka and many toasts, pronouncing so seemingly knowingly, yet so cluelessly, on the success of socialism. At the celebrations of the seventieth anniversary of the October Revolution in 1987, there was a special buzz. Not that there wasn't the usual nonsense, but there was something else in the air for those with eyes to see and ears to hear. I spoke to the cultural attaché, who knew of my book, *Marxism and the Philosophy of Science,* and wondered if glasnost made it possible for it to be published in the USSR.

Just after that was an event, a dinner dance, celebrating the seventieth birthday of Mick O'Riordan, the general secretary of the Communist Party of Ireland (CPI). He was always proud of the fact that he came into the world at the same time as the October Revolution. There was an odd pre-glasnost tone to it and yet glasnost still hung uneasily in the air. There were ambassadors, politicians, trade union officials, political activists at it. He was given awards by the GDR and USSR. The Soviet ambassador praised him for "the glorious deed of his full of historical events life." A few months after that came the eightieth birthday of Sean Nolan, party treasurer. An even stranger atmosphere pervaded this event in a restaurant in Ranelagh. Sean was even more taciturn and aloof than usual. Mick O'Riordan officiating was even more cold and clichéd than usual. Jimmy Stewart, deputy general secretary, having a fair bit to drink already, tried to lighten the mood, referring to "all this restructuring" going on under perestroika and gestured to us as "the revisionist corner over there." We commented that we were pioneers of "pre-glasnost glasnost." The Soviet ambassador presented Sean with a shell case from Stalingrad. The fellow travelers, the sort who held on to an idealized view of the party—achieved by never joining it—were showing the most enthusiasm. When I was asked why I was writing on a napkin, I replied that I was making notes for characters in a novel I might write. The characters would be amalgams, I explained. A running joke of the evening then was speculating on who would be amalgamated with whom. It was all somewhat surreal. Sean died not long after that. Party property was in his name and he died intestate, leaving many problems for the party.

The CPI mostly ignored the new developments in the pages of *The Irish Socialist*. In conversation, party members veered between opposition, confusion, and support. When I asked how it was going with the International Lenin School, an international party school in Moscow where I had done two stints in the 1970s, I was told that they were reconsidering sending comrades there. "It's a disaster. They come back foaming at the mouth with glasnost and perestroika." There was increasing debate within and between communist parties. Paradoxically, the most pro-Soviet parties were having the most problems with the turn taken by the Soviet party. The Workers Party (WP) was also caught up in these debates. There was a faction wanting to pull away from the USSR and socialist countries and to move in a social democratic direction. Eoghan Harris, a prominent media personality moving from left to right, made the arguments most explicit in a tract titled *The Necessity of Social Democracy*. It was put out as a WP publication, after which it was repudiated by the WP. In 1989 elections, the WP won seven seats in Dail Eireann and a seat in the European Parliament.

It wasn't only in the Soviet Union that the winds of change were blowing. Throughout Eastern Europe, there was a groundswell of rising expectations, both in response to developments in the Soviet Union and an unleashing of pent-up questions, hopes, and fears. Here, I had many close-up engagements with the forces in motion.

With Sam Nolan, trade union official and political activist, I went on holiday in the Balkans every year from 1987. We gravitated to Yugoslavia primarily, but also Bulgaria. These were what we called our "4-s holidays": sun, sea, sex, and socialism. Although we enjoyed swimming, eating, drinking, dancing, we took every opportunity to probe the politics, to talk to as many people as possible about what they were thinking and experiencing. We had long talks in beautiful places with contacts that I had made through my political-academic work. My friend Srdan Lelas, a philosopher of science at the University of Zagreb, was holidaying in Split when we were in Poreč and Rovinj, and Miodrag Vlahović, president of Montenegro, was at his summer home in Tivat when we were in Herceg Novi and Budva. We also got to know the mayor of Budva, Dušan Liješević. These conversations were particularly honest and revealing. We also went to naturist resorts. Sam enjoyed regaling his trade union colleagues with these tales, as they listened with shock. I was a bit shocked at their shock at naturism, thinking they would be well beyond that by this stage.

We found the atmosphere in Bulgaria very different from that in Yugoslavia. Whatever corruption and black-market activities were going on in Yugoslavia, they were not so obvious or ubiquitous. In Bulgaria it was all blatant, constant, and aggressive. All through the day, wherever we went, we were hustled about currency transactions. The official rate was £1=2.7 leva, but the unofficial rate was 7.5 leva. Most foreigners went for it. To get served in a restaurant in a reasonable time and with decent food, it was necessary to bribe the waiters. I refused these practices, so we functioned with an unfavorable rate of exchange, waited hours to be served, and got whatever they chose to give us, regardless of what we ordered, and were overcharged in retaliation for not paying bribes. Some of the food was so awful that I became violently ill. The polyclinic where I went for help was not exactly an edifying example of a socialist health service. Again, this was down to my going by the rules and not offering bribes. One night we were sharing a restaurant table with a family from the GDR: a factory worker, a secretary, and their two sons. After hours of waiting, one of the boys started crying from hunger and frustration. For them, bribery was not even an option, because they had no hard currency. We met them on subsequent occasions. The holiday had cost them a whole year of a secretary's salary. Yet they were in a hotel at a distance from the beach, got a bad rate of exchange, and were offered even worse service. One day on the beach, the mother felt sick and I brought her to our hotel room to lie down. She was awed by our nice room with a balcony overlooking the sea.

I spoke with Bulgarians at every opportunity. They were keen to speak with foreigners. They expressed many points of view, some expressing hope for a renewal of socialism through perestroika, while others saw no redeeming features in socialism and wanted capitalism. With the latter, when I revealed that I was a socialist, their attitude to me changed. There were different reactions: arguing the toss, subtle psychological withdrawal or, on one occasion, sudden disappearance, as if by magic. We spoke with others from socialist countries holidaying there. Again, they expressed a range of positions. We spent an evening with Russians from Siberia. As usual, there was the probing of countries visited, wages received, living space occupied. Their attitude to perestroika was dependent on how it would impact on these matters. Gorbachev had recently addressed this attitude with a variation on the famous JFK speech and pleaded with Soviet citizens to ask not what perestroika could do for them, but what they could do for perestroika. As to the visual iconography, there was more of Mickey Mouse and Madonna than of Lenin or Dimitrov. One night, Sam wore a Marx t-shirt. Those at the gathering from socialist countries looked at him curiously and said nothing. One guy from Belfast asked who it was. I said, "A nineteenth century German philosopher."

Holidays were always a good time for reading. I always tried to find reading appropriate to the setting, so as to keep focused on where I was. On this trip in 1988, I was reading *Rates of Exchange* and *Why Come to Slaka?* by Malcolm Bradbury and *Bech* by John Updike. These captured so many of the ironies and contradictions of East-West interactions in those days. They helped me to see the funny side of what didn't always seem so funny. I also read *Sophia News* when I could get it. There was a good article on perestroika and how it was being implemented in Bulgaria. When I tried to get subsequent issues at the local kiosks, vendors looked at me as if I were crazy and offered me the *Times* or *Herald Tribune* instead. A seaman I met on a boat trip told me of recent changes in his job in the direction of self-management. He thought the Yugoslav system best. This trip made me think about the difference between the two countries. In Bulgaria, there was a sense of being forced into a system they hadn't chosen, of being dominated by a bigger power and never having tried to bring anything distinctive to it. The Yugoslav president, Tito, once spoke about coming to power after descending from the mountains after fighting with the partisans, in contrast to other communist leaders who arrived on Aeroflot planes with pipes in their mouths. There was a dignity to Yugoslavia that was absent in Bulgaria, I thought.

My most intense experiences of Yugoslavia and other Eastern European countries were for work. In 1988, I received an invitation from the League of Communists of Yugoslavia, the ruling party, and the journal *Socialism in the World*, to come to an international roundtable in Cavtat on the theme of "Socialism and the Spirit of the Age." They asked for my paper on this theme to publish in advance of the conference. I thought very seriously about what I wanted to say and how I wanted to say it. I was searching for a new form. I wanted to write a philosophical paper, but more concretely, more passionately, more narratively. I wanted to return philosophical ideas to the flow of experience from which they came. I decided to write a zeitgeist narrative, an experiential account of how I had evolved my worldview, how I found my way to socialism, and how I characterized the current conjuncture. I pondered over my first sentence. I started, "Sometimes I feel as if I have lived epochs in a matter of decades." Once I started, it flowed out of me in a torrent. I gave it to Michael D. Higgins, who read it on the Dublin-to-Galway train and called me late at night when he got home. He said that he had been tired and depressed and my paper brought him to a high level of energy and stimulation, as he raced from page to page as if it were a thriller. He thought it fused history and biography, philosophy and psychology, in a way that was powerful. It dealt with complicated issues by going right to their core. This was exactly the response I was seeking. Still, I had taken a risk with form and I wondered how it would be received at the international conference. This invitation meant a lot to me, because it meant that I had not cut myself off from the gatherings of the international communist movement by leaving the CPI.

I set off for Cavtat via London, Zagreb, and Dubrovnik in October 1988. In London, I joined with Monty Johnstone, Ralph Miliband, Ellen Meiksins Wood, Robin Blackburn, Ken Coates, and Simon Clarke, and in Zagreb with still others, such as Bogdan Denitch, a Yugoslav professor in New York. His booming commentary about matters theoretical, political, and logistical filled the air and dominated the rest of the journey. I received some positive comments on my paper en route, but it was only when I got to Cavtat that I could see what the response was. Never had I experienced such a wave of affirmation. So many people wanted to talk to me. The conference was televised and reported in newspapers and other periodicals. I met with the director of the conference, Miloš Nikolić. He told me he had made a lot of efforts to find me after reading my book, in order to invite me there. No Googling in those days. His field was history of Marxism and he considered *Marxism and the Philosophy of Science* to be one of the best books in this field. He said there was great excitement in the office when my paper arrived, because it was unlike anything they had seen. A young female philosopher, who wanted to interview me, said that the talk a month before the conference was that my paper was the most interesting, and that it made her so proud that these men in this male-dominated scene would say that about a woman.

On the first full day of the conference, I woke up in my hotel room in the Hotel Croatia, went out on the balcony, looked out at the sea, breathed in the warm autumn air, and felt as well as I have ever felt. All though the day, I felt so alive, firing on all cylinders, my whole worldview in play. There was such existential edge to the discussions. It was our task to feel the pulse of the times, not as detached academics, but as participating intellectuals. The atmosphere was glasnost itself. The format assumed that all papers written for the conference were already read. The session was introduced by someone summing up the points in a selected group of papers for further discussion. I spoke at the opening plenary session and several more times in response to other people throughout the day. Basically, I argued that Marxism was still the most coherent, credible, and comprehensive mode of thought, capable of coming to terms with the complexity of contemporary experience. The countertrends were unraveling it at the core, taking something full-blooded, integral, and rich with unrealized possibilities and substituting something insipid, fragmented, and decadent. The crisis in Marxism, I contended, was due to the detotalizing pressures of advanced capitalism as well as the fossilized totalities of certain experiments in socialism.

At the evening plenary, the president of the presidency in the collectivist post-Tito leadership, Stipe Šuvar, addressed the conference. He opened his speech quoting me. At first, I didn't realize what was happening, because he was speaking Serbo-Croatian and I was puzzled by everyone looking at me and the cameras zooming in on me. Then I heard the translation in my earphones and turned scarlet at this unexpected attention. In the course of his speech, he also quoted other papers from the conference in a very intelligent and up-to-the-minute analysis of the prospects for the renewal of socialism. He was playing an important role in struggling for a reformed democratic socialism in a unitary Yugoslavia, combating nationalist tendencies pulling in a separatist direction, not only in the nation, but even within the party. He was a most attractive face of socialism.

The conference was full of luminaries of the international left intelligentsia, such as Luciana Castellina, Constanzo Preve, Samir Amin, Paul Sweezy, Harry Magdoff, Daniel Singer, Enrique Dussell, Göran Therborn, Georges Labica, Ralph Miliband, Ellen Meiksins Wood, and others. Many of the leading intellectuals from Yugoslavia and other socialist countries, whose names were not so well known abroad, were there too. I was honored to be among them. After my solitary swim in the mornings, every moment of the day was filled with the most intense interactions. Although speakers addressed major philosophical and political debates on a global scale, there was a sharp focus on Eastern Europe, especially as we were there, articulating a sense that things could not continue as they were, and anxiety about what would happen next. There was a sense that the ground was trembling underneath these experiments in socialism. There were many points of view at play and many issues at stake, but a basic point of tension was whether the core concepts of Marxism offered a clear vision for the future or whether other positions, such as liberal humanism, social democracy, or postmodernism (or some modification of Marxism in these directions), were the way to go. There was a pulling away from class analysis and class struggle in the name of universal human values, and an impetus to de-ideologization of culture, politics, and economics. It was a retreat from socialism. This trend was coming primarily from the higher party intelligentsia in Eastern Europe. Those arguing back were also from this party intelligentsia, but also and most forcefully from outside these countries. "Western leftists are all theory and no practice," declared Jiang Chunze, a Chinese economist. I wondered how many of them would have found their way to Marxism, or joined communist parties, if they were not in power. Now power was shifting and it was becoming clear. We complained that they idealized capitalism, while they countered that we idealized socialism.

I came into the discussion at formal sessions in strong polemical exchanges, in particular clashing with comrades from Hungary, Slovenia, and the USSR. There were many ironies. I told György

Márkus, Hungarian philosopher, that he was emphasizing only the positive in the social democratic tradition and the negative in the communist tradition. I noted that I was saying it as someone who felt forced out of a communist party and was currently a member of a social democratic party. Last thing that night, I sat in the lobby reviewing the deliberations of the day with Monty Johnstone, Ellen Wood, and Ralph Miliband. Ralph said that Márkus and I personified the two poles of the debate that day. The next day I had breakfast with Paul Sweezy and Harry Magdoff and began a relationship with *Monthly Review* that would continue into the next decades. All day I was involved in further polemics. I spoke at a session on feminism, where I argued that too much of the discourse about women was dominated by consumption disconnected from production. It was all about wanting, demanding, taking and not enough about working, doing, giving. There was a negative atmosphere, more than strong counterargument, from the women who were there as wives, one of whom had been sitting next to me, fussing and fidgeting and giving out about men being allowed to speak at a session on women. There was a positive response from women who were there in their own right, especially Sonja Lokar, a feminist and a party secretary in Slovenia. I chaired a session on philosophy that didn't quite spark, despite my best efforts. The initial report was an uninspired thud, so I responded with an extempore counter-report, underlining the major philosophical points of difference in the papers under discussion, in contrast to the blandifying introduction glossing over them. The debate was Marxism versus liberalism versus postmodernism. After that, I was feeling a bit of cabin fever, as I hadn't been outside the hotel in days. Others were taking the afternoon off to go to Dubrovnik, but I declined and went for a short walk to Cavtat village. I heard that I missed a really lively debate on civil society.

On the afternoon of the fifth day, there was a final plenary and, in the evening, a party. Unfortunately, I was whisked away during the final plenary, although there were things said to which I wanted to respond, and I was not happy to miss the farewell party. However, I had been invited to speak at two further conferences while I was in Yugoslavia. I was brought by car to Sarajevo, stopping on the way to see Mostar Bridge and a monument to the Yugoslav partisans. There were other comrades from Cavtat speaking at this conference, too. It was on nationalities and nationalism. We, all different nationalities, walked around Sarajevo when we arrived and stood on the street where the famous assassination of an Austro-Hungarian archduke took place and sparked a world war. We took in the sights and sounds of what seemed to be a cosmopolitan city of diverse nationalities living together to common purpose under socialism. We then went to dinner and a reception in the Hotel Europa where we were staying. Michael Barrat Brown told us that he had met his wife, a medical doctor, and fallen in love in that very room. After that, Georges Labica and I went out to walk the streets of Sarajevo at night. Others were still drinking and talking when we returned, and we joined the lively company. The next day, I spoke, as did others. It was not so polemically energetic as Cavtat. Most speakers seemed to agree broadly on critically preserving traditional cultures while combating separatist nationalism. It was impossible to imagine on this day the separatist and nationalist forces that would engulf this city in the time ahead.

After the morning session, there was a three-hour interval. Herbert Ushewokunze asked me to forgo the conference lunch and go somewhere else in the city. We found a restaurant in the Muslim quarter, where the food and wine and service were excellent, although it was deserted but for us. We talked about the ideas and people at Cavtat, the prospects for perestroika, as well as telling our telescoped life stories. Strangely, I had just read a novel called *News from Nowhere* by David Caute and Herbert's bio matched almost exactly that of a character in the novel. Herbert was a medical doctor, who had left his thriving medical practice to go into the bush to fight a liberation war. He was a founder and politburo member of ZANU-PF. He was an MP, the first minister for health in Zimbabwe and subsequently minister for home affairs and then transport. His current job was minister for political affairs, which involved the merger of the Zimbabwe African People's Union (ZAPU) and the Zimbabwe African National Union (ZANU). It was ironic that Zimbabwe was moving toward a one-party state, just as the rest of the world was moving away from it. He assured me that "the masses want it." I doubted that, but I was in no position to claim otherwise. He said that he loved the strong way that I spoke and wanted me to come to lecture at the ZANU party school. "If our girls would hear you and speak like you, that would be the end of sexism." I doubted that too, but it was flattering to hear him say it. He took my hands and wove his black fingers around my white ones. "It's beautiful," he said, "like a piano, ebony and ivory, you need both to make the best music." After the long lunch, we walked back to the hotel. He had his arm around me. Several men stopped in their tracks and made a show of disapproval. As soon as the next session ended, I was whisked away, again missing the final session and farewell party.

There were a few of us speaking at all three conferences. We were taken to Sarajevo airport, where we flew to Zagreb and then were driven to Kumrovec, the birthplace of Tito and site of the Tito Political School. The higher party school was a splendid purpose-built modernist building with offices, classrooms, restaurant, library, residences. We also visited a humble house where Tito was born and raised. Next to it was a big bronze statue of Tito in his uniform, boots, and great coat, pondering the future. At this conference, I had interesting, if disturbing, encounters with the younger generation of the party intelligentsia, as well as more time to speak with colleagues who came from Cavtat. Two of them were women. They were opposites. Jiang Chunze from China was an economist in both senses of the term. She seemed only interested in prices and availability of consumer goods. She replied to every macro political question with a microeconomic answer. Pirrko Turpeinen from Finland was a psychiatrist. She was preoccupied with life stories and interpersonal relationships. She spent much of the time in Cavtat and Kumrovec collecting life stories. She quizzed me about my relationships and all sorts of things that I had not addressed in my autobiographical paper. Even when she spoke about the parliament and politburo, as a member of both, it was in terms of the quality of interpersonal relations. The reaction of Chunze to the Turpeinen lecture, which was all about alienation, was curious. Basically, she thought that Finland had a standard of living that was the envy of the rest of the world, so why should anyone be alienated? With so many consumer goods, why would anyone be a communist? I got on best in Kumrovec with Georges Labica. We were both philosophers. Although he was an Althusserian and I was anti-Althusserian, we seemed to agree about almost everything except Althusser. We were sitting next to each other during the Chunze lecture. When we compared notes, we had written nearly identical comments, such as "generalization based on one example!"

The conference was on Marxism and culture. My talk was a polemic against postmodernism and against the retreat from ideological analysis of culture. It did not go down well with the younger party intelligentsia, who were the majority of the audience for these lectures. They had a "down with the old and in with the new" attitude. Marxism was old and postmodernism was new. Gerald Raulet, another French philosopher, who, I contended, gave too much ground to postmodernism, was much more popular with them than I was. Between the lot of us, the guest lecturers, the staff and students, we had some very robust exchanges. In the evening, there was a ceremony in the library and presentations to the speakers. Finally, I got to stay for the end of a conference and the party. We talked and drank and sang the "Marseillaise," "Avanti Populo," "Solidarity Forever," and "Red Flag," all with great fervor. At all three conferences, the male-to-female ratio was high. I found the men very respectful of women as colleagues and comrades, but late at night some of the Yugoslav men became difficult, not giving up after a firm but polite no. On the final night, I thought that my pursuer would push in if I opened my door. Although I hated to play damsel in distress, I knocked on the door next to mine, instead of reaching for the key to my own. Georges Labica saw what was happening and asked me into his room. My pursuer then apologized to him, not to me.

The next day, we said our goodbyes after breakfast and headed for Zagreb, where I spent time with Srdan Lelas, a philosopher of science I knew from other conferences. We walked and talked for hours before he brought me to the airport. We discussed the various debates at Cavtat and his own analysis of the problems of Yugoslavia. He had a very clear mind and a list of reforms that were necessary, including new forms of social ownership and separation of party and state. When I got to Zagreb airport, I was exhausted.

After being on overdrive for so many days, I was heading for a crash. Unfortunately, it was not a peaceful flight. There were no aeronautical problems, but my fellow passengers were irritating and intrusive Medjugorje pilgrims. Catholics from around the world were flocking to the village in Bosnia-Herzegovina where Mary, mother of Christ, was said to have appeared in 1981. They were all around me and running up and down the aisles with "messages from Our Lady." I was trying to write notes from the conferences and a nun knocked over all my papers without bothering to help gather them again. When we landed in London, the priest ostentatiously kissed the ground, as the pope was inclined to do at the time. When I got home to Dublin, I was somewhat overwrought. It was a combination of exhaustion and withdrawal. Whenever I was away and living and interacting at that level of intensity, I found it hard to readjust to normality. Sam said that I was in a daze, that I wasn't really back yet. We went to a union social and I had to keep myself from screaming at a non-working wife who talked nonstop, as if the mundane details of her life were at the center of history.

The next day Herbert Ushewokunze phoned me from Harare, as he did often after that. I followed Zimbabwean politics even more closely and had many questions for him. We also spoke much about Eastern Europe, where events were moving rapidly and dramatically. There was to be a meeting of the council of ministers in

Zimbabwe to discuss the implications of glasnost and perestroika. He asked me if I would write notes for him for the occasion, which I did in a thorough and conscientious way, even if much of it was what he didn't want to hear, because things were going badly, as I saw it. Basically, I thought there were indications that many people in Eastern Europe neither understood nor wanted socialism. I believed that socialism could only be built on understanding and consent. At the same time, I didn't want socialist regimes to give up power. Instead, I hoped they might yet build understanding and consent, but feared that time had run out and it would no longer be possible. In late 1989, Herbert was disturbed at a party congress when commitment to socialism was questioned by those who asked why they should hold on to it when those who begat it were abandoning it.

I was reading and thinking a lot about Africa. I stepped up my activity in the anti-apartheid movement. I often spoke to Marius Schoon, the first Afrikaner leftist I had ever met, although I would eventually meet many. He had suffered terribly for his politics. He was involved in the armed struggle and arrested as a result of infiltration of his group. His wife committed suicide while he was in prison. On release, he went to Angola, where his second wife and daughter were murdered by a parcel bomb meant for him. Marius was a communist hardliner. I respected his convictions and understood his worries. He was not impressed by Gorbachev, glasnost, and perestroika. We often argued about it. We also spoke of the unfolding situation in South Africa. I walked around Ireland, increasingly preoccupied with Eastern Europe and Southern Africa, thinking about the implications of what was happening in Eastern Europe for the rest of the world. The whole global balance of power seemed to be shifting and that would have more drastic consequences than anyone was yet saying. I was afraid of what it might mean for Africa. Our sunny story now seemed to be turning into a darker tale.

In the summer of 1989, we went back to Yugoslavia on holiday, this time to Montenegro. Most of the people on holiday in

Herceg Novi were Yugoslavs, many of them Serbs. Aside from all the images of Mickey and Minnie Mouse and logos of Coca Cola, there were now pictures of Milošević everywhere: on windscreens of delivery lorries, on pennants hanging from car mirrors, on windows of kiosks, on 1990 calendars, on covers of magazines and books. Not an image of Tito anywhere. When we went to visit Miodrag Vlahović in Tivat, we remarked upon it. While Miodrag was tentative, his wife, Vera, was enthusiastic about Milošević, saying that it was possible to be proud to be a Serb again. At this time, there was a struggle for power in the party between Stipe Šuvar and Slobodan Milošević, symbolizing the forces at play. Although Milošević contended that a strong Serbia meant a strong Yugoslavia, it was clear even then that it was not so. I was for Šuvar and all he represented. Another worrying indicator was rampant inflation. I changed $50 when I arrived and became a millionaire for the first time in my life. We spoke to many people and found much uncertainty about what was to come. Otherwise, it was pleasant to be in the sun—eating, drinking, swimming, reading, dancing.

Meanwhile, Hungary had begun dismantling its border with Austria and GDR citizens on holiday crossed it. In August 1989, nine hundred rushed the border in one day. In October, the GDR celebrated its fortieth anniversary and its citizens showed unrestrained enthusiasm for Gorbachev, who was there for the occasion. The body language between Honecker and Gorbachev showed severe strain, especially when Gorbachev warned that "life punishes those who come too late." Watching on television, I was shocked to see Frank Loeser, a philosopher I knew, commenting on these events as a defector from the GDR. In Hungary, there was a party congress, where the party changed its name to the Hungarian Socialist Party, disbanded its workplace branches, announced the separation of party and state, the end of the one-party state, and plans for multiparty elections.

In the midst of all this, I was back in Yugoslavia and mixing with a multiplicity of players in this monumental drama. I had received an invitation to come back to Cavtat in October 1989. This time, I wasn't so much the exotic new one, and it was obvious that I was slated to be one of the Cavtat regulars. The atmosphere was even more urgent this time with a sense of speeded-up history sweeping this world away even as we were standing upon it. The format was more streamlined and the debate was even sharper. The theme was socialism and democracy. Instead of many papers, there was a single platform, drafted by Miloš Nikolić, to be debated. The key sentences were: "There is no socialism without democracy. There is no democracy without socialism." It was a seductive formulation, and my first reaction was to affirm it, but further thought raised many complexities. There had been genuine, if inadequate, democratic gains under capitalism, such as multiparty elections, trade unions, public debate, especially under pressure of progressive movements. These were not to be taken lightly, even if full democracy could only be achieved under socialism. Conversely, there had been real strides in the direction of socialism, such as expropriation of the expropriators, national planning, more equal distribution of wealth, in societies that were undemocratic in many respects. Most participants recognized that the one-party state was on the ropes. It had few defenders, even from those who were there from the parties of one-party states. The imperative was to find a democratic socialist path into the future. The rough consensus was for separation of party and state, autonomous trade unions and civil society, freedom to travel, freedom of expression, multiparty elections, even if it meant communist parties ceding power. Indeed, this had just happened in Poland with the communists ceding power to Solidarity, and it was about to happen in Hungary.

Milan Matouš of Czechoslovakia wanted, not only to defend the one-party state, but to restore the old discursive boundaries where no party could criticize another. Let each participant speak of the problems of his own country, he suggested. That was so familiar to me after my dispute with World Marxist Review in Prague. No, the time for that was over. The gloves were off. Everyone felt they could

say whatever they wanted to say about Czechoslovakia or anywhere else, and they did. These were common problems, caught
up in the same sweep of history. Another reminder of my difficulties in Prague came when I turned on the news one night during
the conference. The longtime editor of Pravda, Viktor Afanasyev,
had fallen and was being replaced by none other than Ivan Frolov,
of Gorbachev's inner circle. This great champion of glasnost had
enforced the opposite of glasnost upon me a decade earlier. The foreign correspondents at the press conference all seemed impressed,
but I was skeptical. There was no getting away from glasnost at
our roundtable, though. One tactic of hardliners was to respond to
questions about lack of free expression with a barrage of facts and
figures about industry, agriculture, and employment. All roads
of retreat were blocked. In a confrontation of Anton Bebler from
Slovenia with Milan Matouš from Czechoslovakia and Hans Luft
from the GDR, Bebler said to them: "I tell you that your countries
are like concentration camps and you tell me that you have full
employment. There is full employment in a concentration camp,
but it is not socialism and it is not democracy." In a debate as to
whether participation in next year's conference should be opened
up to alternative movements in Eastern Europe, Marek Kuczynski
opposed inviting Solidarity, and Milan Matouš did not take too
kindly to the suggestion from Monty Johnstone that Alexander
Dubček be asked to participate.

Most were trying to face up to the challenges of the inevitable.
Marek Kuczunski was struggling to come to terms with the defeat
of his party, but defending their acceptance of the democratic
process and the party's continuing role in preventing a return to
capitalism in Poland. He found himself in something of a dilemma:
as a Pole he wanted the new government to succeed in solving
Poland's economic problems, but as a communist he wanted his
own party to come back to power as the guarantor of the socialist
character of the social order.

While in Cavtat, the international news announced: "Hungary
buried 40 years of communism today" on the day that Hungary

declared itself to be a republic, not a people's republic. Political scientist Gyorgy Szoboszlai put up a strong defense of the position taken by his Hungarian Socialist Party. Hungary's earlier attempts to introduce economic reform had failed, he argued, because its political structures were too rigid. There needed to be a reduction of the role of the party in the state, and a reduction of the role of the state in the economy and in the society. It would be a difficult time, he admitted, because communists had forty years to transform society and people wanted an alternative. There were now more than thirty parties and he speculated that Democratic Forum would win the coming election. Still, he believed there was strong support for socialist values in the society. A number of the alternative parties were also socialist, including a new communist party. He admitted that there was the possibility of a transition to capitalism in a capitalist world order.

Others too, including Miloš Nikolić, took a positive approach, despite their anxieties. He contended that a multiparty system was not only inevitable, but might bring better results for socialism. There was a lot of anxiety, though. I found a number of Yugoslav communists of the generation who fought with the partisans and built socialism in Yugoslavia quite depressed, asking if it was all falling apart. They were wondering if they had failed in the cause to which they had given their whole lives, yet they were still struggling not to fail. Oleg Teofanov of the USSR spoke of the alienation of the masses of working people from power and property, and saw perestroika as a revolutionary redistribution of power and property transferred from the party back to the people.

Most of the worries and warnings expressed about all this came not so much from hard-line communists in the East but from critical socialists in the West. Luciana Castellina raised questions about Eastern Europe looking to political pluralism and parliamentary practices to solve their problems, when these were declining in power and becoming more and more of an empty shell. "Abstract rights of citizens cover over class dominance," she argued. An active participant in the debates myself, I too expressed concern over a failure to focus on where real power was in the world, over a preoccupation with the obstacles to democracy in socialist states to the point of obscuring the most formidable obstacle to true democracy in the world, which was the international capitalist system. All the emphasis was on freeing the economy and civil society from the state and on freeing the state from the party, which was fair enough, but it was obfuscating the need to free the economy, civil society, and party from the hegemony of global capitalism, especially at a time when forces in socialist societies were running headlong toward it.

Teofanov, reflecting the current popularity of convergence theory in the East, asked if the distinction between capitalism and socialism was obsolete. I admitted that most existing societies were hybrid forms, but argued that it was still crucial to name the systemic alternatives. I feared that the backing away from this in Eastern Europe could be a cover for those who wanted to see a peaceful transition from socialism to capitalism without wanting to say so. Darko Strajn, of Slovenia, speaking of the need to free civil society from "so-called socialist states," said he wanted to avoid the very term socialism, however much Western leftists liked it. Ernesto Laclau reacted negatively to all talk of systems and classes and parties, preferring a postmodernist plurality of subjectivities to "old platitudes about class." The issue of whether what was happening would go in the direction of a return to capitalism was taken head on. Harry Magdoff, of *Monthly Review*, went so far as to speak of a counterrevolution on the part of Eastern intellectuals, who wanted to live like their Western counterparts. Hosea Jaffe, in long exile from South Africa, remarked that the crisis of capitalism was being brought into socialism. It was clear to most of us that socialism could only survive through radical democratization. It had to play itself out, whatever the risks. Socialism had to be based on consent. This had been short-circuited in the one-party state. We thought what would come out of it would be something much better or much worse than anything we had yet seen.

Our discussions were world-historically serious, whether speaking formally in the conference hall or conversing informally while having meals, walking along the harbor, swimming in the sea, sunbathing on the naturist beach, or drinking slivovitz late at night. This is not to say that there weren't moments of light relief, when I felt like a character in a David Lodge novel. Hans Luft, from the GDR, was having trouble dealing with it all. News came through that Eric Honecker had resigned and Egon Krenz was now general secretary of the party. Hans said it was because Honecker was ill. If he did think that, he was the only one. He seemed to think that pacifying the youth with greater freedom to travel and pornography might solve the problem. It could even be good, because "we too like to look at naked girls." He liked the availability of porn in Yugoslavia. This time I wasn't whisked off to other conferences. I was able to stay for the farewell party, where the post-Marxist Ernesto Laclau surprised me by singing with great gusto many of the old Marxist songs. I even had an extra day to spend in Cavtat. I went down to the naturist beach with my notes and started on the conference report I was writing for the *Irish Times*. I didn't get too far before Hans Luft and then Leo Panitch arrived. We got into a conversation about possible trade deals between Canada and the GDR, which got reduced in the telling to exchanging tractors for porn, which got funnier and funnier the more Leo and I told the story afterward.

We all took leave of each other, full of plans for future conferences, not knowing how quickly and how drastically it would all come unraveled and make this conference the last. On the flight from Dubrovnik to Frankfurt, I was again besieged by Medjugorje pilgrims. These were even more aggressive, being American and not British. One woman from Brooklyn insisted on proselytizing me, despite my polite but firm declaration that I was an unbeliever. When she persisted, I told her that I had been a serious believer, studied philosophy, worked my way through the arguments with great care and wasn't for turning. "Forget all that," she said. "Everything you have ever learned is hogwash." To clinch her case, she told me of seeing a swirling sun with the face of the boy in the seat behind us, and then a human heart. She proceeded to draw the heart for me. It was like a valentine chocolate box, not a biological organ.

I flew farther west to Dublin, but my mind stayed in the East. The dizzying pace of events continued and accelerated. On November 7, the government of the GDR resigned. On November 8, the politburo of the Socialist Unity Party (SED) resigned. On November 9, the Berlin Wall came down. I took in every detail, flicking from one channel to another, clipping one newspaper article after another, phoning Berlin to find out what my contacts thought. Then, still in November, the action turned to Prague. Masses were on the streets. Dubček returned to Prague and waved at the crowds. Some felt that the promise of the Prague Spring might come to fruition in this autumn, but others had other ideas. It all seemed up for grabs. From one city to another, one country to another, this wave spread and surged. People were on the street, united in demanding change, but divided as to what change they wanted. Some wanted a renewal of socialism, while others wanted a return to capitalism, while still others wanted a restoration of monarchy. By the end of 1989, the GDR was governed by a roundtable headed by Hans Modrow as prime minister, Václav Havel was president of Czechoslovakia, and Nicolae and Elena Ceauşescu had been executed in Romania. We saw most of it live on Sky, which had come on the scene as a 24-hour news channel in Europe.

All through 1989, I felt the tremors of this groundswell and struggled to conceptualize its meaning in world-historical terms. Earlier in the year, Attic Press had approached me with their project of reviving the pamphlet form and asked me if I would write one for the first batch to launch the series. The title I proposed was *Has the Red Flag Fallen?* I was responding to the mass media barrage presenting a picture of socialism being dismantled on a grand scale. I wasn't yet ready to concede this, but I felt the full force of the torrents cascading in that direction, and needed to write my way through it. It unraveled before me like a nightmare: a vision of the Kremlin being conquered without a single marine opening fire, without a single ICBM being launched. Perestroika was meant to bring a renaissance of socialism, not its demise. However, I witnessed the alienation and anger in the population, no longer reticent about articulating its disaffection. I heard the voices of the spoiled children of socialism, who took for granted everything that socialism had given them and railed against it for all that it had not delivered. They idealized free enterprise and pop culture, indeed capitalism itself, seeing only the consumer luxury and ignoring the exploitation upon which it was based. In opening up to the West, they went wild for Coca-Cola and McDonald's hamburgers. They ignored feminism, but embraced first ladies, haute couture, and beauty contests.

Within the capitalist world, the socialist voice, challenging from within, seemed to have gone silent. Some ex-socialists spoke of seeing the error of their ways and some left parties moved so far to the right as to jump center, learning not only to live with the market, but to love it. There was a new designer left that scoffed at talk of production and labor and class struggle and international solidarity, because it was all so boring. They spoke of individuals with plural identities, of market segmentation, of milieu groups, of floating signifiers with no signified, as they fancied the sophisticated sound of their post-everything pastiche. This fatal shift from production to consumption, from class struggle to declassed citizenship, was a shift from left to right, whatever they said. Looking to the South, I saw deep dark eyes wondering if the beacon they had seen shining was going dim. It looked as if they were being abandoned, as third world liberation movements were no longer in fashion with the new-look left in Europe, at the same time as the USSR was declaring itself for a de-ideologized foreign policy.

I asked: Would the new emphasis on universal human rights be a bland blanket to smother the burning exigencies of class struggle? Would the euphoria over market forces block out the sight of the devastation they engendered? Would the lists of piecemeal,

short-term reforms replace the goal of expropriating the expropriators? Was it for this that comrades gave their sweat, their
tears, their blood, their lives? Was it for this that they led clandestine, hunted lives or were shot in the streets? Was it for this they
endured prison or exile or died of dysentery in the bush? Was it for
this that they stormed the Winter Palace? Was it for this that they
buried their dead in the valleys of Spain? Had the red flag fallen?

I wanted to be a countervailing voice. I admitted that capitalism prevailed, showing itself to be a far more formidable, far more
resilient, system than we had imagined. Yet our critique of capitalism had not been refuted. From there, I set out a clear outline of
what was capitalism, what was socialism, and how we might get
from one to the other, an alternative path between reformist evo-
lutionism and revolutionary insurrectionism. The pamphlets were
reviewed in various newspapers and periodicals and discussed in
various forums. Mine was predictably controversial. I received
praise from those who already agreed or thanked me for clarifying
so much for them. I took stinging criticism from those who didn't
agree, although they sometimes hid it behind accusations of my
being too emotional or too caught up in symbolism. The main line
of attack was that I was defending the indefensible, that I should
give up and realize it was all over.

Soon the red flags were not only falling; they were being ripped
down and burned in the streets. Such a fierce backlash, such a
ferocious wave of anti-socialist reaction. I was not so shocked as
some on the left, but I was surprised at the escalating vehemence
of this backlash and its ever more reactionary character. I had
overestimated both the passivity and progressiveness of these
populations. I had believed that support for socialism was stronger. My sympathies were with some of the protesters, but there
was still a wrenching in me as each government fell. I did not
grieve for Honecker or Zhivkov or Ceaucescu or the lesser-known
cynics or careerists who kept them in place, but I did grieve for
the honest communists who lived and died for this movement.
I grieved for something in myself as well. Events in the GDR hit

me hardest. I was not impressed by those who joined the exodus, especially doctors leaving behind the sick and bringing the health service into crisis, but I was impressed by those who stayed and demonstrated. I felt strong sympathies simultaneously both for the SED-PDS (the ruling party in transition from one form to another) and New Forum, a movement for democratic reform, but soon the voices of both Hans Modrow and Jens Reich were drowned out by other voices. Both the forces of reform communism and forum politics had come to ascendancy too late to prevail. They were being overtaken by other forces, darker forces. In other countries too, such as Hungary, those who initiated the reform process, such as Imre Pozsgay, had already been discarded by it. I began to see that the same might come to pass for Gorbachev, as well as for his opponents. Those who took to the streets were not the same as those who were taking power. All through the events of 1989, I clung to the belief that the promises of perestroika could be fulfilled.

By 1990, I could see that what we were witnessing was the restoration of capitalism and not the renewal of socialism. I did not think that this was the death of socialism, despite the headlines screaming at me that it was, but I did accept that it was a massive defeat. This was a most dramatic upheaval, not only politically, but psychologically. My whole sense of history was built around the idea of a transition from capitalism to socialism. Yet I saw the opposite happening before my eyes. Many on the left were finding it disturbing and disorienting. I was preoccupied with thinking it through and refusing the easy answers, whether from right or left.

When in Ireland, I was thinking, talking, and writing about Eastern Europe. I had many invitations to speak about it in universities, at political meetings, and on the mass media. I had endless conversations about it. One night, Slava Boius, first secretary of the Soviet embassy, came to our Dublin flat, as did other ex-CPI comrades. There was a searching debate about whether the USSR would survive. Sadly, I argued that it would not, while Slava argued that it would, but with a tone of desperation. Another Soviet diplomat, whom I met regularly, was Vladimir Minderov. One day I read in the *Irish Times* of a new book, published by a defector from the KGB, Oleg Gordievsky, which revealed that Minderov was the "KGB rezident," i.e., the head of the KGB in Ireland. I was surprised, but not shocked. From the beginning of my activism in the 1960s, I assumed that some of the people I knew worked for various security services, although it was rare to find out exactly who. My attitude to the KGB was different than to the CIA. It was hardly the stuff of spy novels, in any case. Our conversations were about public political developments, such as the conversations I had with many others during this time.

I was surprised at the extent of Labour Party engagement with all this. I received many invitations from LP bodies to speak on it. I was co-opted into the international affairs committee of the party. There were a number of different positions on it, as there were throughout the international left. One was a social democratic triumphalism, but it was counterpointed by a more complex position refusing to rejoice in the downfall of the communist project, a position especially taken by those of us who had been members of communist parties, including Justin Keating, who had been a government minister. This committee stepped up its activity, having many discussions among ourselves, as well as meetings with visitors from abroad, such as Gyula Horn, Hungarian foreign minister and later prime minister, and Jiří Dienstbier, Czechoslovak foreign minister. Another visitor was Peter Schultze of the German Social Democratic Party (SPD) and Friedrich Ebert Stiftung. The FES had much funding to be distributed and wielded it arrogantly, even imperially, veering between a blandly technocratic discourse masking their ideological position and a blatantly anti-communist venom. When I spoke of the new Party for Democratic Socialism (PDS), they made it clear they wanted to wipe it from the face of the earth. As to the GDR Academy of Sciences, they thought it should be razed to the ground, along with everything else about the GDR. I asked Michael D. Higgins, as our international spokesman, if he might speak up more on these matters.

Any speaker from Eastern Europe attracted avid audiences. I got LP and trade union support to bring Gyorgy Szoboszlai to Dublin, where he spoke at LP meetings, as well as at various universities, and was interviewed by newspapers and on radio/television stations. He was very conscientious in all these engagements, but I was disappointed in his stance in that he answered every broad question in such narrow terms. When people asked about the future of socialism, he responded with details of electoral procedures, constitutional changes, all within an orthodox political science framework. He was factual, but steered away from anything polemical. It was the opposite with me. I was arguing a position that, as I expected, was attacked from different sides, but there were some surprises. At a Labour Youth school in Kerry on the theme "Is socialism dead?" I spoke, as did Emmet Stagg, a prominent politician on the left of the LP. He was disappointed with the position I had taken and we argued all through the night. He said he depended on people like me to analyze what was happening abroad, and now I had let him down by conceding too much to the criticisms made of the socialist countries. Another person, with whom I had great rapport, who took issue with me, was Herbert Ushewokunze, who wrote a long letter, full of stale jargon, pointing out my errors. On the other hand, I was on a platform at UCD and the speaker following me was none other than Mick O'Riordan, who started by saying that he agreed with everything that I had said. I was even more shocked at that.

In the spring of 1990, I set off for Berlin, Budapest, and Prague. Elections were underway. Parties were proliferating. Many visions of the future were competing and colliding. There was much media attention to what was happening. I wanted to ask the questions that no media reports were answering for me. I wanted to contest the dominant discourse that was drowning out voices and ideas I thought should be heard. I wanted to know how those living in this cataclysm were coming to terms with it. I proposed a series doing this to the *Irish Times*, who gave me an advance that paid my air travel. I mobilized my contacts and made a plan. I was told that I no longer needed to get visas through London embassies, but I could just show up at the respective airports and get visas on the spot. Off I went.

In Berlin, I presented a letter of invitation from the GDR Academy of Sciences, where I was to give a lecture, organized by Herbert Hörz. The first thing I wanted to see was where the wall had been. After all the dismantling I had seen on television, I was surprised to discover how much of it was still there and then how colorful it now was. However, the city was not so oriented toward the wall as it was a few months ago. The euphoric champagne cork-popping and hugging among East and West Berliners was over and what seemed so sweet had started to go sour. Too many cars, too much noise, buying up subsidized goods, dealing drugs, maybe next AIDS, they said in the East. Undoubtedly, there was another set of complaints in the West. I roamed the streets, alert to every image, every event, every encounter, as carriers of world-historical significance. I noted the slogans on posters, the titles in bookshops, the plots of street theater. The atmosphere in Berlin was charged with a palpable sense of ideological struggle. It was full of ironic juxtapositions, I reflected, as I walked down streets, still named after Karl Liebnecht and Rosa Luxemburg, plastered with anti-socialist slogans. Not that many Berliners paid heed to them. "Berlin is red," my informants insisted, while conceding that "Dresden is black." So confirmed the election results on March 18 and 25. Bookshops featured authors previously banned. Works by Rudolf Bahro, Wolfgang Harich, and Robert Havemann were being displayed, reviewed, and discussed as if they had just been published. Bahro and Harich returned to the GDR, to much attention and acclaim, although Havemann was dead. There was particular respect accorded to those who were honest socialists, who had argued for an alternative path and suffered for it.

"We are a new party" proclaimed the Party of Democratic Socialism (PDS). They were, but they were also an old one, heir to the Socialist Unity Party (SED) and Communist Party of Germany (KPD) before it. "It was the ruling party of the GDR, the party of

Erich Honecker, disgraced and democratically pushed from power. "But this is also the party of Marx and Engels, of Rosa Luxemburg and Karl Liebnecht, of Wilhelm Pieck and Ernst Thälmann," Hans Modrow reminded them in the process of settling accounts with their past. These were the last days of Hans Modrow as prime minister. He moved me with his modest manner and determined conviction more than anyone else coming out of the maelstrom of this period of history. I was also really impressed by Gregor Gysi, the new party leader. He stepped into a role for which nothing could have prepared him. He was like a cross between a stand-up comedian and Old Testament prophet. I did a profile of him for the *Irish Times*. Of all forces emerging out of this turbulent turn of history in this part of the world, the PDS most credibly and energetically embodied a synthesis of the old and the new for me. They took a critical view of the communist tradition, but wanted to carry forward what was positive in their past into a radically new future. Older party members found their world turned upside down. Some had committed suicide. Others lived on in a world they no longer understood. I asked my friend Nina Hager about her father, Kurt Hager, a politburo member expelled from the party. "He was not corrupt," she insisted, "but people recognize him on the streets and tell him he should be in prison. He is very depressed." At the same time, Nina's son got very involved in the PDS election campaign, getting into a scuffle with other young people, who wanted to take down the flag of the GDR on election day. Young people were coming into the PDS.

There were strong communist traditions crossing generations here that had not breathed their last. I felt it acutely in the home of Bernhard and Erika Tschernig, who shared their Pankow flat with me. Bernhard was press officer for the Volkskammer, the GDR parliament, and Erika was a librarian in the party academy. They were both staunch communists, who got up at 5:00 a.m. to go to work in the morning and stayed up late at night playing Ernst Busch records and discussing politics with me. Erika was from a proletarian communist family and proud of it. Her uncle was on the central committee and high up in the Stasi. "He was not corrupt," she insisted. "He can't understand what has happened. He is without hope. His spirit has narrowed." As we entered their daughter's Treptow flat, which was covered with political posters, I got a strong feeling that this tradition was transforming itself, but had a lot of life in it yet. In many ways, these young communists were facing a situation nearer to that of their grandparents, going back to being in opposition, communists under capitalism. The middle generation too was realizing that it was now a part of a left much more like the left in the West and they showed a new interest in the left in the West.

But why, I asked over and over again, could the force that was now the PDS not prevail sooner within the SED? Each person to whom I put this question responded as if it were a question they had not fully answered for themselves. Each had a list of turning points showing where the party had taken the wrong turn. The years 1968 and 1985 were on all lists. All were opposed to the intervention in Czechoslovakia and supported glasnost and perestroika. But what did they do about it? "We discussed it. We could write what we wanted in our academic publications, but not in *Neues Deutschland*. We could say what we wanted in the Academy of Sciences, in the universities, in our own party meetings, but not on television. We had freedom, but it was the freedom of fools," said Herbert Hörz, vice president of the Academy of Sciences. Once again, I gave a lecture arranged by him in what was, by any standards, a no-holds-barred atmosphere. Members of this party were judging both themselves and others, sometimes quite harshly. Nevertheless, there was a determination to carry on. "Comrades, our vision is restricted when our heads are bowed. Only an upright position will allow us to face up to the issues ahead," Gregor Gysi exhorted.

One night, Bernhard and Erika brought me to their party branch meeting in Pankow. Workplace branches were being disbanded and members were moving into new neighborhood branches. There was a red flag flying next to the flag of the GDR.

As I entered, sixty or seventy people were milling around and playing their party cards. I sat down next to Ursula Kapzenstein, a scientist, who compressed her long life story into the five minutes before the meeting came to order. Then there was a proposal to accept a new member, who followed the speech proposing him with a speech giving a synopsis of his life story and an explanation of why he had not been a member of the SED. At first, he was rejected because he was too critical and then because he was too old. Various neighbors then got up and spoke about him, saying that they always regarded him as a comrade. Then a vote was taken to accept him into the party and he was presented with a bunch of red carnations. After this, various members who had transferred from workplace branches got up and introduced themselves. The meeting then settled into a discussion of the program for the local elections on May 6 and all the problems they were facing. "Everything we have is endangered," said one to the others, who were living in buildings being reclaimed by previous owners and were doing jobs that could be terminated any day.

Being a party member was a very different thing from what it was only a few months ago. Far from being a career advantage, it had turned into its opposite. This had taken a heavy toll. Some had even gone all the way to the right of the political spectrum. "Radishes and beetroots," they declared. Some were red on the outside and white on the inside, while others were red all the way through. While those moving from workplace to local branches were forming closer bonds with their neighbors, other bonds were being broken. There was a new tension in workplaces, where people had suddenly changed their colors as power shifted. There was a new alienation in neighborhoods too. One evening a comrade was bringing me home for dinner. As we walked from the train to the apartment block, she said that the way people carried themselves on the street had changed. Before the *Wende* (the great change), everyone looked their neighbors in the eye and nodded greetings, but now they averted their eyes and said nothing.

The atmosphere was edgy with a sense of a new order as I

attended the first session of the new Volkskammer after the national elections. Bernhard had got me a ticket for the gallery. I saw the right taking power before my eyes. The right was on the right and the left was on the left. Opening proceedings, Lothar Piche of the DSU spoke belligerently: "God protect our German fatherland." Standing in this place with the emblem of the GDR still over him, it was quite shocking. The right clapped and then rose in a triumphalist standing ovation. The left (PDS, Alliance 90, and even SPD) sat sternly in their seats. The Christian Democratic Union (CDU) had won the election and the SPD went into coalition with them, enabling the election of Lothar de Maizière of the CDU to be the last prime mister of the GDR.

It was becoming clear that the days of the GDR were numbered. There was an election for president of the Volkskamer. Gysi proposed Modrow, but only the PDS voted for him. In fact, not even all of the PDS. They had 66 MPs, but he got only 65 votes. I asked Bernhard why. He laughed and said that would have been Modrow being too modest to vote for himself. During the day, I spoke to MPs of various parties during breaks when MPs mingled with the press and diplomatic corps. I was especially keen to speak to Jens Reich, a leader of New Forum who had often been interviewed on international television and impressed me with his sincerity. I asked about unity of the left. "It will be on the streets and not in the parliament," he replied and referred to the decision of the SPD to go into coalition with the right. About the PDS, he felt that every proposal they made now had to be met with the question: "You had forty years. Why have you not done it before now?" He reproached Modrow and Gysi for having been implicated in the old order for so long, but then he said that this was a reproach he also put to himself. He was sorry that he did not defend Havemann. As a scientist, he had a positive view of Marxism as philosophy of science. About Marxism generally, he said, "Marxism without a strong subversive element is not credible to me. This was what was wrong for so many years." About the communist tradition: "They have taken an old and honest tradition and made something other of it." He thought that I had an overview of the terrain that was lacking in those in the middle of it.

I then got into a conversation with an SPD MP, who defended a coalition with the right. Word was going around Berlin that Ibrahim Böhme, the SPD leader who had resigned that week, after *Der Spiegel* accused him of being a Stasi informer, had attempted suicide. His replacement by Marcus Meckel had tipped the balance from left to right in the SPD, divided on the issue of coalition. I wondered if SPD members in the East had assimilated anything of the values of the GDR and would retain any distinctiveness in an all-German context. Members of the SPD in the West to whom I had spoken wanted to annihilate any trace of the traditions of the GDR. They were especially keen on sequestration of PDS property. The PDS had already voluntarily handed over the premises of the party school to them. "Why are you in the PDS and not the SPD?" I asked John Erpenbeck, who had formed a social democratic platform in the PDS, which had five hundred members. "The most intelligent and progressive people are in the PDS," he answered. "The social democrats have no ideas about social democracy." That week Gregor Gysi wrote a letter to Willy Brandt requesting observer status for the PDS in the Socialist International, although not all PDS members welcomed the idea.

"The biggest mistake we made," Herbert Hörz reflected, "was not to be a real socialist unity party." The SED was formed in an amalgamation of the communist and social democratic parties. "We shouldn't have kept calling it communist all the time." Taking up the same theme on the day I visited the central offices of the PDS, Hans Weingold said that it was time to do now what they should have done then. "We want to continue communist traditions, but also those of the wider socialist movement." There would be room now for factions holding different positions within the party. I visited what was once the higher party school, now divided into offices of the SPD on the one side and the PDS on the other. There was a strong sense around Berlin of a newly diverse and vibrant left. The House of Democracy, also property given over by the PDS to the new forces, was occupied by the Greens, Democracy Now, the United Left, and a host of other groups, and had a new-left feel about it.

The atmosphere around Humboldt University made me feel as if I were back in the Sixties. Lively posters revealed a welter of socialist, feminist, and green events. Masses of students were gathering for a demonstration "against decline." A student wearing a mask of Chancellor Kohl was cracking a whip. Thousands of them marched through the streets carrying the flag of the GDR, which had already become a protest symbol, in one of many ironic reversals of the times. Later in the week there was another demonstration of one hundred thousand of all ages and walks of life. Outside the Volkskammer, speakers demanded a 1:1 exchange rate.

There were enormous adjustments ahead in the lives of those I was visiting. So much uncertainty beset them as they faced the next days and years. Helga Hörz had been elected president of the UN Commission on the Status of Women, but was uncertain if she could continue, as it was conditional on the existence of the GDR. Herbert was tackling the complicated task of reorganizing the Academy of Sciences, which had to be drastically reduced and restructured. It was clear that the new order would not support the same number of intellectuals, and those it would support would not be the same ones. Nina Hager, a professor of philosophy, who was not going to be a Marxist one day and something else the next, feared she might be one of the first to go. So many who had professed Marxism were now renouncing it. Colleagues I visited at the Academy of Social Sciences were already clearing their offices. Birgid Gysi and Renate Ullrich, cultural researchers, outlined to me how theater, television, and the arts would be transformed in the new scenario as they did so. Hans Luft too was clearing his desk, while planning to stand in the local elections. His wife, Christa Luft, had been minister of finance in the Modrow government and was now a PDS MP.

I went to a dinner party at the home of Jack Mitchell, a professor of English literature at Humboldt University, who was hard to recognize as the same person I knew when he stayed in our house in Dublin. It was the strain of the *Wende* combined with aging and failing health, I thought, as well as the murder of Mairead Farrell while on an IRA operation in Gibraltar and the gunfire at her funeral in Belfast. Jack's daughter Jenny was married to Niall Farrell, Mairead's brother. The night kept changing tone abruptly. Jack's son was humorously characterizing GDR culture in terms of the passivity of a crowd, who would put up with anything until one person protested and then they were all up in arms. We were all laughing and then a judge burst into tears. She did so periodically through the evening in her anxiety about the future. Jack recited a poem he wrote about the British army and Gibraltar and spoke as if British armed forces would burst through the door and gun him down at any time. There were other times when extreme stress expressed itself in conversations, but what most struck me during these days was the extraordinary composure and world-historical scope of their consciousness. "Quo vadis?" asked Bernhard Tschernig late one night. No one in this world of flux knew the answer to that, but nowhere more than in Berlin was the question being asked in the same way.

I took my leave of Berlin and flew to Budapest. My colleague, Györggy Szoboszlai, put me up in his house, arranged many meetings for me, and provided constant commentary on Hungarian society at this juncture. Although I arrived in Hungary at an equally crucial moment in its political life, the scene in Budapest was much more low-key than that in Berlin. Perhaps it was because the reforms had begun earlier here and were initiated by the ruling party, but the process was less convulsive, less dramatic, less polarized. Perhaps it was also the Hungarian character, more moderate in temperament, that explained why everything felt less energetic, less sharp-edged, less far-thinking than in the GDR. There was very little ritual surrounding the elections. As the results of the second round came in, most people, even activists, were, in the privacy of their own homes, watching them on television. It was a decisive result, with the Hungarian Democratic Forum (MDF) emerging as the largest party with a wider margin than had been expected against the other major contender, the Alliance of Free Democrats (SZDSZ).

Hungarian politics were not so easily described in terms of left and right as in the GDR. The main cleavage was between Christian, nationalist, populist elements, and liberal (often Jewish), westernizing, urban elements. There was a spectrum of right-to-left positions within each of the parties on either side of this divide, and parties crossing this divide had factions leaning to either side of it. Most positions commanding any significant support were clustered around the center. "The natural temper and main political instinct of Hungarians is centrist," said Gyula Kodolányi, editor of *Hungarian Review* and a founder of MDF. I asked him about the "third way" that MDF had been seeking. He explained that he was against the extremes of the liberal free market and socialism. Certain ideas of social justice had become ingrained through Marxism, and he felt it was important to retain what was positive in the past forty years. He wanted to see capital investment create a dynamic economy, but also to have a social safety net and subsidized culture. He was especially against a laissez-faire cultural policy.

The MDF-SZDSZ divide was between one more grounded in the values of family, church, and nation and the other more oriented to international capital. The USA and the IMF were backing SZDSZ, but would have no trouble working with MDF. The US ambassador had been dismissed in suspicious circumstances having to do with his degree of involvement in the SZDSZ campaign. No one believed that the present party structure was definitive, predicting that it would evolve along other ideological lines, which would more clearly reproduce those prevailing on an international level.

There was a rush to fill the space for social democracy. I felt as if I were being given a summary of a particularly dense and far-fetched thriller, as György Markus told me the sorry story of the Hungarian Social Democratic Party (MSZDP) from the inside as a member of its council. It first moved against reform communists and other leftists, then adopted neoliberal policies and sought an alliance with SZDSZ. Then its leader, Anna Petrosovits, became very Catholic and sought an alliance with the Smallholders and Christian Democrats. Members were embarrassed by her adoption of a Thatcherite persona and the photo opportunities she took in the market, buying paprika, wearing furs, and distributing bags with photographs of herself. She went on television saying that God was with the Social Democrats. They didn't win a single seat. During the campaign, there was an occasion on which various party leaders in the Socialist International (SI) were put on display to show their support. They were given a paper instructing them: "Dear Guests, Please don't use the terms 'democratic socialist' or 'comrade.' We are in Central Europe." After the election came the bloodletting, including the suspension of the party leader, rumors of her attempted suicide, and her return with bodyguards outnumbering delegates, in an ongoing struggle for power.

"The Hungarian Socialist Workers Party (MSZMP) in its worst days was more democratic than this," said Markus, regretfully. His final thought was: "I like 007 stories, but not to be in this one." After the polemical polarity between Markus and me in Cavtat, I was surprised that we had such easy rapport now. It wasn't that we agreed. I asked him how he became a social democrat. He explained that he had been working in the party research institute and undertook to study social democratic ideas and he began to identify with them. "The trap of Gorbachev is to try to reform communism. You can't reform it. You have to change it." "To what?" I asked. "Capitalism. There is nothing else. A systemic alternative is utopian. A practical alternative is better. The best you can make of capitalism is what social democrats do. Maybe in a hundred years, there will be another option." I admired his clarity, but still resisted his conclusion. Meanwhile, others were moving in on this terrain. Everyone believed that there was potentially an enormous vote there for social democracy being dissipated by the poor quality of the MSZDP, and there were various formations contending for alignment with the SI. Moreover, MDF, SZDSZ, and FIDESZ all had social democratic wings. I was surprised to discover how far to the left the ideological spectrum within SZDSZ and FIDESZ went. SZDSZ encompassed not only Gaspar Miklos Tamas recommending high Toryism to Hungarian peasants, but also members of the Budapest School, former new left Marxists, who had returned from exile.

Out of the former ruling party, the Hungarian Socialist Workers Party (MSZMP), there emerged the Hungarian Socialist Party (MSZP) and a new MSZMP. The MSZMP did not want to go as far in distancing themselves from communist traditions as the MSZP, whom they regarded as wanting to reject the political legacy of the former ruling party, but not its property. Imre Forgács, head of the internal affairs department of the MSZP, wanted to see the party joining the SI, but worried over the prospect of the party moving too far to the right to do so. "We must have integrity," he told me on the day I visited the white house on the Danube, shortly to be handed over to the state and vacated as party head-quarters. Looming was competition on who would gather the forces of the left. Andrea Szego of the official trade union organization argued that it could not be the MSZP. The problem was not only that they were too identified by the communist legacy on the left, but also that they had moved too far to the right as their government, under Miklós Németh as prime minister from 1988 to 1990, implemented Thatcherite policies. "There are two problems," she said. "It is not only that they were whores, but that they were bad whores. Western countries would have paid a high price for a change of system, but they didn't even ask the price."

Hungary was rearranging its relation to its past. "For the next forty years everything will be blamed on the last forty years," said György Aczel, former politburo member. People were speaking nostalgically of the Habsburgs and were milder in their critique of the fascist Horthy than of the communist Kadar. The Avenue of the People's Republic was about to revert to being Andrassy Street, named after a count, who was foreign minister under the Austro-Hungarian empire. The Hungarian Democratic Forum (MDF) announced that many other streets would be renamed. Attila Agh, professor of economics, presented me with his card, pleased that he had the foresight to have the "Karl Marx" eliminated from what was the Karl Marx University of Economics, but had let Dimitrov Square, named after Georgi Dimitrov, Bulgarian communist who headed the Communist International from 1935 to 1943, go by, so he still had thousands of obsolete cards. Meanwhile, the Voice of America broadcast from Budapest and McDonald's sponsored television programs. Kiosks displayed the most explicit pornography I had ever seen.

"Socialism was a violation of these people," György Szoboszlai said to me as we crossed Vôrôsmarty Square, looking into the passing faces. On another day, after answering yet another barrage of questions from me, he put one to me: "Why look to such underdeveloped countries as this and ask why we failed to build socialism? It is a question I put to the Western left." György Wiener of the MSZP also put a strong emphasis on underdevelopment. "The main problem was not the one-party state, but the lack of preconditions for socialist development. What was surprising was that we had some successes, not that they collapsed."

"What is left of the past forty years? Has it all disappeared without trace?" I heard a woman from a UN research team ask a group of social scientists. It was a question I asked many times myself in my encounters there. Negativity, indecisiveness, and sidestepping characterized most replies, even on the left. I did not get the same feeling of the left having gone down and come up fighting as I did in the GDR. What was left of the left was too dissipated, too clustered around the center, and sometimes too indistinguishable from the right to know if and how it might regroup and challenge the society emerging now that the statues had been smashed and the red stars ripped down and the soup kitchens opened up. While pondering these matters, there were moments of light relief. One day I was sitting in Vôrôsmarty Square collecting my thoughts and writing notes when I witnessed twenty or so people who lined up single-file behind an unsuspecting person or persons imitating his/her/their every gesture until switching to another person or couple. It was hilarious to watch. After that, I always looked behind me when walking in public.

Then I flew from Budapest to Prague. This time it was not so easy at the airport. I was taken aside and interrogated. I was asked the purpose of my visit. There were various answers I could have given, all true, which would play differently, depending on whether I was dealing with the old or new order. Thinking it was the old order, I said that I was visiting *World Marxist Review*. My interrogator made various phone calls, then walked me through customs and baggage reclaim, hailed a taxi and instructed the driver to take me directly to *WMR*. I had no idea why I was singled out, because Prague was swarming with all sorts of people whom the old order would not have allowed in Prague. I had arranged to stay at *WMR*, which I found to be a very different place from my interval there in 1978. I had a lot to think about as I walked down the long corridors of this building, which was once a seminary and soon to be one again. The Czechoslovak government had ordered the journal to leave. International members of the editorial board were packing up and booking flights home, although some were members of illegal parties and had nowhere to go. Some assets were up for sale locally, while others were being shipped back to the USSR. The Catholic Church would take possession of the building.

There was a flurry of activity as a last issue was being produced before closing down. Under glasnost, *WMR* transformed itself almost beyond recognition. Every issue brought new surprises, especially to those acquainted with it for many years. Published since 1958, for years every issue was full of formulaic pronouncements on peace, disarmament, and proletarian internationalism, full of bitter denunciations of bourgeois ideology and socialist revisionism. Anything written with life in it was drained and distorted into an empty and unshapely shell. I was not the only author to object, although others were more resigned to their mutilation. However, when it changed, it did so for real. The Letters pages not only praised articles, but took issue with them. There were honest

articles on Trotsky and Bukharin. *WMR* opened its pages, not only
to critical communists, but to non-communists criticizing communists. There were articles, not only by Alexander Dubček and
Milovan Djilas, but by John Kenneth Galbraith, Andrei Sakharov,
even Zbigniew Brzezinski. There were articles articulating
positions against which the journal had published fierce denunciations. There was a particular attraction to articles arguing for
convergence of communism and social democracy and even convergence of capitalism and socialism. V. L. Shelepin, Soviet editor
of the journal, told me that he thought that class struggle was a
bad thing. He wanted economic efficiency, social justice, consensus, solidarity, democracy. He was keen on Civic Forum and the
pluralism of positions within it.

Everything was opening up just as it was closing down. When
the announcement *of WMR*'s closure came in March 1990, I
had written an article about it in the *Irish Times*. The sub-editor
had titled it "Marxist Journal Reforms Too Late," which was fair
enough. I was sad to see it ending just as it was starting to be interesting. Being there as it was being dismantled made me see vividly
how the communist movement was coming apart and also how
weak were some of the bonds that held it together. My conversations with Stanislav Schegolsky were jolting and memorable. I had
known him in Moscow a decade earlier. He was a Soviet interpreter
who had accompanied me in my research visits to the Academy of
Sciences and Lenin Library in Moscow. He seemed harder now.
He spoke more freely. He was very critical of the modus operandi
of the journal and the role played by representatives of the various
communist parties there. They were paid a lot of money for very
little work, availed of the best of health care, including luxury spa
treatments, and did not want to know how the mass of people in
socialist countries actually lived. He did not think the CPI distinguished itself there. He had much to say about life in both Prague
and Moscow, where he was soon returning. He said that his parents were finding it all hard to comprehend.

I walked the streets of Prague trying to grasp the contours of the change that was convulsing this place. On the surface, it was like a fairy tale. Crossing Charles Bridge at night with the castle lit up on the hill, listening to the groups of young people playing guitars and singing on the streets, seeing the smiling face of the symbol of Civic Forum everywhere, Prague seemed so charmingly cheerful. However, noticing the nuances in the political cartoons, standing at the mound of multicolored wax in Wenceslas Square, and reflecting on what happened here, the cheerfulness took on an ironic and bittersweet quality. Then hearing the stories of people's lives and penetrating level after level, made me question the cheerfulness and realize how mixed it was with confusion, regret, panic, guilt, fear, deceit, betrayal, settling of scores, and struggling for power. "In November it was beautiful, but now it is not so nice"—this was said to me, but I was asked not to name the person who said it, which told something about Prague under the surface, Prague after the world's television cameras had gone. The Velvet Revolution had begun to show its claws. It was also the legacy of many waves of turbulence in this most vulnerable crossroads of European history.

The streets seemed dangerous at night. People warned me about walking alone, because prisoners had been released, and there was a lot of anger and alcoholism in public places. Whenever it seemed menacing, I looked around and saw no police in evidence. On one occasion, a drunken group set upon me, because I was wearing a Russian shawl. At one point, it became obvious that I was being followed. One night when the narrow streets of Hradčany were relatively quiet, I became aware of a shadowy presence and shifted directions several times, trying to remember how it was done in spy novels, but I would not have been a good spy and it persisted. I wondered who and why, but kept my eye on the bigger picture. I needed to get around and make good use of my time. I had appointments in offices by day and invitations to homes by night.

High on my agenda was checking out Civic Forum, the force that led the demonstrations against the old order and was making leading the way in shaping the new order so far. There was a high moral tone and promise of reconciliation emanating from it, but this was mixed with other forces it had unleashed. Civic Forum was far from the makeshift operation seen on the news a few months earlier. It was busy, but not brusque, and highly organized, with departments and files and computers and photocopiers. I asked Jan Urban, a leading figure in CF, about the problem of forum politics. It was one thing to unite people in what they were against, and another to unite people in terms of what they were for. The spectrum spanned the distance from reform communists to religious revivalists. He expressed his belief that, after a long period of alienation and atomization, it was necessary to keep the coalition together to foster the rebirth of politics from below. It would be bad to break apart into parties too soon. In the future, the political spectrum would look quite different. Eventually, there would be a place for a strong left, right, and center, but in the present situation, people were tired of "isms." To my argument about the necessity of naming the system, he replied: "On a sinking ship, you look for any lifeboat and start to quarrel over what color it is only when you can see the shore." Although there was a particularly negative reaction to the concept of socialism now, he was a socialist and saw a future for socialism. He spoke of the strength of socialist traditions, which would inevitably resurface. There would be a pendulum effect. I asked how he related to communist traditions. His parents were honest and idealistic communists. His father, an ambassador under Dubček, died in 1988 after three interrogations.

There was a radical overturning reaching into every corner of this society's life, not just in its overt politics. Of course, it was only right that the professors purged after 1968, who became boiler stokers and window cleaners, should now become professors again and that those who had taken their places should become boiler stokers and window cleaners. Evidently, Milan Matouš was facing such a fate. It was also understandable that those who compromised were being held to account for their compromises. They were not sure what would come next and how far it would go. They were afraid, not only of what they admitted was justified criticism, but of unjustified criticism as well. All sorts of things were being resurrected and reinterpreted. If a person did not get a promotion or had an article rejected for publication years before, they were claiming now that it was not for scientific reasons.

"Nobody will say it," one professor said to me, "but the monopoly of Marxism in an unacceptable form is now being replaced by the persecution of Marxism. Before, those who were not Marxists had to make it seem as if they were. Now those who are Marxists have to make it seem as if they aren't." Neither was a healthy situation. The shakeup of intellectual institutions was far more drastic here than in Hungary or the GDR. In Hungary, the Academy of Sciences, the universities, certain journals, and even the media were already bases where dissident intellectuals could function. In the GDR, there was more of a convinced Marxist intelligentsia, who found ways to function with intellectual integrity, even if they had their blind spots and failed to bring their critical spirit to play upon the structures of power or to allow space for a wider range of views. In Czechoslovakia, anyone of real critical intelligence was either purged or compromised by consenting to the purges. Some even did the purging. In all of these societies, however, it was now difficult to be a Marxist. "Let them get a taste of their own medicine," some said. However, most of the cynics, careerists, and conformists abandoned Marxism the first moment it was advantageous to do so. Those who professed it now, who would get the full force of the backlash, would be those who least deserved it. Joe Duffy on RTE News reporting from Prague related an incident in which communist books were being sold and crowds were grabbing and burning them. He thought it was great fun. I didn't.

There was still so much fear. "We are like an emaciated and beaten animal, released from the zoo, and looking untrustingly at open country," was how economist and later president of the Czech Republic Miloš Zeman described the situation. It was the only place where people asked me not to mention their names in anything I wrote and were even nervous of my taking notes. One man I went to see, once a prominent intellectual and political figure, who had been purged and interrogated and now scratched a living somehow, was like a frightened animal. It was one of those encounters that haunted me for a long time afterward. Now that years have passed and he is dead, I'll reveal that was Karel Kosik, prominent philosopher of the Prague Spring. He invited me to his flat. I asked him questions about his life and thought. He asked me not to interview him or take notes, but instead, "Let us speak together as philosophers." He was back teaching at the university, but was still uncertain about how things would unfold. He argued that the starting point for critical analysis of our times was the philosophy of Martin Heidegger. The task was liberation of subject from object. He asked what I thought about what was happening. Could it be true that we were witnessing a transition from socialism to capitalism? Yes, I replied, I was afraid so. After a while, some friends of his arrived. One was a Parisian fashion designer, who showed her drawings of extravagant outfits that would only be worn on a catwalk. It was surreal watching Kosik, who had been talking about Marx and Heidegger, search for a vocabulary for these fashions. Then we went to a tavern for dinner with a wider group of people. I got into an interesting conversation with a Czech photojournalist for Associated Press, who had been a philosophy student of Kosik's in the 1960s. He said that he almost became a communist then. His parents were social democrats. His father emigrated and his mother went to prison for three years. Now he saw the future in Civic Forum. He was also into exploring religion. At one rally, people recited the *Pater Noster* together, which was a significant moment for him.

I missed Radovan Rictha, also a leading philosopher of the Prague Spring, my best contact in Prague. He had been dead for seven years. I spoke about him with logician Karel Berka. We discussed various philosophers we both knew and what was going on under the surface at philosophy conferences where we had met. During a long evening in his flat, he unfolded his life story and his analysis of the present situation. When young, during the Nazi occupation, he had been interned in Terezin. He had lived his whole life in fear. He believed in the party in 1945, but lost faith in it at the time of the Slánský trials, a 1952 show trial stemming from a wave of anti-cosmopolitan purges. He was expelled from the party in 1951 over an article on dialectical and formal logic. He was not a Marxist. He didn't believe in dialectics or ideologies or class struggle, but he couldn't say so. He was back in the party and partially rehabilitated in 1956. He made many compromises and signed things he didn't want to sign, especially during the post-1968 "normalization." He left the party only recently. Basically, he admitted, he joined the party because he was afraid not to join it and left the party because he was afraid not to leave it. He was torn between relief at not having to pretend anymore and fear at being held to account for things he did while pretending. He didn't find the intellectual atmosphere that much freer now.

There was a new orthodoxy now. It was one form of monopoly being replaced by another. Now, instead of Marx, it was Heidegger. The dominant worldview was now religious phenomenology. More attracted to Bertrand Russell than to either Marx or Heidegger, Berka still felt he could not pursue philosophy in his own way. "The students are now in charge in the university, pointing fingers and cancelling courses," he added. At the time, he asked me not to mention his name in anything I wrote, but, as he too is now dead, I'm doing so after all these years. Another philosopher I met, who had no problem about my using his name, was Jindřich Zelený, a Marxist by conviction and still a communist. Telling me how he had caught fire with it as a student in 1945, he proceeded. "We have to admit to failure, but it was failure of an attempt to make something great." He was convinced that there would be a decade of dissolution and then the time for the socialist vision would come again, but it would be very different from anything we had seen until then. Everywhere I went I saw pictures of Václav Havel, John Paul II, Tomáš Masaryk, first president of Czechoslovakia, but none of Karl Marx or even Alexander Dubček. Dubček had returned to Prague to cheering crowds, but had been sidelined as too associated with communism, even if a critical kind.

There was so much guilt here. The system worked in such a way that everyone was implicated. Much of the lashing out against others was an attempt to displace people's own guilt. I also began to get hints of another mechanism. So many people said to me: "Only Havel is clean." Eventually, having been a Catholic, it started to sound to me like "Lamb of God who takes away the sins of the world," as if there were some level on which Václav Havel was taking on and purging this guilt in the collective psyche. Others objected to the canonization of Havel at home and abroad, highlighting his personal faults and intellectual contradictions. Besides, Havel was not the only one. Others had stood up and suffered prison, exile, or marginalized manual labor. They were looking to find their places in the scheme of things now. Many exiles made another life for themselves abroad and were trying to decide what to do now. I met with Jan Šling, who had been active in oppositional politics here before going into exile. I had previously encountered him at the Communist University of London (CUL). He was the son of Otto Šling, a communist leader who was tried and executed with Rudolf Slánský in 1952. He expressed severe disappointment at how far his former comrades had moved to the right. He was especially disconcerted to hear them express such admiration for Thatcherism. When he stressed the social cost of it, they didn't give a damn. He thought that Civic Forum was fudging the issues. He regretted that reform communism, which had made the running in oppositional politics, was being overtaken.

As for the Communist Party, it had lost over a third of its membership, but still had over a million members and was therefore a serious force in the elections. What sort of people stayed in communist parties when the tide turned against them? There were two sorts: those who were too implicated to have any place else to go and those who believed in it. The sort of people who joined the party to advance themselves lost no time in joining Civic Forum and new parties. The Communist Party of Czechoslovakia (CPC) had reduced its apparatus, closed down institutions such as the higher party school, withdrawn from workplaces, elected new leaders (only four of one hundred of its central committee were reelected), allowed platforms, opened dialogue with expelled members and other groups, and changed its style of work. Even Václav Havel commented that he found Rude Pravo, the party newspaper, interesting to read. While I was there, the procurator of Prague called for the Communist Party to be banned. As far as others are concerned, banning would be too good for them.

Back at *WMR*, I met Lubomir Mlynar of the CPC, who was exploring the possibility of a successor project to the journal. There were proposals for an international broad-left publication. As for his party, it had lost its leading role, much of its property, and many of its members. His attitude was that one historical period of socialism had ended and now another one must begin. "If we meet again at the beginning of the next century, we won't be talking about communist parties and social democratic parties. We need new ideas and new organizational forms." I reflected on these words that V. L. Shelepin, the Soviet editor of *WMR*, had just spoken to me. "All that is solid melts into air," wrote Marx and Engels, but air still exists and we breathe it all the time.

So many times in these months I heard talk of "starting again at zero," of scrapping forty-to-fifty-to-seventy years of history and starting over. There would be no starting over and certainly not from zero. This vast experiment in human history failed to fulfill the hopes it engendered and the edifice it constructed was collapsing, but I felt that it had cut too deeply into the psyche, into the rhythms of history, to disappear without a trace. Whatever way this legacy would play out, it would be in a drastically transformed environment. I believed that the turn to the right in Eastern Europe would, paradoxically, bring the greatest need for the left that this part of the world had ever known. After the euphoria would come the exploitation, and eventually the discovery that freedom was not so simple nor so accessible as it seemed.

The people of Eastern Europe would have to get the hamburgers and Coke and jeans and beauty contests and faith healers out of their system. I did believe that Eastern Europe was better for what dramatic democracy it had achieved. Who could resist the righteousness of the reversals of prisoners becoming presidents and presidents becoming prisoners? Who could not welcome the fall of the Berlin Wall, the election of factory managers and parliamentary representatives, the reassertion of suppressed thought in the universities, the reappearance of books of banned authors in the bookshops and libraries, television worth watching, radio worth hearing, newspapers worth reading? Who could say Eastern Europe was not better for glasnost and multiparty elections? Who could believe the world was not better for disarmament and the end of the Cold War? But, I asked, was it progress to see Leningrad become Saint Petersburg again, to see Modrow replaced by de Maziere, to see Walesa, a trade union leader, selling his country's workforce as cheap labor for foreign exploitation, to see enterprises held in social ownership being privatized, to see a world of relative equality transformed into one of five-star restaurants for some and soup kitchens for others, to see educated and employed women going back to the home, to see people with a secular and socialist education longing for miracles and monarchs, to see people who lived together in peace at each other's throats? These countries had formed an alternative base of power in the world, which set limits on the hegemony of international capitalism and on what US foreign policy could do in the world. What they couldn't get with their guns and bombs and nuclear warheads, they could now walk in and buy at cut-price and be begged to do it and praised for doing so.

I was back home for May Day, but my attention was still on events abroad. Visitors from abroad kept us constantly connected, as did other forms of communication. Nelson Mandela arrived in June, only months after being released from prison in South Africa, and attracted a massive crowd on the streets of Dublin. One boy, on his father's shoulders, got very excited and shouted "Look, Dad, it's Paul McGrath," confusing him with a Black Irish soccer player. A delegation of Moscow trade unionists was hosted by the Dublin Council of Trade Unions. There was much drink and many toasts to proletarian internationalism, but not much insight into what was happening to the thing toasted. Some trade union- ist engaged intelligently, but the blustering and bluffing behavior of others was embarrassing. Some were worried about the Soviet delegation coming to a DCTU meeting, because Trotskyists might ask the "wrong questions." They had no grasp of glasnost. At a social during this period, I recited Brecht's *To a Waverer*, a poem that spoke to the uncertainties of the time.

Each month brought new elections, most resulting in defeat of communists. There was a wrenching in me as each government fell. In Romania and Bulgaria, reformed communists were elected. Some leftists thought the tide would turn quickly back again, but I didn't think so. The CPI was still not coming to terms with what was happening to socialism and was retreating into nationalism. Some were considering merging into Sinn Fein.

In July we were back in Yugoslavia, combining a holiday with my working on articles for the *Irish Times*, which was how I sub- sidized my holidays in those years. The small town of Budva had never experienced such a large influx as in the summer of 1990. Its beaches and narrow streets were teeming and its telephone lines and water supply were strained beyond capacity by a population swelled to many times its normal size. The reason was not just that it was a charming coastal town along the glorious Montenegrin Riviera, but that Yugoslav holiday patterns had undergone a sig- nificant shift as a result of the heightening of ethnic tensions in the past year. Previously, much of the population of Belgrade migrated to the Croatian coast in the summer, but Serbs who dared not ven- ture into Croatia with Serbian license plates were swarming into Montenegro.

In the aftermath of the victory of a Croatian nationalist in spring elections in Croatia, stories were circulating of Serbs (as well as Croatian communists) being purged from government, media, and educational positions; of a huge rally proclaiming the autonomy of Serbs within Croatia; of incipient paramilitary formations among both Serbs and Croats. There was a revival of Ustasha tendencies among Croats, and the Chetnik movement among Serbs, right-wing nationalist trends thought long dead. A commemoration of Mihajlović, leader of the latter, was held in Belgrade for the first time in forty years. On the eve of the World Cup, Croatian football fans turned their backs on the Yugoslav flag, booed during the national anthem, and cheered Holland against Yugoslavia in a friendly match in Zagreb. TV Zagreb then refused to cover the matches of the Yugoslav team as they progressed to the quarter finals. "It is like 1941 again," a Macedonian street trader said to me. "It is not just nationalities splitting apart, but in the same family, one brother is a fascist and the other a socialist." It was no wonder that some of my friends here, who fought with the partisans and moved on from the struggle against fascism to build socialism, were feeling bewildered and betrayed, seeing so much of what they had built being dismantled.

The League of Communists of Yugoslavia (LCY), the communist party that ruled for the four decades that Yugoslavia pioneered its independent path of self-management socialism, had collapsed. In its wake came, not one successor party, but many, formed within the disparate republics, and not on the best of terms with each other. The opposition parties were even more splintered, however, as the transformation of Yugoslavia from a one-party state to a one-hundred-plus-party state proceeded. There were still some tenuous threads holding together what was once whole. I phoned Zagreb to find out what was happening to the Tito Political School in Kumrovec, where I had lectured. It was in suspension, Jelena Nenadić, who worked there, told me. Croatian communists were still in there after their defeat, she assured me, as a strong and serious opposition. I phoned Belgrade to find out more about the plans, outlined to me in a letter from Milos Nikolić, to form a new international association of left-oriented intellectuals, now that the annual roundtable on socialist theory and practice would no longer be held in Cavtat, and that the institute organizing it had been closed. He was hopeful that the journal *Socialism in the World* and an international conference could be relaunched on a new international basis. Meanwhile, he was trying to organize a roundtable of left parties in Yugoslavia, although for the first time in his adult life, he belonged to none of them.

The opposite was the case with another of my fellow philosophers in Belgrade, Mihailo Marković, who, like others of the Praxis school, had been on the outside of party politics for years, had been elected vice president of the new Socialist Party of Serbia (SPS). After winning a referendum deciding the question of whether multiparty elections or a new constitution should come first, Marković was convinced that the SPS would remain in power after elections. He believed that their policy represented the best solution to the problem of social property. Stocks would take the form of workers' shares and would not be sold on the open market for 10 percent of their value as in Poland and Hungary. It would not be as in Slovenia and Croatia either, he said, where bourgeois parties had won and were committed to dismantling social property, noting that it was an unprecedented situation to have two different systems in the one country. The president of the new SPS was Slobodan Milosević, who was spoken of fervently as having restored pride to Serbs and was very popular in Montenegro as well as in Serbia. Many who had supported the Praxis philosophers from abroad were bewildered by Mihailo's association with Serbian nationalism.

Communists were still in power in Montenegro, and they too were forming a new socialist party. There were seventeen parties in Montenegro at this stage, but polls showed 25 percent support for communists, more than for any of the opposition parties. I did not encounter the bitter anti-communism here that I had elsewhere in Eastern Europe. Various young people I met outside my network of political and academic connections spoke of the communist tradition as honorable but over. "It was perfect on paper, but it just didn't work," was how more than one person put it. Among the most diverse people I drew out, there seemed to prevail a desire for something new, which would combine the economic efficiency of capitalism with the humanistic values of socialism. They were looking for a third way. I went to the island of Ostrovo Cvijeca to visit Miodrag Vlahović, retired now after being president of Montenegro and a member of the presidency of Yugoslavia. Sitting under the fig trees and grape vines, sipping slivovitz and eating fish he had just caught that morning, we went over events since I had been there last summer, interspersed with attempts to sum up the larger movements of history converging here. "We had the chance to prove that socialism has a human face," he reflected. "It is gone now, but there are seeds which can be preserved for the future."

Back in Budva, I had the same sort of conversation with Dušan Liješević, major of the town and involved in the social, political, and industrial life of Montenegro. While drinking in the open air as night fell, he gave what was nevertheless a most sober assessment of current situation. To my toast, "To the future of Yugoslavia," he replied, "Do you think so?" "Do *you* think so?" I said, throwing it back to him. Despite everything, he did think so. In the end, he thought that the exposés of Tito, the ethnic tensions, the right-wing reactions, all would run their course, and that both Yugoslavia and socialism had some kind of future. There was a new mood of confidence following a currency reform, bringing the convertibility of the dinar and zero inflation, which had tourists complaining about higher prices and struggling with 1,000,000 dinar notes, now worth 100 dinars, but had, for Yugoslavs, reduced much of the economic anxiety.

I had planned to go to Albania by hydrofoil from Yugoslavia, but when I went to buy the ticket, I was informed that it had been canceled from the Albanian side, "because the safety of passengers could not be guaranteed." So I stood at the Albanian border and looked from the top of a mountain into miles of Albania that did not look much different from Yugoslavia. The nearer to the border with Albania we went in Yugoslavia, the more Yugoslavia began to look like Albania. Only it was not like contemporary Albania, but an older Albania, an Albania that existed before either Albania or Yugoslavia chose the socialist path. The women in towns like Bar and Ulcinj were wearing white veils and layers of long skirts and balloon pants. As I walked among them in the Balkan heat in my cotton minidress, I remembered summers I had spent in the heavy black serge and white starched linen of a Catholic nun. The women were color-coded. You could tell by what color they wore if they were Albanian or Montenegrin, Muslim or Catholic or Orthodox, married or single. On market day in villages like Ostrovos, the single women were brought to market with the fruit and vegetables and rabbits and chickens.

There had been a number of illegal border crossings in this area. It had intensified the problem Yugoslavia felt as a major crossroads for refugees from south to north, from east to west, from poverty to wealth. With the prospect of a democratic revolution sweeping Albania, and with the conflict between Kosovo and Serbia heading toward irreconcilability, there were worries about aspirations for a greater Albania encroaching on Yugoslavia. What surprised me most, speaking to both Serbs and Albanians, was how impenetrable these people still were to each other, even after living side by side for so many years. At night, I listened to Radio Tirana. It told of conferences and scientific research and gave the Albanian version of world news. They had reestablished diplomatic ties to the USSR, but took a harsh view of Yugoslavia, especially on Kosovo. In between all this, there were Albanian folksongs and classical music. After every program, there was the "Internationale."

On our last night in Budva, Dušan informed us that Iraq had invaded Kuwait, a development that would also shape our political lives, necessitating intensified protest against US domination of the international arena, as it weighed in with Operation Desert Shield and then Operation Desert Storm. Once again, my family and I would be on different sides of a war. On the flight home, there were Medjugorje pilgrims, this time Irish ones, some of them quite young. Sam and I speculated about who had come to pray and who had come to sin.

In September, I went to Vienna. Once again, I had a strong sense of wending my way through world-historical crosscurrents. The first thing I did was to seek Adam Schaff, a Polish Marxist philosopher I much admired, but discovered he had been in hospital and was now in a rural rest home. I left him a note and wished that I could talk through this conjuncture with him. Walking the streets of Vienna, I thought of the many layers of history that had left their deposits here. Grandiose cathedrals of Catholicism and palaces of the Austro-Hungarian Empire, mingled with the institutions of Red Vienna. Streets named after monarchs crisscrossed streets named after socialists. I remembered the Second-and-a-Half International seeking a third way between "terrorist Moscow and impotent Bern," which seemed relevant again. How much was left of this tradition of Austro-Marxism, I wondered, as I contemplated the fate of these two streams within the socialist movement in the years since, and asked if there was some sense in which they were converging again at this new turn in the historical process. After all, people who had come through each of these two traditions were coming together here in Vienna to assess the meaning of the events in Eastern Europe and to discuss a way forward from them. From East and West, former communists and current social democrats were arriving for a conference on "The Democratic Revolutions in Central and Eastern Europe: The Challenge for Social Democracy," hosted by the Renner Institute and the Socialist Party of Austria, which was in government at the time. They were MPs, party leaders, academics, and writers. They were from old social democratic and labor parties from the West and new socialist parties, resurrected social democratic parties, and reformed communist parties from the East. From some ex-communist countries, there were competing parties seeking affiliation to the Socialist International. It was especially fierce in Hungary. I met Györgö Markus again, who filled me in on the latest in this saga.

There was a discernible gulf between East and West. Western social democrats were a bit bewildered by their Eastern counterparts. They had somehow expected, when these new social democratic parties had been formed, that Eastern social democrats would be just like them. That they could not and should not be like them did not seem to occur to them. That the rhythms of decades comprising a different history had cut too deeply into the society and into the psyche for them to be the same; that these people might bring not only problems but also positive traditions; that they might bring not only new numbers but also distinctive perceptions, escaped them. Social democrats were wary. Old wounds had not yet healed and new ones had opened. They felt that the backlash against communists had rebounded on them. They were at pains to distance themselves in the eyes of electorates who had not distinguished among the forces of the left and swung to the right. It was this that made Franz Vranitzky, Chancellor of Austria, put such a strong emphasis on the divide between communists and social democrats in his opening address to the conference. "Between these two standpoints there can be no compromise, no third way," he declared, repudiating the earlier traditions of his party. Austria was in the middle of an election campaign and Vranitzky's handsome face was on election posters everywhere. The Socialist Party had been in power a long time and there were anti-socialist slogans on the posters of the other parties. Willy Brandt, the distinguished president of the SI, poignantly expressed a certain bitterness at democratic socialists having to pay the price for the crimes of communists. He nevertheless displayed a highly nuanced and open attitude to the revolutions in Eastern Europe, which, he argued, were much more differentiated and contradictory than expected. The party landscape would be drastically different from what it was at that moment, he predicted, and spoke in favor of broad contacts with the new forces, without neglecting traditional ties.

The next speaker was Yuri Afanasiev, a high-profile member of the Supreme Soviet, who struck a very bleak tone. He had left the CPSU, but could not see his way to joining another party. He did not consider himself a social democrat. It was not possible to instill new life into socialism, he argued, and all hopes of socialism with a human face, from Garaudy, Gomulka, and Dubćek to Gorbachev, had shown the futility of it. Perestroika had failed. Homo Sovieticus was an animal who wanted to consume as much as possible, steal a bit, but change nothing. He did not believe that the influence of Marxism had ended. The vision of socialism would continue to serve humanity in a kind of convergence, which would generate contradictions in capitalism, without being able to transcend it. There was a role for social democracy in maintaining equilibrium in an ocean of interests. That was all. "The Soviet Union tried to put into practice a dream of mankind. For proving that this dream cannot be materialized, mankind owes a debt to it," he sadly concluded.

Almost equally bleak was the scenario described by Joze Pucnik, president of the Social Democratic Party of Slovenia, which was in government within the center-right DEMOS coalition. "There is no great paradigm for Slovenia," he declared, "only clearing away rubble." Others, however, were more positive. Jiří Hajek, foreign minister of Czechoslovakia in the Dubček government of 1968, now supporting Civic Forum, spoke of the need for a strong democratic left to play a leading role in the reconstruction of civil society. I asked him later how he felt about the prospect of the restoration of capitalism. "When you take a wrong turn, you have to go back. Socialists should be the most far-seeing about this." He seemed to see far enough to envision a chance for socialism on the other side of this. Silviu Brucan, a communist politician, journalist, ambassador, and more recently a leader of the Romanian revolution, highlighted the international context for the Eastern European revolutions. There had never been a true choice between capitalism and socialism, he argued, because the world economy was a hierarchical system in which socialism was always under the domination of capitalism. Stalinism was the brutal reaction of an inferior economy to the power of the West. Pursuing the consequences of his argument with him afterward, he said he felt that too many were capitulating to this domination. Pal Forgacs of the independent trade unions of Hungary asked, "Did we fight against communism to restore capitalism?" He expressed his fear that it would be a special Eastern European capitalism, which would take only the dark side of capitalism and make this area the poorhouse of Europe. He fought for the celebration of May Day in Budapest, reasserting the traditions of the left.

In a session on national conflicts, the main clash was between those asserting their claims to national independence and others urging them to transcend their nationalist claims. "Where does it all end?" Igor Tschubais of Democratic Platform saw national conflicts as rooted in non-national causes. He cited a song then popular in the Soviet Union: "I would like to believe in something . . . no matter what . . . I want to believe in something." Much of it was reaction to a vacuum, to the loss of a unifying vision. Here at this conference, however, it was good to meet a threesome who seemed to be best of friends, a Serb, a Croat, and a Kosovar, showing in practice that a unifying political ideology transcended nationalism.

One of the few women to speak cut much closer to the bone than many men would have dared. Eugenia Kazewa of the USSR went to the podium and said, "I don't expect your applause when I finish. I'll be happy if I don't get the catcalls I would get at home. I am a communist. I have not left the party, at least not yet. I joined the party as a young girl and never had any privileges as a result of my party membership." She still lived in hope that socialism could be reformed. She asked why did those, such as Yuri Afanasiev, leave only now. If they could not live in the CPSU under Gorbachev, how could they live in it under Chernenko, Brezhnev, and even Stalin? She did get applause. Social democrats, said Peter Jankowitsch, chairing the session, were a tolerant audience. Perhaps not tolerant enough to open up to this enormous source of energy, this painful self-criticism, this earnest search for another way that was emerging from the ruins of the communist movement. An exception to this, a young Austrian woman in the ruling party's Socialist Youth, told me that they often found reformed communists much more interesting than social democrats.

The best of these honest communists did not come cap-in-hand, begging for acceptance on any terms to become identikit social democrats. However, some of them did. They had made their careers as conformist members of communist parties and left as soon as these parties were losing power, denounced everything about the communist tradition, and groveled before the social democratic one. I was appalled, listening to them. When I got up to speak, I said so. It was a strong polemic against social democratic triumphalism and a defense of what was defensible in the communist tradition. It was a plea for a new intellectual synthesis and political convergence of the best of the social democratic and communist traditions. I evoked the tradition of Austro-Marxism, taking an opposite view of it from what Vranitsky had taken in his opening address. Willy Brandt was sitting right in front of me, paying curious attention. Heinz Fischer, chair of the Socialist Party parliamentary group, who was chairing the session, said that I reminded him of the Irish soccer team. Jack Charlton, the team manager, was famous for saying "Put them under pressure." Silviu Brucan assured me that I did, and it disturbed them. He said that I said what needed to be said, but it was hard to believe that it came from an Irish woman. A number of people, mostly from the East, spoke to me strongly and warmly about my ideas. Among others who approached me was Jochen Reinert, covering the conference for *Neues Deutschland*, who recruited me as a writer for that paper. Miloš Nikolić asked me to come with him to a meeting at the Renner Institute about forming a new network of left intellectuals. Although his institute had closed in July, he continued to work in his office, until one day when the locks were changed. The invitation to this conference in Vienna had not been sent to me personally, but to the Labour Party in Ireland. Nobody, except a few people who already knew me, expected a speaker from a social democratic party in Ireland to take such a position. I reported to the international affairs committee when I returned, knowing that I had articulated a position that was not the official position of the party, although a number of party members would agree with it. They didn't seem too bothered by it, presumably because it was a gathering of intellectuals and not a body making official decisions.

I was aware all through September that these were the last

days of the GDR. On October 3, it was subsumed into a unified Germany. The international media presented it as joyous occasion, a victory for democracy, whereas those I knew were experiencing it as a massive hostile takeover. They accepted that German unification was inevitable, but not in the way it was happening. It was a blitzkrieg, trashing every aspect of their lives. I was determined to go back to Berlin and play a part in contesting the version of the victors by conveying the voices of the vanquished. First, I went to London, to a conference on the media representation of Germany, organized by the British Film Institute and the Goethe Institute. There were searching questions articulated, such as what histories were being remembered or repressed. There were multiple perspectives in play and the legacies of the GDR were not totally trashed, so it was a thought-provoking event. At night, I went to a Wolf Biermann concert with Monty Johnstone, who was dealing with the fracturing of his own party as well as that of our whole movement

While in London, I spoke at a "Futures" event, organized by the Communist Party of Great Britain (CPGB) where this fracturing was on full display. At a packed session titled "Marxism and Beyond," the debate centered around the question of whether any kind of unifying philosophy or project was possible. It reflected a severe loss of confidence in any sort of overarching vision linking all the various issues and projects concerning the left, reinforced by the ascendancy of postmodernism in various intellectual and cultural circles in Western Europe, and the massive rejection of Marxism in Eastern Europe. I gave a sweepingly historicist and polemical analysis of the current conjuncture and future possibilities for the left. The chair responded sarcastically that she admired my "combative confidence." Ralph Miliband, also on that panel, agreed with me, but the audience was full of people denouncing intellectual "totalitarianism" and praising pluralism. Monty Johnstone insisted that they could move beyond accepting that Marxism has been discredited by the revolutions in Eastern Europe to using Marxism to understand these revolutions. There were many references to *Marxism Today* as "a glossy magazine whose contents rarely reflect its title." After the session, an older woman came up to me and said that no one had ever reminded her so much of J. D. Bernal. It turned out that it was Margot Heinemann, herself an eminent Marxist writer, who had been one of Bernal's lovers, and she was delighted that I knew of him and had written about him.

Emotions ran high during another session called "Is the party over?" It was becoming clear that it was. To survive or not to survive, to renew or to liquidate, was the choice facing the CPGB at its special congress coming up in December. "This is a very emotional debate," one member admitted. "It is our identity at stake, not only our own, but others, including those who have died." Permeating many speeches, there was a mood of despair, a sense of standing in the wreckage of failed utopia. Margot Heinemann sketched her many years in the party, full of high hopes and many disappointments. The communist movement had been shaken by crises many times before in its turbulent history and the CPGB had been torn asunder by every one of them. The years 1939, 1956, and 1968 had especially painful connotations for those who lived through them. What made this time different was the strident assertion that this was the terminal crisis. According to Martin Jacques, editor of *Marxism Today*, the era which began in 1917 ended in 1989, and it ended in disaster. At a session titled "Socialism after the Berlin Wall," he asserted that 1989 meant the end of any systemic alternative to capitalism. It meant that capitalism was triumphant. The energies of oppositional movements in the future would be directed to changes in the capitalist system. It also meant an end to the rivalry between the two main traditions on the left, the communist and social democratic traditions. The communist parties were over and the social democratic tradition had prevailed, as he saw it. That was not how others saw it. It was cowards flinching and traitors sneering. "Many years ago, I joined a communist party with fire in its belly," wrote Arthur Mendelsohn in a recent party publication, regretting the impotence he felt overtaking the party. There were still those arguing that the vision of socialism was not dead, nor was the party. "For me, comrades, the party is not over," declared Mhairi Stewart, a young Scottish woman with an air of defiance.

Even in the debate about whether a unifying vision/project was possible, there was a breadth of vision and depth of political passion, which had characterized the political culture of communist parties, which was qualitatively different from that of other parties of the left or right. Members of the Labour Party present at Futures seemed to be most acutely aware of it, and several remarked to me of how stimulating the atmosphere was and how bland the Labour Party was in comparison. It reinforced a strong sense of a need for a position to the left of social democracy. If this were to disappear, something vital would be lost and the political culture of the left would be severely impoverished. The event ended with Billy Bragg singing his new version of the "Internationale." Addressing the question of why he rewrote it, he said that for his generation, "Arise ye starvelings from your slumbers," did not mean much today. The real question, he knew, was why rewrite it at a time when everyone was saying that its culture was collapsing? His voice raised in song was a force standing against such collapse.

Meanwhile in Ireland that autumn, there was a presidential election. It was the first time that the left contested this office. Mary Robinson was nominated by the Labour Party and Workers Party. It was good to see cooperation between these two parties. As the campaign proceeded and a scandal surrounded the Fianna Fail front-runner, it began to look as if we might win and see a left feminist president. I had known and liked Mary for the previous decade, but I did not like her transmutation during the election. She changed her whole look, which was fine, but she was becoming haughty and conservative. On *Today-Tonight*, a current affairs program, she responded to a question about socialism with a flat denial that she was a socialist and distanced herself from the left who were supporting her. It wasn't that I expected her to launch into a full-blooded defense of socialism, because she was a lawyer, who was not strong on the level of political philosophy, but I found her negativity in the face of the socialism-is-dead atmosphere of the time to be opportunistic and infuriating. I wrote to her telling her that I would no longer campaign for her, but I would vote for her, although with far less enthusiasm. Actually, I probably campaigned more effectively for her after that than if I had been on the door-to-door canvass, because I persuaded a number of leftists, who were also furious after her performance and threatening not to vote at all, that they should vote for her nevertheless. I was glad that she won and I attended the victory party. When I had occasion to meet her when in office, it was across a great divide. She became ever more regal and distant from the left. She seemed more comfortable conversing with monarchs and oligarchs than with those who campaigned for her election. However, it played at home and abroad as a victory for the left. When I was abroad in the immediate aftermath, I found international leftists excited about it and congratulating me on it.

Only weeks later, I was again in London for the congress of the CPGB. I covered it for both the *Irish Times* and *Neues Deutschland*. There were three options proposed: renewal, association, or twin-track. The association option was the most drastic. "Better to go out with a bang than a whimper," according to its advocates. It involved dissolving the party into a looser association, open to members of any political party or none. It would be decentralized, based on individual membership, but could organize local or interest groups. It would not contest elections, but it could organize journals, conferences, and events. Some would join the Labour Party, whereas others talked of the possibility of it evolving toward a new political party. Still others sang the praises of forum politics. The renewal option was to renovate the party, perhaps to relaunch it with a new name, certainly to recast its structures and methods of work. "We shouldn't sacrifice what we have got for something amorphous, weak, and nonexistent. The assets built up for generations should be kept under the democratic control of the party," said Monty Johnstone. He was not against a wider socialist formation, but believed that the way should be prepared for it over a longer period of time. Betty Reid warned against "nebulous networks . . . down blind alleys with no way back." The twin-track option was to combine the positive proposals of the other two: to renew the party and also to form a new broad left association. Its advocates claimed that this duality was part of the tradition embodied in the British Road to Socialism of combining work in the party with building a broad democratic alliance. This was the position of the party secretary, Nina Temple, who claimed: "There is no surer way to liquidate the party than to carry on business as usual. We either develop a new culture of radical socialist politics or we die with the old Bolshevik era."

There were over one thousand amendments from six thousand members. The election to the national executive dispensed with the recommended list, but did elaborate guidelines to ensure a balance in favor of comrades from Scotland and Wales, comrades who were female, Black, youthful, gay, and disabled. The white, male, heterosexual, able-bodied Londoner would soon become a new minority needing positive discrimination, a candidate in that category wryly remarked to me. The election addresses read like personal columns: "white, male, twin-track, keen on networking, rock 'n' roll, rock climbing, haven't paid poll tax." Late at night at the top of a double-decker bus with two long-standing members of the party, we met a young student, who had just joined the party in September, who was standing for election. We asked him what he thought. He proceeded to give know-it-all answers to every question, as if he were a great sage, and without any sense that anyone else might know more than he did. We played along with it, until we got off the bus and Irene Fick, my friend and comrade who was putting me up for the night, and I doubled over with hysterical laughter. In the light of the next day, it was serious again. Speeches were passionate with charges of dogmatism and complacency being countered with charges of recklessness, liquidationism, and asset-stripping. Although the compromise position of twin-track was adopted, the reality was liquidation.

As 1990 ended, it was the end of so much that had become important, not only to me, but to the history of the world. The communist movement had lit up the twentieth century, clarified the contours of capitalism, set out to build a systemic alternative to it, shifted the balance of power and distribution of wealth in the world. These experiments in socialism played out in a world dominated by an ever more dominating capitalism, and they did not prevail.

Before 1990 ended, I stepped into the new unified Germany, observed the all-German elections, investigated overturned lives and pursued the question, "What remains?"—also the title of a much-discussed work of author Christa Wolf. Even as the world was still turning upside down, I was stepping into the new world order. The USSR still stood, but I knew that its days were numbered. The drama of how it would end and what would come in its place had yet to reveal itself. I was planning another trip to Yugoslavia, not yet knowing what tragedy would engulf it. As I moved into the 1990s and beyond, I would continue to chart these currents and to navigate massive new waves sweeping my world.

CHAPTER 2

The New World Order

IT IS DIFFICULT TO DRAW a sharp line between the end of one era and the beginning of another. Even as the dismantling of the previous era continued, the new one had begun. The era in which socialism was a serious countervailing power in a world dominated by capitalism was giving way to one of capitalism prevailing. My clearest step into this new era was in November 1990, when I arrived in a very different Berlin than the one I left only months before. It was my first entry into a post-socialist society.

The "New World Order" had been heralded by the US president George H. W. Bush in September 1990 as an age of unified global governance now that the Cold War was over and communism had been defeated. This chimed in with Francis Fukuyama's proclamation of an "end of history," because liberal capitalism now stood without any credible challenge. I did not see it that way, but I did have to face a massive defeat for my side and think through the consequences of this world-historical transformation. I could not accept the international media soundbites, articulating the triumphalism of the victors, so I found myself on the terrain of the vanquished.

Not that the counterrevolution was complete. The world was

still turning upside down, and it was difficult to achieve equilibrium or even to discern the velocity or direction of the upheaval. The USSR still stood, but it was no longer the mighty presence that it once was. Although it was not clear how it would end, I could see that the end was nigh. Whole countries would be wiped from the map of the world as this New World Order took shape.

The first to go was the German Democratic Republic, as it was dissolved into a united Germany. The last days of the GDR weighed heavily on me, because I knew the country was something more than the gray prison it was portrayed to be. I watched the live television coverage of the "unification" of Germany on October 3, 1990. The picture of German unification filling the international media was one of a fantastic street party, full of champagne and song, the realization of a dream, a victory for democracy. That was history as being written by the victors; I was interested in history as experienced by the vanquished. I saw the vanquished as not only as the deposed politburo but the majority of the population as the eastern part of Germany. It was their stories I sought when I returned to Berlin in November 1990.

According to this alternative version of history, even as it was unfolding, it was a brutal *Anschluss*. "It has been a *Blitzkrieg* operation. They have behaved like an occupying army, without grace, without generosity, without sensitivity," was the gist of many tales I was told using terms stemming from the Nazi period. It was not that those saying this were altogether against unification, but they insisted that it should have been negotiated on more equal terms and on a more protracted time scale, leading to a new constitution and a new social order, drawing from the institutions and traditions of both states. As a legal entity, the GDR might have ceased to exist, but in the social psyche it persisted. When I arrived in the new unified Germany, the phrase I heard most was *ehemaligen DDR* [former GDR], which filled every conversation and news report, and reverberated on the street and Strassenbahn. "What remains?" was the question I constantly put to myself and to everyone to whom I spoke, a question not answered by Christa

Wolf's controversial book of that title (*Was Bleibt*), a question that would take time and deep reflection to answer.

What didn't remain was all too obvious. The Palast der Republik stood empty with a disturbed space where the hammer and compass had been stripped away. GDR state television was off the air. The Praktika camera factory was closing down. The Academy of Sciences was being dismantled. *Abwicklung,* meaning "winding up," was the word of the moment. The argument about the Academy of Sciences, for example, was that it must go, because there was already one in the West. This was despite the fact that the one in the East was three hundred years old and the one in the West was only three years old, its vice president and my friend Herbert Hörz pointed out to me, still hoping that something of it could be saved. The same argument about the universities and other institutions was taking place as well. Although Humboldt University was much older than the Free University or the Technical University in West Berlin, its future was less secure. Departments in which the subject matter was considered to be ideological, such as the social sciences, were being "wound up." The funding for the completion of the publication of the Marx and Engels collected works was cut off. Even books and film were being destroyed, with the excuse that there was no space to store them. "At least when the Nazis were burning books, they did it openly," Michael Kann, a now unemployed filmmaker remarked bitterly. The new masters were moving to eradicate every trace of what the GDR ever was.

The tragedy of the *Wende* (great change) was that it opened everything up and then closed it all down again. During the period of the Modrow government and the roundtable, a time of disturbing dislocation as well as remarkable creativity, people were beginning to shape the sort of society in which they had always wanted to live, to make the sort of television programs they always wanted to watch, to write the sort of articles they always wanted to read, to sing the sort of songs they always wanted to hear. I was there in the spring of 1990, just at the end of this period, just as the Deutschmark was casting its dark shadow over it all. On a stretch of the wall still left, called East Side Gallery, there was a mural of a people crossing a sea that parted for them and then, once they had irrevocably embarked on their journey, flooded over them. It was the most truthful and powerful image of what was happening before my eyes.

Those who took to the streets opened the way for forces larger than themselves, forces that they couldn't control or even fully comprehend, the external forces of a globalized market economy moving in on any sphere outside its hegemony, and the internal forces of capitulation. IG Farben and Krupps, last seen here during the Third Reich, were coming back. Junker aristocrats were reclaiming vast estates. Even descendants living in New York, who couldn't speak a word of German and never set foot on German soil, were claiming vast properties. This land and its natural and built resources had been people's property, but people brought back the expropriators who had been expropriated and welcomed them to expropriate it again. It was to me as if history were moving backward. Although I had some previous experience of dramatic social change, I had never seen such a deep and drastic undoing of a social order. People had the ground go from under their feet, and their whole world turned inside out. Some were too stunned to know what had happened to them. I felt at the edge of history here. My sense of the trajectory of history was being challenged by what was happening here and I was irresistibly drawn to it, to feel the pulse of it, to know up close the living texture of it, and to find out what it meant in world-historical terms.

All-German elections were set for December 2, 1990. I attended many election events, especially those of the PDS, the party I supported. I observed the electoral activity most closely in the Pankow area where I was staying. One day I passed a somewhat lackluster SPD rally and moved toward the much more vibrant PDS scene in Pankower Markt, where the bitter cold and dark were lit by red lanterns saying *Mut zum Träumen* (courage to dream) and filled with the live and video images, words and music of such dreams. At all of their events, I found the imagery, the candidates, the music

to be fresh and forthright, showing, speaking, singing of a society
struggling to come to terms with itself and of a force with energy
and purpose and direction in the face of the task. The biggest event
I attended was a PDS rally in the Deutschlandhalle in West Berlin.
The party leader, Gregor Gysi, spoke at it. Although he was a tiny
speck on the faraway stage, a huge video screen magnified every
nuance of facial expression and created a uniquely intimate sense of
presence, combined with the power of a mass scene. Leaning over
a high table as if it were a bar with only an ashtray on it and not a
scrap of notes, he was like a stand-up comedian one moment and a
biblical prophet the next. It was as if he were born for this moment.
I saw him then as combining the best traditions of the communist movement with a fresh voice for the future. His extraordinary
mixture of jokiness and gravitas brought a new sense of fun as
well as a sharp intelligence and polemical style to the heavy stuffi-
ness of German politics. On television current affairs programs, I
took great delight in watching reaction shots of Kohl, who seemed
puzzled and off guard in the face of Gysi's quick quips. David and
Goliath imagery irresistibly suggested itself.

On election night, I went to the Haus am Köllnischen Park
to watch as election results were revealed. Disappointingly, the
Christian Democratic Union (CDU) won the election, but the PDS
did win 17 seats in the Bundestag. Discussing the results on television during the *Elephunten Runde* (the elephant round, where
the leaders of all parties in the new Bundestag formed the studio
panel), Marianne Birthler of Bundnis 90 (the alliance of organizations of the people's movement, including New Forum) asserted
that the people voted against their own interests. Naturally, Kohl
and others came down on her fiercely. Those who were heralded as
heroines of the revolution were heroines no more. She was quoted
often and everywhere during the next week, both with approval
and disapproval. I thought she was right. The people voted for the
Deutschmark and for the Western standard of living. What they
received was a society of higher prices and lower wages, pensions,
and unemployment benefits for the *ossies* than for the *wessies*. Yet

even those in unemployment queues, some of whom would never work again, voted for the CDU.

It was not a matter of clapped-out industries needing to be bailed out from outside. It was a project of undermining even thriving enterprises like Praktika, to get a knockdown price for the entire hostile takeover, and to be thanked for doing so. Eastern shops were taken over by Western chains. A viable agriculture was undercut by this pattern in produce. So was publishing. The chains that took over the big bookshops had quotas on the number of Eastern books that could be on sale, which were regularly checked and enforced. It was a third world pattern. As for the environment, many of the complaints about Eastern pollution were justified, but it was also true that the recycling systems for paper, plastics, glass, and metal were ended. On every issue, there was another side to the story.

When I was here only months earlier, most people I knew were still bustling about with the day-to-day routines of their working lives, although some were already clearing out their offices when I visited them. This time most of them were unemployed, and those still working felt that their days were numbered. Some were paralyzed with depression. Some busied themselves with a welter of new forms on tax, insurance, unemployment benefit, retraining schemes, and job applications, desperate hopes of new careers, recriminations against colleagues and fellow citizens. Some examined their consciences and analyzed the new social order. Some counseled others, despite being in a bad situation themselves. Some were determined to fight and involved themselves in trade unions, social movements, or left parties. Many did all of these things in turn.

It was becoming obvious that there was widespread unemployment, but *Berufsverbot* as well. People were being denied the right to pursue their profession, because of their past service to the GDR and their present political convictions. Only getting what they deserved, some said. The problem was that those bearing the brunt of it were those of greatest critical intelligence and moral integrity. Throughout Eastern Europe, those who had the hardest time in the old order would have the hardest time in the new one as well. Many of those most compromised and corrupted under the old regime were the most opportunist about finding themselves a cozy place in the new regime as well. In some sectors, all existing contracts, such as those for school principals, were canceled, and all had to reapply for their positions. The new public service forms asked not only about membership in the SED, but detailed questions about functions in the party and contacts with Stasi, the GDR intelligence service. In many jobs, there was a certain open, inevitable, routine contact with Stasi, but there was also a shadowy area in which no one really knew exactly how much contact with Stasi they did have in their working lives. I listened with fascination as some colleagues tried to reconstruct it and told me what they did and didn't write in reports about their contacts with me in years past.

Bernhard Tschernig, when I was last in the GDR, was head of press and information services in the Volkskammer, the GDR parliament. Before unification, it was said that only competence would count, not political affiliation, that it might even be better to have honest people who were openly in PDS. Then came unification and an interview with the head of personnel of the Bundestag and the verdict: "You were an exponent of the system. We cannot use people such as you." All GDR ambassadors were by definition exponents of the system; therefore they were ineligible to work in the public service, even as postmen. It applied to many people who occupied many positions. An ironic twist in how it all worked was revealed to me by a teacher, who, as a student, had been more interested in Marxism than her classmates, often asking questions and bringing in other texts, who received lower marks than the others. When the Western assessors came, this went in her favor.

What most disturbed me was the revelation of just how far the social fabric was coming unraveled and how some people were unraveling from within. The loss of solidarity in this society, in which this solidarity once seemed so strong, not only in general, but in groups and persons I knew, some for many years, really got to me. I was prepared to see the CDU win the elections, to see Federal police patrolling Marx-Engels-Forum, Karl-Liebnecht-Strasse and Rosa-Luxemburg-Platz, to see Alexanderplatz looking like Atlantic City's boardwalk, but not for this degree of social and psychic dislocation. It was not only a society where no one was sure what exactly the public rules were anymore, but one where very few even knew what their own criteria were. However, some did know and had stood up remarkably well against all odds. Some, whose social or professional situation was worst, were best within themselves. Helmut Böhme, who was director of the Institute of Genetics, was deposed and forced into early retirement in very unfavorable conditions before the *Wende* for being critical of the party leadership. Now, he was the only one of the six hundred who worked in that institute to be a member of PDS. He was socially isolated and professionally blocked, but psychologically together and politically determined. Jens Reich, another scientist, a leader of New Forum, now sidelined, told me that they retained the ideals of their movement, which sought to change the rules of the political game, "even though the wind is blowing very chilly on our faces."

I believed that the values of this ill-fated experiment in building socialism had entered too deeply into the psyche and into the social order, even in those who are now voting CDU, to be as totally eradicated as some might think. How this would play itself out remained to be seen, but already there were some small and simple signs: teenagers wearing t-shirts saying "Born in the DDR" and draping their bedroom walls with the flag of the GDR, playing a new, upbeat version of the anthem of the DDR, which people were singing with tears in their eyes. Much had changed, not all of it for the worst. Fighting against the odds brought out very different qualities than being secure in power. Although many thought that the last word on the legacy of the GDR was being written, I didn't think so. I continued to follow this story closely and in 1991 the *Irish Times* ran my article "German Unification: The Other Side of the Story" as a major feature covering a whole page.

A major marker of the New World Order was the Gulf War, which raged in the early months of 1991. As Operation Desert Storm bombarded Iraq, there was no major countervailing force standing against US domination of world affairs. I was as outraged by this as I had been at any US war since Vietnam, and took every opportunity to protest against it. In the spring, I traveled to the United States, the center of this New World Order. It was the first time I had been there in ten years. Because of this, I saw the country in sharper relief than at any time before or since. On my way, Shannon Airport was overrun by US soldiers returning from the Gulf. When I arrived at JFK Airport in New York, I showed my US passport (which I only used to travel to the US). The passport official broke into a friendly smile and said, "Welcome home, Helena," which I found strangely disorienting, because I didn't consider the US to be home anymore. New York City was littered with the paraphernalia of war, and the airwaves and streets were full of the discourse of war.

The conference I attended there was full of analysis and anxiety about the nature of the New World Order. "After the Flood: The World Transformed" was the ambitious world-historical theme drawing me to the ninth annual Socialist Scholars Conference in New York. Perhaps nothing that could happen in three days could really fulfill the grand expectations such a title engendered, but the conference did make a fair stab at it. At first, it was a bit overwhelming. Looking through the program at the number of panels—over a hundred, more than twenty taking place simultaneously at any given session, and some with very intriguing titles—there were impossible choices to make. Wandering around the bookstalls, with so many new books and journals, again with such enticing titles, how could I possibly read them all? So many people were buzzing about, both inside the theaters and corridors and classrooms of the conference and outside on the streets of Manhattan. It seemed so teeming with bodies and books and bustle, I wondered how I would make my way amidst it all. I made my choices as best I could and resigned myself to the fact that I couldn't attend sessions on "Warring Stories: Reading and Contesting the New World Order," "Constructing the Enemy," "Unknown Secrets," "What Are the Alternatives for the 3rd World?," "Communist Regimes: The Aftermath," "Multi-Culturalism," "Marx: The Video," "Playing Fields of Democracy," "Feminism, Post-Structuralism and Critical Theory," "Culture Wars," "The Soviet Disunion: The Hour of Thermidor?," "Post-Fordism: Flexible Politics in the Age of Just-In-Time Production," "Has Postmodernism Superseded Marxism?," "Cuba and Vietnam: Last Chance for Socialism?," and many more. I was curious about "Plato for Progressives" and "New Paradigms for Mathematics," but life was too short. I didn't mind missing "Ireland: Censoring the Revolution" and "Ireland's Unfinished Revolution: 75 Years On," although, when I imagined what would probably transpire, I did feel a bit uneasy at leaving the field uncontested.

At "What's New in the New World Order?" the venerable Paul Sweezy regarded it as "the new world disorder." Those who ruled in advanced monopoly capitalism had no idea of where the process was going, he argued, because they didn't understand their own system. North/South rivalry had been complicated by East/West rivalry, said Samir Amin at the same session, but now the South was reverting almost to colonial times in its subservience to the North. There seemed to be a new trilateral structure of power: United States, Europe, and Japan. One of the hidden aims of the Gulf War, he argued, was to give a further blow to the European project. Taking a long view of the capitalist order, he asserted that hegemonies were short-lived, whereas rivalries were the rule. As to the East, there would be increased chaos. There was still a question of whether some socialist dimensions would survive.

The panel on "Germany Reunified: Prospects and Problems" generated varying perspectives. Marlene Nadel, a New York journalist, commenting on the absence of anyone from the eastern part of Germany, gave the starkest account, one not often articulated outside the eastern part of Germany. German unification was an *Anschluss*. It was colonialism. It was a total closing off of other perspectives. The people of the ex-GDR had their voices stolen, she claimed. Dieter Dettke, the Friedrich Ebert Stiftung representative in Washington, was somewhat uneasy about the arguments of the previous speakers. He went on to say that he was surprised at how easy external German unification was, but the real problem was internal unification. He was challenged from the floor about the responsibility of the SPD for the form of German unification that had been adopted, and there was an argument about whether or not there had been any alternative. The members of the panel "The Yugoslav Crisis: When the Ethnos Becomes the Demos" were introduced as "representatives of the democratic opposition in Yugoslavia, most of whom were, until five minutes ago, the regime." Bogdan Denitch, a Yugoslav who was also a professor at the City University of New York, a citizen of Croatia, but a Serb, was for Croatian sovereignty, but not at the cost of Serbs living there. The transition in Yugoslavia, Denitch argued, should have been the least painful in Eastern Europe, because they had been most open, but nationalists had squandered it all. He knew of no house without arms now. He nevertheless expressed some modest hope that it would sort itself out, because, "After all, the Yugoslavs are no more uncivilized than the Irish."

At the final plenary, titled "After the Flood: The Future of the Left After Communism," Daniel Singer, author of a recent article in *Monthly Review,* imaginatively titled "Prometheus Rebound?," asked if our future was one of capitalism from here to eternity. We were into a period of unprecedented experiment. Arguing against anti-socialist voices in Eastern Europe, he made the point that capitalism was not just Park Avenue and the Champs Elysées. It was also Brazil. "Whatever Boris Yelstin might think," he insisted, "to see a US supermarket is not to see the light." Other speakers focused more on the US. The US moved to a different rhythm, said sociologist Norman Birnbaum. It needed an anti-model for its ever more desperate triumphalism. Cornel West, philosopher and professor, addressing the audience in the stirring style of a preacher, spoke of the spiritual sterility of the *Pax Americana.* The three questions facing the left in this situation were: Where are we? What is to be done? How to do it? West criticized the textual turn of the academic left and incited them to deal with actual historical agents acting in circumstances not of their choosing. The US left had journals, but not mass political organizations. There was a need to muster the imagination and to harness the potential of ordinary people.

I ran into an Irish printer who had been active in my Labour Party constituency, who was working in New York, and was one of the several thousand attending this conference. He found it surprising and fascinating. It was utterly different from anything he had experienced of America until then. Most of what went on was intelligent and stimulating, but one plenary session on the Gulf War was broken up by protesters, who argued that there was no gay person on the platform and that gay people were more oppressed by the Gulf War than anyone else. To my shock, many people in the hall applauded them. I looked at my printer comrade sitting next to me and our faces registered how different this was from the Irish left. I had many intense conversations in my days in New York, at the conference and after it, with old and new comrades of the US and international left. I also visited *Monthly Review.* There was an open invitation to come every Wednesday for a brown bag lunch and seminar in the middle of the large loft in midtown Manhattan, where their journal and books were published. The Wednesday nearest to the annual SSC was considered a gala, because there were always so many people from out of town. They called on me to speak about Ireland, which I did, but I opened it up to the state of the European left. I was interviewed on radio by WBAI about this, too.

I then traveled to Philadelphia, a place that was once home, where I had many layers of connection to American society, to try to get to the bottom of what was happening in this society. The shops were full of all the same sort of collateral kitsch as New York. There were t-shirts with the US flag proclaiming, "These colors don't run" and with George H. W. Bush saying, "Read my lips,

Saddam." If you were thirsty, you could have a "combat cooler,"
a soda in a camouflage can. The country was on a massive "We're
number one" marketing binge. Flags and yellow ribbons were
everywhere. The Gulf War was part of every scenario. It came into
every conversation. It was a topic on every television talk show.
There was a new local angle in every day's newspaper. The war's
iconography was part of every scene the eye surveyed. Yet, the further I got drawn into America, the less real the Gulf seemed. There
was something about the US that made the rest of the world seem
unreal. It was a society so turned in on itself. The discourse about
the Gulf War was far less about the Gulf than about America. The
people of Iraq, the devastated homes, the burning oilfields were
only extras and props in this narcissistic national drama.

All was not as it seemed here. Beneath the bravado, beneath the
massive support for Bush and the Gulf War, there was enormous
ambiguity. I asked one of my brothers, a truck driver, what he
thought of all the flags and yellow ribbons around Springfield, PA,
our suburban hometown. He liked them, he said. Did he think the
war was right, then? No, he said, he didn't necessarily think that it
was right, but he thought that, once it had started and the troops
were in there, it had to be supported. Another brother, a high
school teacher, took a harsher view: "It was scary. The American
people didn't care if it was right or wrong. They just wanted to
win." In a *Cheers*-type bar, where my sister was well known, one
young male after another came to speak to me out of earshot of the
rest to tell me how critical they were of the war, but how difficult
it was to say so. Within homes, people confessed to feeling intimi-
dated about not putting out yellow ribbons.

Noam Chomsky, as active against this war as the one in Vietnam,
argued that support for the war was very thin, that scepticism and
disbelief were barely below the surface, but that each person felt
alone with it, because most had no forms of association that would
affirm or mobilize it. Even within the military, the support was
thinner than might be imagined. A US Marine officer, who asked
me not to give his name or rank if I wrote about him, was scathing

about the war and the politicians who were responsible for it, but left ignorant eighteen-year-old kids to deal with it. There was more critical thinking in the officer corps of the armed services than anybody realized, he told me. In a postgraduate course on strategic studies for military personnel, much of what was discussed, such as exploitation and colonialism, would have been considered treasonous twenty years ago. The country seemed to be riding high, telling itself that it had kicked the Vietnam syndrome, that it was back on center stage after feeling like a spectator to history during 1989, that it had put Europe and Japan and the third world back in their place. But the victory was hollow and everybody knew it, underneath. Already, even before the main victory parade, it had been spoiled by the realization that there had been no real fight, by the pathetic desolation of the Kurds, by the returning parasitism of the Kuwaitis, by the resentment of veterans of bloody combat in the Second World War, Korea, and Vietnam at the glorification of "a few days in a sandbox" as a war.

But these things were the least of it. The truth was that, although the US had reasserted a kind of political and military supremacy and Hollywood had not ceased to assert cultural supremacy, there was no longer the economic base to sustain it. Japan was still buying up Manhattan and Hollywood. The truth was that, as Rev. David Gracie of the American Friends Service Committee said to me, "There is a big vacuum where a sense of national purpose should be." The truth was that, it was a society that did not believe in itself in the way it pretended. It was a society where the symptoms of decline were unmistakable. The Spring 1991 issue of *Dissent* was a special edition titled *Social Breakdown in the United States? Signs of Crisis, Symptoms of Decay*. Articles outlined a scenario featuring the specifics of crime, drugs, aids, homelessness, racism, collapse of cities, crisis in education, financial scandals, declining productivity, but also more general phenomena such as the dissolution of social bonds and norms, an unprecedented collapse of meaning, a monumental eclipse of hope, a wave of palpable unease spreading across the whole spectrum of American society. Introducing the theme, Irving Howe, literary and social critic, wrote of a malaise, a sense of things coming apart, of social problems becoming intractable, of a crisis too deep to be corrected by any normal upturn in the economy or quick fix of government intervention. One sign of breakdown he advanced was the lack of any consensus on what even constituted the problem, let alone a solution. The spurious solutions advanced: 1) to allow the free market to proceed in its majestic mystery; 2) to improve character, especially the character of the poor and oppressed; 3) to acquiesce in the sophisticated resignation of the limits of social policy, all failed utterly to understand the problem. The process of breakdown was accelerated in the Reagan years, the years Barbara Ehrenreich referred to in her book as *The Worst Years of Our Lives*. So many symptoms. Authors came at it from all possible angles and the evidence mounted to a compelling case. The rising popularity of fantasy and the fact that the basic myth of upward mobility was no longer rags-to-riches achievement but winning the lottery, was, according to Jim Chapin, a shift from the psychology of work to the psychology of lotto, a testimony to the irrational side of capitalism and to a deep loss of faith in rationality and in the efficacy of human effort. Todd Gitlin, asked from where did *American Psycho* and *Die Hard 2* and all the murderous stuff that flowed down the channels derive their energy. The culture was beset by a zeitgeist that slashed and burned. It was driven by a cynicism so deep as to defy parody.

I found such sensibility everywhere I looked. The current crop of American films, such as *Metropolitan, Avalon, Where the Heart Is*, to name just the ones I had seen, were pervaded by a strong sense of America having reached its peak and hurling now along a downward curve. Paul Kennedy's book *The Rise and Fall of the Great Powers* described a cyclical process, in which supremacy was established through economic strength, followed by military spending to maintain supremacy, followed by economic decline. The US and USSR were in decline and Europe and Japan were in the ascendant, the argument went. Barbara Ehrenreich's other recent book, *Fear of Falling: The Inner Life of the Middle Class*, was another of many recent titles giving expression to various aspects of the economics, politics, sociology, and psychology of decline. Indeed, I could detect it on every city street, in every suburban mall, in every family gathering, in every professional encounter, in every newspaper, on every television show. Walking down Philadelphia's Market Street one day, a dirty, drunken homeless man tumbled about on the sidewalk as I passed. Passing at the same time were a gang of youths, who argued loudly and abusively with each other for several blocks about whether his condition was his own fault or not. There was such a sharp edge to the argument, perhaps because none of them could be sure it might not someday be them, because none of them really knew whether they could trust this society that their own best efforts would be enough. Talking to Americans of all sorts, especially if daring to probe, revealed an enormous disaffection not far under the surface. Most often it was a list of specific gripes that were combined with a heavy but vague and inarticulate angst that was bigger than all of them. Pressing further went along alternative paths, such as blaming politicians or reducing large-scale sociological problems to small-scale psychological ones, or simply coming up against a wall of impenetrability. I asked one longtime friend, a journalist writing obituaries, what his political philosophy was. "I don't know," he said, "I just know that, when I look around in the world, I don't like much of what I see."

There was still such material plenitude. There was so much living space. There were so many gadgets. Yet there was such massive inequality. The top 20 percent took 50 percent of the income, whereas the bottom 20 percent took only 3.7 percent. The 60 percent in the middle were full of anxiety about how to hold what they had. The class divide was bound up with all sorts of racial and sexual and generational tensions. The generational tension was perhaps most symptomatic of decline. There was a sense that the middle generation, my generation, called boomers (i.e., born of the postwar "baby boom"), were the best educated and most productive, that with us this society had peaked, that we had achieved a standard that surpassed our parents, but would not be reached by our children. This tension expressed itself in various ways. At its most basic, there was resentment in relation to the federal Social Security system, a fear in the middle generation that the older generation, who were living longer, were using up resources that would not be replaced by the younger generation. The tension was not limited to the dynamics of national distribution. There was an international dimension as well. Deep down, many knew that this nation could not sustain the proportion of the world's wealth it had been taking. Much of this country's sickness, Dave Gracie said to me, was rooted in "trying to hold on to a lifestyle that is a scandal to the rest of the world."

There was so much that was just so out of kilter here. There was a long-running saga in my own family about a relative who should be committed, but was living on her own, drugged up, a danger to herself and everyone around her the moment she failed to take her medication. With the trend to deinstitutionalization of mental patients, many were wandering around, destitute and dangerous, on the streets. Side by side with this was the lavish care and attention to the exquisitely tortured psyches of the rich and the psychoanalysis of their pampered pets. This did not feel like a society that had won, a society that represented the victory of liberal democracy after the downfall of the alternative system, a society that had proved that it was number one after an easy military victory. However, there was so much distraction, so much chatter, so much clutter. There were so many television shows, so many things to buy, so many hard-sell-can't-fail schemes to get rich, to know yourself, to find God, to lose weight, to buy sex. There was so much talk about Kitty Kelley's book on Nancy Reagan, about what happened at the Kennedy compound at Easter, about a gay palimony suit against Merv Griffin, about whether the Mets would beat the Phillies. What did these preoccupations reveal about the collective psyche? What sort of society was it that threw up *The Simpsons* and *Mutant Teenage Ninja Turtles* as its dominant icons? A campy, cynical, childish, desperate society. A society in decline.

These topics and images were nearly all there was left of a common culture, and large numbers were utterly alienated from them or related to them only in a cynical, camped-up way. The fact was that, although Americans shared a common space, they shared less and less in the way of a common culture.

There had been a drastic erosion of civil society. There had been a decline in churches, unions, political organizations, even neighborhoods. "There is no community anymore," I was told again and again. There was less and less public space, even for shopping, which seemed one of the last public places where people came out of their separate private spaces. It was not only the big old city center department stores that were deserted, but even the suburban shopping malls. Everyday piles of catalogues arrived in the post, and shopping channels on television paraded a never-ending supply of goods that could be ordered by phone and delivered to the door. Such areas of public space that did still exist were beset with conflict and crisis. The much discussed crisis in education on one level was anxiety about declining standards, about illiteracy and sub-literacy, about abysmal ignorance of basic geography. There were so many levels of irony in the situation. "American students rank near the bottom of the world in skills, but at the very top in self-esteem. Yet our formula for self-improvement is always more self-esteem, not more knowledge," wrote Jim Chapin. On another level, there was a bitter debate about curriculum in which many of the larger tensions of American society were being played out. Although there never was a centralized education system and therefore no common curriculum in the US, there was nevertheless a common worldview underlying its decentralized education systems, and there was a pattern in the diverse debate coming in the wake of the challenges to this worldview in recent decades.

Basically, the right blamed the decline in standards on the left, on the 1960s countercultural critique of white, male, Eurocentric (or Amerocentric, more accurately) education and called for a return to classical texts. Allan Bloom's *The Closing of the American Mind* was an instant bestseller in this mode. There were complaints about the "thirdworldization" of American education and calls for a return to a common culture. There was a backlash against race studies and gender studies and peace studies that was part of a more general backlash against antiracist and antisexist and antiwar movements. The *Philadelphia Inquirer*, when I was there, carried an article by a final-year English student at the University of Pennsylvania complaining about the DWEM-bashing (i.e., Dead White European Males) that she claimed had become the orthodoxy of her faculty. On many campuses, there was a reaction against what was called PC ("political correctness"), and in many institutions there was a reaction against speech codes banning racist and sexist language and against affirmative action and race and gender quotas. The PC debate currently raging was but the latest episode in a long struggle between the explaining and explained classes. The left, which was once a force in American society, at least within the universities, did not speak with one voice on all issues in this debate over the production of knowledge. Many saw the absurdities of instructing students on the irrelevance of canonical texts they hadn't even read and the convoluted poststructuralist and postmodernist texts that had replaced them. They also saw the dangers of an evasive, noncritical and noncommunicating pluralism based on the politics of identity. It was a complex debate about how to include excluded voices and how to allow for cultural diversity, without indulging mediocrity and fragmentation; about how to be critical of received tradition and to open it out, while still preserving some sort of a common tradition and a dialogue within it. This was my position.

Twentysomethings, who had come of age in this flabby, anything-goes world of protean pluralism, complained that they had no bearings, but it was doubtful that any Great Books panacea would bring definition to their diffuse, unfocused, confused selves. There were so few points of common reference anymore. It was becoming less and less possible to talk to anyone who had read the same book or article, heard the same radio program, or even seen the same television program. It was all so fragmented.

American television was so broken up into such tiny little bits, with such constant interruption for commercials, that I found it hard to watch. I found that I actually knew far more about US. television programs than anyone I met there, but it was very different to watch *LA Law* or *thirtysomething* in Europe, where the same programs seemed far more coherent than they did here. Where would it end, I wondered. Some, especially if they were coming forth as candidates in the upcoming presidential election, offered hope of some sort of upswing, but the odds were against it. "More likely," Gar Alperovitz argued in *The Nation*, "is a continuing trend of decay and failure that will slowly destroy all the old beliefs, leading first to ever deeper disillusionment, then to profound apathy, then to de-legitimation of the existing system, then to anger, and possibly after a long dark winter of discontent, to a demand for something different: for perestroika, for reconstruction, American style." I doubted it.

Why was the left such a reduced presence in US society? Outside of certain journals, conferences, and universities, people hardly knew it was there. There was so much disaffection in this society and yet so little evidence of a movement to focus and mobilize that disaffection. Where had all my old comrades gone? I was looking for what was left of the New Left of the 1960s and wondering how they saw the world now. The winds had shifted and blown many of them off the course they set back then. In Philadelphia and New York, I sought them out. Most of them were still there, but with scaled-down schemes, smaller projects, more modest expectations, and without much of a movement behind them anymore. "It is more disorganized, more decentralized, more reformist now," Jack Malinowski told me, now working at the American Friends Service Committee. Also working there was Dave Gracie, who remembered the blaze of our former days but believed that there were "still embers that can be lit into fire now and again." Making inroads into the legal profession for some time now were my friends David Kairys and David Rudovsky, who were celebrating twenty years in their radical civil liberties law practice together.

David Kairys had edited a book, *The Politics of Law*, discussed on many talk shows and used in many law schools. He had just won an important case representing an FBI agent who sued the FBI for racial harassment. Ann Doley was fundraising for left projects. As she saw it: "There are lots of good progressive people out there and there is lots of good work going on, but somehow it doesn't seem to add up to a whole. You can't do community organizing, if there is no community." "I just keep going out of outrage," Ed Herman told me, not knowing whether anything would come of it all, just knowing that there had to be a fightback. Herman was emeritus professor at the Wharton School of Economics, and the author of many books critical of US foreign policy. One, written with Noam Chomsky, called *Manufacturing Consent: The Political Economy of Mass Media*, became a classic. He wrote a column for *Z* magazine and edited another magazine, *Lies of Our Times*. Eric Canepa, a musician involved in running the New York Marxist School and the journal *Socialism & Democracy*, was a dynamo of networking. Otherwise, he thought, "ships might pass in the night" in these days, when the left was so fragmented within itself.

But not all had found such projects to keep going. Some had retreated into private life. Some, especially if they were university teachers in philosophy, sociology, politics, law, psychology or such fields, held jobs that had progressive potential but belonged to no political organizations. Marx Wartofsky, for example, was a professor of philosophy at the City University of New York. He felt that his only way of expressing his critique and commitment was through doing his job conscientiously, but regretted that he had "no political ambience." If something came along that felt right, he would go with it. So would lots of others. There was a massive, unorganized left here that could possibly be activated again. Richard Bernstein, another philosopher, spoke of "cycles of potentiality." He was, after all, around in the 1950s, when things didn't seem very promising, either. There was still the memory and aspiration of the 1960s there, and it was important "to keep alive a certain story." Even the most upbeat admitted to moments of despair. Others had given way to it altogether. Addressing himself to this, Gar Alperovitz wrote in *The Nation* of how easy it was in dark political days to despair and to confuse a difficult moment of history with inevitability. He cautioned against giving away the future by default. Instead, he incited the left "to undertake a long, reconstructive, community-building march through the painful debris of a society in stalemate," to build a new progressive movement that "might write a radically new and dynamic chapter of history in the new century."

I reflected on what I had experienced during the month in America and wrote a four-part series on the US published in the *Irish Times* and a longer analytical piece in in the *Irish Review* called "America: Symptoms of Decline," which did not go down very well with my family. My GI Joe brother was particularly enraged.

Meanwhile, I turned my attention back to Eastern Europe. America might have believed it was back on the center stage of history, but I didn't think so. I saw the center stage to the east. The year 1991 brought much tumult, as the tide of this New World Order swept through the whole of Eastern Europe. Although the structural similarities were most striking, there were distinctive developments in each country. They were all undergoing a transition from socialism to capitalism and an integration into the global system, but the disintegration of existing social relations took more disastrous forms in some places than in others. It was especially brutal in Yugoslavia, as its various ethnicities pulled away from one another with explosive results. In June 1991, Slovenia and then Croatia declared their independence. The Yugoslav army moved against separatist forces. It lasted only ten days in Slovenia, but persisted for four years in Croatia, while spreading to Bosnia and Kosovo for the rest of the decade. I found it especially shocking to see it unfold in places where I had so recently been, such as Dubrovnik and Sarajevo. I kept in touch with people I knew as best I could. Sometimes I even saw them on television, often taking opposite sides. One night I was stunned to see Kathy Wilkes, an Oxford philosopher with whom I had walked the walls of Dubrovnik a decade earlier, witnessing the destruction of Dubrovnik on my screen. My Yugoslav friends told me about their conditions of life: their institutes closed, libraries burned down, colleagues and comrades turning on each other, some rising and others falling in the political scheme of things, some reduced to selling their possessions on the streets to be able to eat. On the news I saw and heard the rhetoric of denunciation of comrades, the destruction of property, the dispossession of refugees, the tales of rape and murder, the dissolution of the social fabric. Although I was no longer starry-eyed about the "new man," I was still shocked at the atrocities inflicted by those schooled under socialism.

Sam and I had been planning to travel to Yugoslavia in July 1991, but, with the country in a state of civil war and foreign ministries warning their nationals not to go there, Yugotours canceled all its bookings there. They offered us alternative arrangements in Bulgaria, which we accepted, although I still wanted to find a way to get to Yugoslavia and hoped to take up an invitation to participate in a roundtable in Subotica in October. Meanwhile, the *Irish Times* had commissioned an article about life on the ground in Yugoslavia but agreed to take one on Bulgaria. Since our last time in Bulgaria, Communist leader Todor Zhivkov had been deposed in a central committee coup, the Bulgarian Communist Party changed its name to the Bulgarian Socialist Party, renounced its leading role, and announced multiparty elections, which it won in June 1991. We arrived in Slantchev Briag (Sunny Beach), previously a thriving international resort on the Black Sea, to find it half empty. Hotel after hotel was closed. There were no queues for dinner and there were loads of spaces on the beach. The sun and the sea were as glorious as ever, as was the luxury of sitting and sipping the local brandy after strolling along in the balmy evening air past the flea market stalls selling matryoshka dolls, carved wooden boxes, red woven bags, and pirated tapes.

However, the consequences for Bulgarians of the decimation of their tourism, in the wake of the collapse of Comecon (the economic system of trade between communist countries), were dire.

The whole economy of this region, not only its service sector, but also its agriculture and manufacturing, had been built around the tourist industry. All transactions between the former socialist countries now had to be made in hard currency, and most Eastern Europeans didn't have the money to pay for a holiday in Bulgaria anymore. Those who did, now that there was new freedom to travel, were using it to go where they had not been able to go until now, not to Bulgaria. Gone were the Russians, Czechs, Hungarians, Poles, and East Germans who holidayed here in summers past. Only the West Germans, Dutch, British, and Irish remained. The resort was a world unto itself for tourists who were only interested in the floor show here, and the food there, and the black-market rate for the lev from day to day. Here, you got the impression that every Bulgarian was a black marketeer. Here, there was little evidence that anyone ever had anything to do with socialism. The only red flags to be seen in Sunny Beach were those warning that the sea was rough.

Outside the resort was another Bulgaria. When I told people I met in the cities and towns and villages that here was the most blatant black market I had ever seen, they said they were ashamed, even though it was not part of their own lives. The demise of Comecon meant that export earnings were plummeting while import costs were skyrocketing. Inflation was spiraling, with the cost of living outstripping wages. Prices were low for Western tourists, as the rate of exchange (both official and unofficial) was very favorable, but for locals more and more commodities were moving beyond their reach. People said they only thought of buying food now, not even clothes, let alone furniture, cars, or holidays. In the nearest town, the ancient and picturesque harbor of Nessebur, where I went looking for the offices of the Bulgarian Socialist Party (BSP), the other sort of red flag was still flying. In through a courtyard, I found a taverna, a lecture hall, a clinic, and upstairs offices. Within a few moments, we were having tea and talking politics with the party secretary and other comrades. A few nights later, we returned for an evening in the taverna courtyard with other comrades to drink beer and brandy and hear further stories and points of view.

As I knew the main lines of the high politics of Bulgaria, I wanted to know how they had experienced the transformation of their society at a local level and in their own lives. They said that they wanted democracy and renewal, but didn't agree with those saying that everything before was so black. They agreed that they made mistakes, but didn't want to see what they had created that was of value be destroyed. They were different ages, sexes, and professions and they were eager to tell their tales of how their lives were before and after, in a way that was full of social and self-criticism, and yet determined and proud. They insisted that the transformation of their party was for real. Because party, state, and trade union were all tied together before, party meetings were dull and taken up with details. There was no real political debate, although there may have been stories or jokes about Zhivkov over coffee. Now, party organization in the workplace was out, along with democratic centralism. The local party organizations were democratic and lively and full of debate. This building where we sat was formerly a closed-off place occupied by fifteen full-time workers. Now, it was wide-open and full of a different sort of activity, although there were only two full-time workers, and space had been given over to a medical clinic. They did not think that it should be forgotten that it was their party that initiated the whole reform process.

Over the bridge to New Nessebur was the office of the Union of Democratic Forces (UDF), the coalition of opposition parties that was in power in this town. In the window were the voting figures for this area from the last election: 55 percent UDF/44 percent BSP. There was also an ad for West cigarettes showing a slim blonde girl offering one to a beefy Red Army general. They spoke bitterly of the past forty-five years. One showed me a map of the detention camps where people were sent for wearing long hair or tight jeans or for telling political jokes. She complained that she was educated to be a lawyer, but could not practice her profession, because her family were not communists. I asked her if she thought there was anything that should be preserved from these years. She replied in the negative. I asked how people could live with it all those years. She swung around behind me and rammed her arm into my back. "With a Kalashnikov at your back!" she exclaimed forcefully. Another spoke in equally negative terms of the communists, but said that the amazing thing was that young people were joining this party. The UDF was severely divided. It spanned a wide spectrum from right to left and it was doubtful how long an alliance of greens, social democrats, and monarchists could hold. I spoke to Bulgarians who wanted restoration of monarchy. One told me of a relation who had come all the way from Australia "to vote for the king." There was discussion in the parliament about having a referendum on whether to be a republic or a monarchy. "Better to be ruled by one wise man than the rabble. When the poor come to power, they rob you. Better to be ruled by somebody already rich." The king, Simeon Saxe-Coburg-Gotha, who had ruled briefly as a child, before monarchy was abolished by referendum in 1946, later returned, reclaimed royal estates, and was elected prime minister in 2001.

In Bourgas, the nearest city to the resort, an hour's ride on the local bus, I found it interesting to find streets named after Marx and Lenin side-by-side with one named after Czar Boris, the father of Simeon, who had allied himself with the Axis powers in the war. Scurrying around were a busload of Canadians wearing t-shirts with "King's Kids" in English on the front and "We love Jesus" in Bulgarian on the back. I asked one of them what king this was and found out it was meant to be Jesus and not Simeon. "God told us to come to Bulgaria," she told me, as she boarded the bus to continue on her mission to sing and speak of her divine monarch to bemused Bulgarians. Campaigning was underway for a September 29 election. Public opinion polls showed support fairly evenly balanced between left and right, red and blue. There were rallies and posters and leaflets being produced, but it was in the media that the election was essentially being fought. The rules of the game in this arena were being hotly contested. Television and radio were blue, supporters of UDF told me gleefully. Socialists complained that small right demonstrations looked massive on television, whereas media coverage of left ones focused on where old people were clustered and picked out a few sentences from speeches that distorted meaning. I was fascinated by live sessions of the Bulgarian parliament on television, as well as by locals crowded around, watching it. The parliament and their audience were packed, and there was a sense that much was at stake. At one point, two MPs, both UDF, came to blows. One night there was intense discussion over the whole historical relationship between Bulgaria and the Soviet Union, and controversy over whether to deal now with the USSR or the constituent republics.

Away from the network of urban intellectuals, which was the usual world in which I moved, I went into the fields, villages, collective farms, and rural homes, where I heard of the coming crisis of agriculture. A struggle between former owners of the land and those who cultivated it all these years was looming. They spoke of how they erected buildings and planted orchards and asked how it could be right that these would be taken from them. The owners didn't want to work the land, but they did want large rents, which would make it difficult for those who worked the land to survive. Agronomists who went into collectivization with great enthusiasm in their youth insisted that life in these villages was 100 percent better than it was before and they did not want to go back. They had lived the difference between capitalism and socialism and didn't want to return to capitalism, the director of a cooperative farm said emphatically. These villages voted heavily for the BSP. In the home of a family of rural teachers, I got a rundown of all the trials and tribulations besetting education at this crossroads from the viewpoint of several generations; from problems of pay (one young teacher showed me the lemonade-making operation he ran to supplement his income) to curriculum (Dimitrov had not only been disinterred but eradicated from the history of Bulgaria). Hearing that I was a philosopher, they informed me that Marxism was out and Kant, Hegel, and Wittgenstein were in. One recent graduate told me that she had just run into her former teacher of Marxism-Leninism and she was in the opposition now. When a machine operator in a petrochemical plant in Bourgas arrived home from work one evening, he addressed me with a most out-reaching and wide-ranging analysis of what was happening in the world and what prospects there might be for socialism down the road. Even after all the disappointment and betrayal that the experiment in socialism had brought to Bulgaria, he reflected that socialism would have to come from developed society, not from an underdeveloped place like this. Moreover, he said, renouncing dictatorship of the proletariat, it would come from intellectuals, not from manual workers. If they were all like him, I would have to disagree.

I left full of anxiety about life here and elsewhere. I couldn't stop thinking about these lives being turned upside down. Despite what many Soviet citizens wanted, the Soviet Union was coming apart. In March 1991, there was a referendum about the future of the USSR in which 77.8 percent voted for the USSR to con-tinue. The authorities in several republics (although not all parts of them) boycotted the referendum, but the majority participated with high voter turnout. In Russia, the result was 73 percent. In Ukraine, it was 81.7 percent. Nevertheless, the USSR was hurtling toward its demise. It was not only the different republics pulling away from one another, but different forces with different visions of what their societies should be.

Paradoxically, the end was accelerated by a move to defend it. In August a group of inept, hard-line communists declared a state of emergency and detained Gorbachev in his dacha in Crimea. Crowds gathered in the streets of Moscow, called for a general strike, and demanded the return of Gorbachev. Yeltsin climbed on a tank and made himself a symbol of this resistance. Within days, the coup collapsed and its leaders were arrested. In Ireland, Michael O'Riordan and Eoin O Murchú of the CPI defended the coup. The Soviet ambassador, Guerman Gventsadze, defended the coup and then twisted and turned when it did not succeed. Gorbachev returned to Moscow, but was humiliated by Yeltsin, giving him orders in the Duma, dramatizing the shift in power relations that would seal the fate of the USSR. Yeltsin decreed the termination of the CPSU and seizure of all party assets. Gorbachev acquiesced and resigned as general secretary. Various republics declared their independence, while others formed a Commonwealth of Independent States, which never materialized. On December 25, 1991, Gorbachev resigned as president of the USSR, declared the office defunct, and ceded its powers and resources to Yeltsin as president of the Russian Federation. The USSR ceased to exist. The red flag was lowered over the Kremlin and the pre-revolutionary flag was raised in its place. I followed these events blow-by-blow via the mass media, with a sense of deep mourning.

Those who thought this would be a happily-ever-after tale of freedom and prosperity were disappointed almost immediately. It was the Wild East. It was economic collapse and social upheaval. It was a raw and ruthless form of capitalism, such as those advocating it from outside had never experienced. It was an orgy of accumulation by dispossession. It was not the expected rise from second to first world, but a plunge into third world. Public assets were privatized. Vouchers were distributed with a veneer of equity, but seized by the various ruses of a rapidly emerging oligarchy. Ordinary citizens were disoriented and dispossessed. This "shock therapy" resulted in millions of excess deaths as well as decline in births. Studies later published by the UN and *Lancet* revealed stark statistics connecting a rise in mortality to this mass privatization, unemployment, impoverishment, and social turmoil. Yeltsin, who rose through stirring up resentment of party authority and material privilege, soon strode the land like a tsar, accumulated wealth, and spawned corruption beyond anything previously seen. People demanded democracy and got mafiocracy instead. I continued to follow the life stories of those I knew into the 1990s. Letters told me that their institutions had collapsed and they had lost their jobs, or that their institutions had been restructured and they kept their jobs, but their communities had collapsed. One wrote to me that he felt "like a man running after an ever-faster train." Another said it was living in a world where "To be is to buy."

Not only were the GDR and USSR gone, but Czechoslovakia and Yugoslavia also disappeared from the map of the world as the decade unfolded. Most tragic were the demise of the USSR and Yugoslavia as they splintered into murderous mini-ethnicities. People who lived and worked together in harmony, even in intimacy, became enemies. I did not believe, as some asserted, that all this ethnic hostility was seething under the surface the whole time. I knew too many people there who testified otherwise and lived in shock as it overtook them. Others gave way in the face of it, and the most shocking thing to me was to find comrades and colleagues, who were by no means closet Ustashe or Chetniks, take positions in nationalist parties and governments that took the place of Yugoslavia. Much of this nationalism was a response to a vacuum, to the collapse of a social order. It was people's retreat into a romanticized past to get their bearings to negotiate their position in the present, within the new social order, that of globalized capitalism. It was a response to dislocation. Those who were railing against Tito and Yugoslavia and pining for their lost kings and national cultures were also flocking to the EU, NATO, Hollywood movies, and McDonald's hamburgers. I argued that nationalist disintegration was riptide and the overpowering wave of the future was integration into the New World Order of global capitalism. Nation-states, however much they multiplied, were more and more powerless against the power of stateless money. As I beheld Sarajevo become a powder keg, and fretted over the fates of those I had met there, I remembered what one of them said: there are higher ways of connecting people to each other than nations. Those of us who discussed all of this in that place were part of that higher way, and I felt compelled to defend that past against so many slanders. Nevertheless, I also had to come to terms with the fact that the ground had shifted underneath us.

I was still doing a lot of public speaking and media debating about all this. I took the occasion of an invitation to be keynote speaker at a conference at University College Galway to address it as "Socialism: A Blind Alley or a Long and Winding Road?" to reflect on the trajectory of history as we were experiencing it. The address was published as a pamphlet by a trade union, along with a response by Proinsias De Rossa, the leader of Democratic Left, an organization formed from a split in the Workers Party, which was torn apart by these historical events. His text was a shambling social democratic distancing from the fate of these regimes.

Another Democratic Left was formed in Britain from the ruins of the Communist Party of Great Britain (CPGB), which ended in 1991. DL was formed as successor organization, initially as a party, but then as a campaign group/think tank, and survived only until 1998. Some members, who refused this path, joined the Communist Party of Britain (CPB), which had broken away from the CPGB in 1988 and took the daily paper, the *Morning Star*, with them. The CPB survived as the truer successor to the CPGB. *Marxism Today* produced a final issue in 1991. Its cover proclaimed in giant letters: "The End." Such splits and new formations were playing out throughout the world as the left struggled to come to terms with this turn of history.

There was much talk of a third way, which meant different things to different people. I was thinking of a need for a third way for the left, a path that would carry forward the best of the communist movement, even as it crashed and burned, and the social democratic movement, which seemed to be on the upgrade as a result of this downfall. Many reformed and renamed communist parties were becoming social democratic ones. This didn't turn out as well as some hoped, because what unfolded through the 1990s was not only the social democratization of communist parties but also the neoliberalization of social democratic parties. What I wished for was some fusion of the systemic thinking of communism with attention to the possibilities of transforming the system from within characterizing social democracy. The communist movement was too perfectionist, too adventurist, too maximalist, too coercive, too willing to sacrifice means to ends. The social democratic position was too unadventurous, too minimalist, too eclectic, too myopic, too pedestrian, too parliamentarist, too accommodating to capitalism, too willing to sacrifice ends to means.

I explored these ideas with Günter Grass when he came to Dublin. His book *From a Diary of a Snail* defended the social democracy from positions to its left. He admitted that the runaway stallion of the Weltgeist was more compelling, but from the point of view of the snail: "Many overtake me and later fall by the wayside." To be a social democrat, he said, was nothing to cheer about, nothing to dilate your pupils. It was to resist the temptation to jump, to leapfrog ahead, to mount the heaven-storming ladder. It was to be inconsistent, to expect only partial achievements, to distrust oneself above all. He wrote of the dark side of utopia and argued that flights into utopia lead from euphoria to depression, from exaltation to resignation. Yet he conceded, "Even in our dreams we sighted no new land. . . . Where is the push if nothing pulls? Something is always lacking. What? Serviceable foundations, a framework, formulations of goals. . . . What should be changed? Not everything at once." Over dinner, I kept coming back to his question: Where is the push if nothing pulls? He was open and engaging about it, but we both held our positions. However, the dominant discourse about a third way was not between different traditions of the left, but between left and right, between capitalism and socialism. The 1990s was the decade of the center, defined by theorists such as Anthony Giddens, and pursued in power by politicians such as Bill Clinton, Tony Blair, Gerhard Schröder. It basically accepted capitalism, not only abandoning struggle against it but a systemic critique of it.

Labour Left continued to organize on many issues, but its big battle was always about coalition with parties to the right. In the 1992 general election, Labour won more seats than ever: 33 of 166, and was in the pivotal position to decide what government could be formed. Labour went into coalition first with Fianna Fail

and then with Fine Gael and Democratic Left. Most members of
Labour Left supported a coalition for the first time, arguing that
Labour was strong enough to bring its policies to fruition. At the
very least, it might stem the tide of privatization and stop the erosion of the public sector. Michael D. Higgins became Minister
for Arts, Culture and the Gaeltacht, which was very popular with
the left. I saw less of him once he became a minister, but he did
launch the new edition of my book, *Marxism and the Philosophy
of Science* in Waterstones. Various left activists, including myself,
were appointed to public bodies. In my case, to the governing
board of Dublin Institute for Advanced Studies. Labour did pass
many progressive reforms, including abolition of university fees.
Labour Left never formally disbanded, but it was the de facto
end. I became less and less active in the Labour Party from this
time and sought projects at home or abroad that gave expression
to my more radical commitments. When traveling, I saw parties
I would join if I lived abroad, such as the PDS in Germany and
Synaspismos in Greece, and wished for such parties in Ireland. I
was involved in such international campaigns as those protesting
the seizure of PDS property, and defending Hans Modrow and
Markus Wolf when they were put on trial in the new Germany.

I was on the executive board of the Tom Johnson Foundation, a
LP think tank modeled on the Friedrich Ebert Stiftung (FES) and
Renner Institut. We had a number of meetings about setting up its
legal structure and making plans for various projects and seminars,
which never came to pass for many reasons, but primarily because
Michael D, who was in charge of it, was too preoccupied with the
demands of ministerial office. The FES was active in Ireland and
elsewhere during this period and drove much of the agenda for
this foundation. I found many of the FES co-sponsored seminars
on such topics as security architecture utterly mind-numbing. It
was blandly technocratic discourse. It was sometimes so abstract
that I could not see the point of it. When I asked who was the
enemy against whom Europe had to defend itself so urgently, no
one could tell me. I found most social democrats so boring. They

spoke vaguely of peace and democracy and equality and solidarity in such a bloodless way, neither in terms of concrete lives nor overall structures. I was still on the international affairs committee, which might have been important, because our party leader, Dick Spring, became Minister for Foreign Affairs, but he took little notice of our views. We especially took exception to his support for Yeltsin. At one point, most of the cabinet was lined up with a red carpet laid out for Yeltsin at Shannon Airport. They waited and waited, but he was too drunk to get off the plane, and flew away without meeting them. At a press conference, when he arrived back in Moscow, he just laughed it off.

I did a lot of freelance journalism. I became Irish correspondent for *Neues Deutschland*. I wrote a media column for *New Nation*. I appeared on many arts and current affairs programs on radio and television. I wrote reviews and cultural commentary for various publications, especially during 1991, when Dublin was European City of Culture. I was invited to its glittering launch at Dublin Castle, because I was giving a public lecture as part of its program of events. I acquired a press pass and got free tickets for many events. I still did features for the *Irish Times*, especially on my trips abroad. I wrote for a number of other journals. Some went the way of *New Nation* and disappeared: *Times Change, Making Sense, Graph, Crane Bag*. Others, such as *Irish Review, Irish University Review*, and *Irish Communications Review*, survived.

I had become quite involved in the Irish Writers Union (IWU) since its inception in 1986 and was on its executive board for several years. In 1992, I was elected chair. We had been campaigning for better contracts and against censorship. We had managed to acquire premises in Parnell Square through lottery funding. I was also on the board of the Irish Writers Centre, which was also home to the Dublin Writers Museum and other literary bodies. We ran writing workshops and had lots of meetings and events here, such as book launches and poetry readings. I found many of these lively and interesting, but others quite tedious. Some of the poetry readings were excruciating, even those by well-regarded poets. A lot of it seemed too esoteric, even masturbatory. My mission during my period as chair was to address the role of writers in society, and I organized a number of events to do this. I received invitations to give public lectures and write articles about this during this period. I was very critical of the lack of vision and failure of nerve in the task of coming to terms with the times, at least with scope and depth necessary, resulting in writers succumbing to the seductions and delusions of the age. There was a basic tension between an individualistic art-for-art's-sake position versus art as philosophical, political, and social expression, although it was rarely articulated so explicitly.

There were several international writers conferences in Ireland during these years. One was on the theme of literature as celebration, and the mood was to repudiate the connection between literature and politics. Most speakers affirmed literature as pure celebration and begged questions as to what to celebrate and why. The audience, on the whole, adopted an utterly idolatrous stance to speakers and clapped most loudly for the most anti-intellectual and antisocial statements, such as proclamations that there is no connection between art and politics and that a work of art evaporates with socio-historical inquiry. When one person from the floor asked, "What's it all for?," the prominent poet on the platform said that this was a dangerous question, a question asked by regimes. The most powerful voice of dissent did eventually come from the platform. Nigerian novelist Chinua Achebe not only embodied something antithetical, but told them that the powers-that-be would be very happy with the division of labor that the writers at this conference had staked out.

After 1990, visiting writers from Eastern Europe were to the fore in affirming individuality and mystification and repudiating ideology and social responsibility. Their audiences gushed at them about their courage and wisdom. I dissented on both counts. Most of them had kept their heads down and made careers under the previous regimes and only spoke against them after the regimes had fallen. They were equally cowardly in their relationship to the new orthodoxies in their societies. Their lauded insights were only echoes of the Western orthodoxy of bourgeois individualism. I don't know if I convinced any writers of my arguments, but Anthony Cronin, cultural advisor to Charles Haughey as taoiseach (prime minister), called my views appalling without articulating any argument against them, during an occasion when we were both speaking at the Kavanagh Yearly in Monaghan. Poet Michael Longley began speaking by saying sorry, but in a way that seemed more sarcastic than sincere. One participant wrote to me after the event to tell me how appalled he was by the sheer aggression aimed at me, along with the general failure to address my arguments. I found engaging in intellectual debate in Ireland very different from America. There was reluctance to confront differences head-on, and to duck and dive and gossip behind a person's back instead. There were people who wanted to change this and I did my best in universities and public forums to push this forward. Some IWU events I organized were very controversial, especially one where Eoghan Harris articulated a peon of praise to Hollywood and caricatured European drama and literature. I disagreed with his position, but was buzzed by the ideas and emotions it brought to the surface. We also held a debate on the *Field Day* controversy, after feminist fury erupted at the publication of a three-volume anthology that underrepresented female writing. We held debates on the role of satire, criteria for literary criticism, postcolonialism.

Another aspect of my role as chair of the IWU was negotiating its acceptance into Services Industrial Professional and Technical Union (SIPTU), the largest trade union in Ireland, as part of its cultural division. Another duty was meeting with Salmon Rushdie during the period in which he was living underground because Iranian supreme leader Ayatolla Khomeini had issued a fatwa against him for writing *The Satanic Verses*. It was all very clandestine. Along with other members of the IWU executive, we met in an upstairs room of the Abbey Theatre. I found him interesting, but utterly self-absorbed, perhaps understandably, given the fraught life he was living. We sympathized with his plight, defended him publicly, and were open to suggestions of what else we might do, but he seemed to want us to drop everything and devote ourselves exclusively to his defense.

Several substantial pieces I published during this time could be categorized as writing about writing. One, "Literature and the Zeitgeist," published in *Irish University Review*, was a polemic against the anti-intellectual assertion of the autonomy of literature and an analysis of the epistemological and ethical paralysis in contemporary culture as it shaped creative writing. Another, "Gender and Genre," argued that the fault lines opened by the social division of labor, in this case by the sexual division of labor, cut deeply into the whole process of writing, not only through the historical exclusion of women, but more profoundly through the psychological severing of human personality according to gender: through identification of the rational, the theoretical, the political as masculine; and the emotional, the experiential, and the personal as feminine. I showed how this psychosexual cleavage shaped writing and traced a certain dynamic in the struggle out of oppression toward liberation, transcending such dualisms to a more holistic vision and deeper empowerment. I later developed this into a theory about the history of knowledge and the effects of exclusion based on class, race, and gender. Both of these articles and the lectures I gave making these arguments were quite controversial. Some people hit against me, but others engaged intelligently and movingly.

I also published and lectured in the field of media studies and received invitations from various public bodies to hold workshops on interrogating the media to see below and beyond the surface stories. I brought media analysis to bear in my paper for a very lively "Imagining Ireland" conference in 1993 at the Irish Film Institute, one of a number of occasions when media producers, critics, and audiences came together. That year also saw the conference of the International Association for Mass Communication Research at Dublin City University. The keynote speech was delivered by sociologist Anthony Giddens, who described the process of globalization as a dialectic of unifying and fragmenting forces. He emphasized how decentered the whole process was, from the breakdown of personal relationships, to the downward spiral of Yugoslavia. He rejected both conservatism and socialism as solutions, and only offered a vague dialogic democracy, a politics of minimizing damage in a difficult and damaged world. Much of the conference continued in parallel sessions in the same mood: post-this, post-that, neither right nor left being appropriate concepts anymore, dissipating any promise of a coherent framework, seeing the world through a shattered mirror. In this atmosphere, media theorist Colin Sparks spoke of Marxism as "the philosophy that dare not speak its name." Taking a similar tone at another conference I attended at this time, on gender and colonialism at University College Galway, literary critic Terry Eagleton spoke of feeling like an endangered species as a male, middle-aged Marxist, fenced off by barbed wire with a sign saying: "Beware: It totalizes and reduces." I too was constantly engaged in polemics against the prevailing postmodernism during this time.

In 1993, I was back in the US. I spoke again at the Socialist Scholars Conference in New York. I was on a panel on the European left with Andre Brie of the German PDS and Luciana Castellina of the Italian Rifondazione Comunista. I was asked to introduce Gregor Gysi at a public meeting in Greenwich Village. I was honored to do this, but disappointed that Gysi didn't export so well, failing to connect with foreign audiences. It became a ritual of my trips to New York to come to the Wednesday lunches at *Monthly Review*. Comrades from many countries converged and related how the world looked from where they were. I had many rich encounters in and around the conference. I got to know people who had formed Committees of Correspondence, a breakaway from the CPUSA, with whom I shared many positions. I went to Philadelphia, too. It was always such a contrast to move from interactions with the New York intelligentsia to my family in suburbia. However, the suburbs were no longer so staid as they once were. Catching up during these years meant unfolding a tangled web of divorce, debt, disappearances, suicide, matters that I never imagined would touch my own family. My brother Joe, now a marine major, had his plans for a military career derailed by the downsizing of armed forces that accompanied the end of the Cold War and the advent of the New World Order. Not that the US was finished with foreign wars. Beginning with the Gulf War and moving to the Balkan wars, I still spent much of my political life protesting them, while my brother still took part in them through the reserves, eventually becoming a full colonel.

Still feeling the lure of the Balkans, Sam and I expanded our travels into Greece and Turkey. I didn't take to Turkey very well. I was nauseous much of the time and broke out in an itchy rash whenever I came into contact with water, whether in shower, pool, or sea. I did find Ephesus amazing. In contrast, I was especially engaged by Greece. During trips to Crete and Rhodes, I investigated the political spectrum and related strongly to the left coalition Synaspismos, although I didn't realize then how intense my involvement with the Greek left would eventually become.

Although I lived precariously, I had great freedom and I led an interesting and fulfilling life. However, in the early nineties, obstacles began to multiply. In Ireland, Sam and I lived in a small flat in Phoenix Court on Infirmary Road. It was also my primary place of work. I had my computer set up by a window overlooking the Phoenix Park. The building passed to new owners, who raised the rent by 50 percent and then undertook extensive renovations, which were extremely disruptive. We were without heat or running water and surrounded by noise and filth on a non-union, black economy building site riddled with theft, deceit, and drugs. At one point, the builder burgled the newly installed boilers and held them hostage for the landlord to pay more money. Next the fraud squad was on the case. Some mornings, I woke up crying with frustration and fury, feeling that there wasn't one square inch of the world where I had any power whatsoever. We endured all that for those months and began to get back to normal.

Finally, they sold the building for vacant possession and issued

us eviction notices. I went into class-struggle overdrive and organized all the tenants in the building to resist. Some of them had
never resisted anything, but they were stunned by this injustice
and all refused to go. I organized a ministerial visitation to the
flats. Emmet Stagg, the minister responsible for housing, told
tenants that right was on our side. Several other left politicians,
including Tony Gregory and Joe Costello, came around and said
the same. There were many pressures and threats bought to bear.
The landlord sued us for overholding, and we were given a date
to appear in court. Meanwhile, several of the tenants—three of
them retired nurses—began to crack. Two of them quarreled and
didn't speak for days, during which one of them died of a heart
attack, alone. Eventually, the emergency services gained entry and
found her body in a state of decomposition. A coroner's inquest
ensued. After this, the will to resist broke, and tenants began to
look for other homes. Only a nun and I wanted to continue. One
tenant found a place around the corner and told us there was a
suitable place for us, which we decided to take. We had a further
battle about our deposits. We agreed to pay back rent for the three
months overholding, minus our deposit. The other tenants were
robbed of their deposits.

During this bruising battle, another problem intensified. I had
been having ever more severe abdominal pains for several years,
and they became excruciating during this period. My doctor was
unable to diagnose the problem. On Christmas Eve in 1993, he
sent me to the emergency department of the Rotunda Hospital,
where I was told there was a large mass obstructing my abdominal organs. I was scheduled for a hysterectomy in January 1994.
During this surgery, I had a cardiac arrest. I came to consciousness
in the intensive care ward of another hospital. I saw no white light
and received no messages from beyond, although my mother, who
had heard many such stories on talk shows, kept suggesting that I
must have. I was still an atheist, but very reflective on the fragility
of life and inevitability of death.

I was living a life at the interstices of many institutions: universities, media, political parties, trade unions—but so precariously. At fifty, I assumed it would always be this way. Despite my high qualifications and hard work, employment security eluded me.

Until it didn't.

POSTCRIPT: ON PERESTROIKA AND ITS AFTERMATH

Ever since these years, when I was preoccupied with events in Eastern Europe and the world-historical overturning they set in motion, I have kept coming back to this period, sparked by its continuing resonance. My reflections have been set off often by the deaths of protagonists, the discovery of archives, the publication of new sources or conflicting narratives of the past coming into play in the present. The death of Gaspar Miklos Tamás reminded me of his renunciation of the neoliberal views he held in the 1990s and his subsequent return to Marxism. The deaths of Mikhail Gorbachev and Hans Modrow made me think about the different stances and parting of ways that occurred among communists. A colleague called my attention to the diaries of Anatoly Chernyaev, Gorbachev's chief foreign policy advisor, now held in the National Security Archive, because there was a paragraph about me during his period of working in the international department of the CPSU dealing with foreign communist parties. These diaries were full of intricate detail about Soviet life, especially within the party apparatus, intelligent reflection, and gossipy evaluation of people I knew. I became caught up in tracing his development from being a critical communist who believed in socialism while hating the empty jargon, the economic inefficiencies, the unnecessary restrictions, to giving up on socialism and taking the capitalist road, sometimes pulling against Gorbachev still speaking of a socialist path. By 1990, Gorbachev, Chernyaev, and those around them chose to cut loose from international communist parties, national liberation movements, and other socialist countries and found their preferred partners in their former adversaries, taking pride in their rapport with Bush, Thatcher, and Kohl. When deciding the fate of the GDR, it was Kohl rather than Modrow with whom they wanted to deal. However, the fate of millions was decided by their deliberations and decisions, which set in motion forces they did not foresee and could not control. Books, such as *Secondhand Time* by Svetlana Alexievich, and documentaries, such as *TraumaZone*, based on BBC footage edited by Adam Curtis, have vividly shown the devastation wreaked in so many lives forced into this capitalist transition. All of these sources have added much detail to my knowledge of this period, but nothing has changed my analysis of it. Even though the Soviet Union is so long gone, the lies about it continue and in a way that is meant to mobilize this negativity about the past for present purposes. For example, during the Russia-Ukraine War, it has become common to refer to Soviet Ukraine as if it were nothing more than a previous Russian occupation of Ukraine. For so many reasons, it continues to be important to tell the truth, the full and difficult truth, of this time.

CHAPTER 3

Another Brick in the Wall

FINALLY, AFTER SO MANY YEARS of much work but little pay and no security, I got a full-time, well-paid, and secure academic job. It was at Dublin City University, where I had been working part-time for fourteen years already. It was the time of the "Celtic Tiger." Universities were experiencing the boom along with other sectors of the economy and society. This rising tide did not lift all boats, but it did lift mine. There were new degrees and new positions. There was also the fact that, in the post–Cold War mood, Marxists didn't seem so dangerous anymore. Of course, I was highly qualified, with a doctorate, a public profile, and two big books, but that had not been enough before this to keep me from being bypassed in favor of less qualified people.

I was fifty in 1994 when things finally fell in place for me. Although the women of my generation, the baby boomers, arrived at menopause with a rash of books and a lot of fuss, I was too busy to take much notice of it. I threw myself into my job. I put in far more hours than anyone could have asked of me: designing new courses, preparing lectures, marking assignments and exams, supervising and examining theses, attending meetings, talking to colleagues and students, visiting students on work placements, and many more tasks. I arrived early and came home late, often exhausted, but sometimes blissfully happy, at having such purposeful and secure work.

It wasn't altogether smooth sailing, though. DCU was the new type of university that was designed to break from traditional academic disciplines and to adopt new modes of teaching, research, and administration more precisely aligned to the needs of the market. I embraced the interdisciplinarity, but worried about the marginalization of history and philosophy and other traditional disciplines. I was in favor of innovation, but actively opposed much about the new orthodoxy reshaping universities and driving objectionable and even nonsensical innovation. My agenda was formed more by 1960s liberation movements than by 1990s neoliberalism.

I was glad that attention was being paid to methods of university teaching. It had once been assumed that all that was required was to acquire knowledge of a subject and then go into the classroom and impart that knowledge. I knew that it was a far more creative and challenging task. I experimented with new teaching methods. Some, such as peer evaluation, I abandoned after one go, but others, such as course websites, learner diaries, and multimedia slideshows, I continued. I was involved in a number of task forces, pilot projects, brainstorming sessions, and committee meetings at DCU addressing the quality of university teaching and learning. In what was considered to be international best practice, there was a shift of emphasis from what the teacher was teaching to how the student was learning. The clever way of putting it was to say that the job was no longer to be the "sage on the stage" but the "guide on the side." I agreed with the basic thrust of this shift, but I did not agree with the downgrading of lecturing. I still felt that a well-prepared and well-delivered lecture could and should be a profoundly powerful part of student learning. I wanted to be the sage on the stage as well as the guide on the side. Another change was a requirement to submit module (or course) descriptors, which set out a structure and week-by-week plan, assessment procedures, and desired learning outcomes. There was some resistance to this, especially among those who just wanted to make it up as they went along and didn't want to be accountable to anyone. I agreed with this requirement and felt that this information should be available not only to students, but also to the university and the public. What I did find problematic was the narrowness and shallowness of some modules, which were so commercially driven. Students were given assignments involving designing celebrity websites or presenting branding campaigns. Some of the practical exercises were quite valuable, though, such as "news days," where students would design a national daily newspaper or evening news broadcast in real time.

The university itself was engaging in branding campaigns to sell itself that I found odd and alienating. One outside commercial company presented us with a branding strategy that threw around empty adjectives like "friendly," "networked," "innovative," but none of them to do with knowledge. At one workshop, we were asked to align all Irish universities with retail stores, so Trinity was Brown Thomas and DCU was Dunnes. It didn't end there, either. Students were referred to as "customers" and started to act like customers, too. Some treated university staff as servants and expected lecturers to be at their beck and call. They wrote presumptuous emails demanding that lecturers brief them on what they had missed when they didn't attend lectures, and rude ones complaining when they didn't get the marks they wanted. Students were also incited to regard themselves as brands. There were workshops instructing them on "how to build your own brand." I made it clear that I didn't regard students as customers and I refused to enter into quasi-commercial relationships with them.

Not all students were like this. Many were eager to learn and to take responsibility for the world. They were open to weighing contending points of view and working out their own positions and preparing to make their own contributions to the world. However, the dominant culture shaping them gave the edge to individualism and commercialism, and the dominant ethos in universities was going more and more in this direction. I felt constantly embattled by it, not only in dealing with the everyday consequences, but in articulating and opposing it on a wider scale. Others agreed with me, but hesitated to express such overt opposition to it.

I believed that the primary purpose of university education, particularly the undergraduate years, was to arrive at epistemological criteria for sorting out contending claims to knowledge, to scrutinize existing worldviews, and to lay the foundations of their mature worldviews. The absence of departments of philosophy, history, sociology, and literature in universities such as DCU was not conducive to this process. However, there was still scope, particularly in such public institutions, to bring these dimensions to bear in other ways. The courses (which came to be called modules during this time) that I introduced, of which I am most proud, were my undergraduate History of Ideas module and my postgraduate Worldviews module. These were taught to students doing degrees in communications, journalism, international relations, and development studies. My History of Ideas module covered the history of philosophy from the pre-Socratics to postmodernism, with a strong emphasis on the sociohistorical context of major intellectual movements. I also gave two final lectures, which went back on the whole canonical history and asked questions about who/what/where was included/excluded, focusing on exclusions of class, race, gender, and geography. I also taught different versions of a course on science, technology, and society to students of engineering and journalism. Here, too, I put a strong emphasis on sociohistorical context and critical questioning. At the postgraduate level, I taught philosophy of science to students focusing on science communication, most of them having science degrees, even doctorates.

Another area for my teaching was media studies. I taught a module on social history and television drama, focusing not only on narrative, but also on questions about what stories are told and what stories are not told. I also taught critical analysis of news and current affairs journalism for journalism students. In conventional news reporting courses, students were taught to structure their stories about who, what, when, where, why, and how. I turned this around and asked them to turn their critical scrutiny on the whole construction of the news agenda and to focus not only on the presences but the absences: to ask what was and was not in the news, who was in the news and who was not in the news

Some students found this eye-opening and thanked me for getting them to think in a whole new way. Others resisted it, complaining that worldviews didn't get them jobs, that there wasn't time in a newsroom to ask such questions, or that they would lose their jobs if they questioned the news agenda. I countered that everything they did was shaped by a worldview, but the difference was whether it was an off-the-shelf, ragbag, unreflective one or a serious and coherent one of their own that would tie together whatever they knew and bring everything they did to a higher level. I told them they were not in a newsroom now but at university and they did have time for questioning, and that the best journalists were the ones who thought about such questions. Those who were willing to question and to consider alternatives were the ones who eventually became editors of national newspapers, high-profile presenters, and correspondents and university professors. As for those who resisted, I rarely heard what became of them.

Students came to their studies with all sorts of problems and pressures. Because I had them write journals and because I was available to talk with them, I learned a lot about the obstacles they were facing. I was very shaken when a student attempted suicide, when another died in a road accident on her way to class, when another was attacked and stabbed with a needle and lived in fear of HIV infection. Others lived lives beset by drug addiction, prostitution, pregnancy, debt. I was as sympathetic and helpful as circumstances allowed. At the same time, I was wary of messers summoning excuses, even lies, about work they hadn't done. I dreaded opening my email when an assignment was due. So many computers crashed, disks corrupted, illnesses contracted on that day. Some students never asked for extensions, while others constantly did so. With one, I wondered how many grandmothers could possibly die during a three-year degree. A contrary example was a student who became pregnant during her studies, then asked for reading lists and assignments in advance, so she could use her summer to start her autumn work.

Some of the rituals of Irish and British academe still seemed strange to me. In the US, teachers simply submitted their marks to the central administration and that was that, whereas we had program boards, where we would scrutinize students' marks across all of their modules. It was interesting to see how my marks compared to those of others for the same students, but it wasted a lot of time for those who attended, because some colleagues didn't submit their marks on time and were not present to discuss how students were doing. At final exam boards of the year, there were external examiners who oversaw the quality of the curriculum and the fairness of marks allocated. I had the task of doing this at other institutions from BA to PhD level.

I marked rigorously. I gave clear guidelines about assignments and criteria to be used in assessing them. I could see that a lot of what students wrote was derivative and often undigested transfer of lecture notes and readings into essays with no real comprehension or reflection. Sometimes there was even out-and-out plagiarism, despite explicit university policy and my own warnings against it. Some lecturers let it go, because the bureaucracy of taking disciplinary action was so tedious and time-consuming, but I pursued it. The same lecturers never failed anyone either, no matter how bad the quality of student work, because they didn't want the bureaucratic hassle or the negative blowback on student feedback forms. Because of these issues, but especially because I wanted students to produce work that was more original, reflective, and meaningful, I began to move away from exams and term papers to the journal form. They were to write five hundred to six hundred words a week giving an account of lectures, seminars, and reading and their own reflections on the themes involved. In addition to this, at the start of philosophy modules, they were to write a thousand-word intellectual autobiography, outlining their worldviews and how they had evolved, which gave them a baseline for considering if their worldviews had developed in any way as a result of exposure to many alternative worldviews covered in the module. These assignments produced some fine writing and reflection. I published the best ones on the Web. Year after year, students expressed a strong response to existentialism. The degree of angst in healthy, smart, good-looking young men was striking.

The journal form also meant that students took lectures more seriously, because all the dimensions of the course were organically connected through this method. Of course, I tried to make lectures interesting enough to make them want to attend. I prepared my multimedia slides, adding bullet points to get to the core issues, accompanied by images to make the subject matter as vivid as possible. Sometimes I used video inserts that dramatized the issues. For my history of ideas classes, I arrived early to set up the projector and had music playing as students gathered: Gregorian chant for the medieval period and Vivaldi's "Spring" for the lecture on the making of the modern mind. But I found it hard to find anything suitable for positivism. For Marxism, I was spoiled for choice: the "Internationale," "Red Flag," "Banks of Marble," and "We Have Fed You All for a Thousand Years."

While it was well known that I was a Marxist, it wasn't necessarily known by students at the beginning of their courses with me. They found out sooner or later, although I preferred it to be later, because of the prejudice against Marxists for having an agenda that somehow distorted some centrist truth. When lecturing, I was careful to represent contending positions, because I thought it was necessary knowledge and also because it was more pedagogically stimulating. In discussions, I did declare my own positions, but made clear that these did not constitute orthodoxies for the course and that students could take any positions they could justify with solid arguments. I respected students who pushed against me, if it was done sincerely and not to show off, and I marked down students who pretended to agree with me only to get better marks.

One student once began an essay with the sentence, "Karl Marx is my favorite philosopher." Aside from it being a childish thing to say, especially for a postgraduate, she had done nothing to indicate that she had acquired enough of even an introductory knowledge of philosophy to have a favorite philosopher.

I was involved in university-wide committees and task forces on teaching innovation, web development, and research promotion. The area where I was most at odds with colleagues was on research. DCU was dominated by scientists and engineers, who operated with a very different conception of research than that prevailing in the humanities. However, the conception of research in the humanities was changing in their direction, narrowing into the categories of quantitative and qualitative and going increasingly for bean-counting content analyses, audience surveys, focus groups. A well-regarded book, covering a wide area of knowledge and conveying serious reflection, by a single author, that might take years to write, was becoming more and more marginal. At one meeting, where forms of research and how they would be evaluated were being listed, I mentioned books. One scientist responded that, of course, there would be textbooks, but textbooks were not original research. No, I said, I mean original books, not textbooks. They looked at me oddly. It was when I first went for promotion that I saw what a wall of incomprehension stood between us. I was told that my work, all my historical research and philosophical analysis, was "all opinion."

There was also increasing emphasis on bringing in external funding for projects of international teams and publishing results in multiauthored articles in peer-reviewed journals, which were beginning to be ranked. Promotion became more and more dependent on the metrics of funding and ranking. This did not suit me, because I did not see why I should have to hustle for funding or to co-author Euro-pudding texts written only to score points for promotion. I definitely did not want to write in the alienated and alienating mode of this version of academe, and to be buried in journals that hardly anyone read. I wanted to write for a wider and more engaged audience about themes that mattered to them and to me. I stuck to my own vision and I was eventually promoted, but I did so in a more embattled way than others, who played the expected game and sailed onward and upward. Others less qualified and committed were promoted ahead of me.

I tried to emphasize the positive and to do what was in my power to do. It was part of the long march through all the institutions of society, and universities were important institutions. Although my vision of what a university and academic work should be was marginalized, I still had considerable room for maneuver to challenge the dominant position and do things my own way in my own courses and projects. Because the academic job involved so much autonomy, it also provided possibilities for teaching and research that dumbed down the curriculum, as well as covered for those who cut every corner. They canceled lectures, marked carelessly, fiddled expenses, failed to attend meetings, or to keep office hours. I was often seething with resentment at the lack of a work ethic among my colleagues. Some did work hard, think seriously, teach conscientiously and publish significantly, but many in my own school did not. Some were high-flyers who played a game of bluff, while others were low-flyers who slipped through the cracks. I rarely saw some of them. Some of them received research leave, but produced no results. Those who did not publish did not get promoted, but, beyond this, there were no sanctions.

What made me even more angry was that our universities were public institutions where a public service ethos was dying and being replaced by individualistic attitudes that allowed people to receive public salaries while producing nothing of public value. Both students and staff were shaped by the sensibilities of the times indulging, even valorizing, celebrity culture, positivist myopia, postmodernist incoherence, and market-driven ruthlessness. There were also institutional mechanisms that increasingly allowed the private sector to parasite on the public sector. Commercial companies were increasingly determining the course offerings and research projects that were pursued and rewarded.

The awarding of honorary doctorates veered from esteeming pursuit of knowledge to aggrandizing commercial success.

Despite these problems, DCU was still a good place to work. It gave me scope to work in an interdisciplinary way, to use the latest technologies, to contest the dominant agenda, to create courses and pursue projects for which I could make a reasonable case. I had to compromise in various ways, but never on matters of principle. There were too many immediate tasks sometimes, which made it hard to do any long-form writing. In addition to the traditional aspects of the academic job, there were additional assignments, such as visiting students on their work experience placements in media organizations and even visiting them abroad in their Erasmus exchanges. There was also a campus radio station where I sometimes made programs with students. I got on really well with students who took their studies seriously. Among colleagues, there were others who felt the lack of philosophy in the university, and we formed a philosophy discussion group that met regularly.

During these years, I had to deal not only with the questions raised by my own students but by a barrage of queries from students all over the world as well. Because I was an early adapter and created websites for my courses and publications, I received a torrent of email from students and professors elsewhere, engaging with this material. Actually, the email came from all sorts of people in and out of academe. Most of it I welcomed. Indeed, it gave me a great buzz to be reaching a whole new audience with my ideas. The best emails were those from people with a reflective response to my writing, who told me about their own development or research. Their range was wide, from a retired engineer in India reflecting on life, to a professor of philosophy teaching Marxism in post-Soviet Ukraine, to a postgraduate in Norway writing a thesis on the Soviet philosophy of science, to a teenager in Britain who became a Marxist on his own and wanted to communicate with someone sympathetic to it. Others were prompted by my convent experience. Some messages were from other ex-nuns who wanted to share their experiences. One was from the daughter of a Jesuit priest and nun, who later had a relationship with a Marxist philosopher who died by suicide—all of which she recounted in great detail. Another consulted me about becoming a nun. I even entered into a correspondence with the Web editor of my former order. I discovered that, of the ninety postulants who entered with me, there were only thirty-three nuns remaining. She sent me an address by the Mother General (called "Peg") which she had given at an event where those who had left the order had been invited to join with those who stayed, to celebrate a milestone of the order.

Some of this email was annoying, though. It came from students, spoiled brats really, who had come across something I wrote but couldn't be bothered to read it and wanted me to repackage it for them to meet the exact terms of their assignments. One actually asked me to bullet-point my article for her. One told me she needed a paper of five to seven pages on an event, a person, or an idea, and how it was relevant to history. Many asked questions of such generality that it would have taken many hours or days or indeed whole books to answer them. Some told me to hurry up, demanding immediate and urgent responses, because their assignments were due, making no allowances for anything else I might have to do and assuming that I was at their beck and call. I did not answer most of these, although I was tempted to explain some elementary facts of life that their parents and teachers had apparently neglected to explain to them. One, which was refreshing, if satirically apposite, began "Greetings, Professor Sheehan: Such ease of access seems improper when contacting a personage of your intellectual gravitas. Supplicants should fast, meditate, ford raging rivers, pass through forests primeval, breach mighty fortifications and ascend daunting peaks...or at least pass muster before the basilisk gaze of a gatekeeping functionary to gain an audience, but I digress. . . ."

Some of this correspondence was hate mail, telling me that my "glorious movement to take over the world has been crushed to the depths of hell." Another email started in the same vein, then proceeded to advise me: "If you have any ethics left, you should go to your local priest and ask for forgiveness. And here is even better advice, pack your belongings and go to North Korea or Cuba instead of spreading lies and poisoning minds of young people with Marxism-Leninism." I left these unanswered, but I never applied any blocks or filters, and felt I had to take the good with the bad and not cosset myself from whatever came. I received a very long email from a Tanya Lysenko in Florida defending Lysenkoism and denouncing all international commentators on it, which I did answer, although my position was already clear from my publications about this trend in Soviet biology.

I embraced the Internet in a big way. I frequented all sorts of Internet spaces, which seem quite primitive looking back from what the Internet became, but amazing and groundbreaking then. At first, I accessed the Internet at a computer terminal via a mainframe VAX computer, although I was delighted when a PC was set up in my office. Before Google, I did searches via Veronica. Before the World Wide Web, I retrieved documents via Gopher. Before Facebook and Twitter, I engaged in social interactions via Internet Relay Chat (where I set up a zeitgeist channel) and via MUDs and MOOs, which were multi-user sites that created virtual spaces through text alone. One I checked out was a virtual online university. You could enter through a lobby, check the bulletin board and go through to classrooms, library, medical center, café, green space, or cemetery. Another site was devoted to postmodern culture, very broadly defined. I wrote a short, anti-postmodernist manifesto for my character description. I also subscribed to a number of eLists, where messages arrived via email. Some of the communication was of high quality, but these lists were often swamped by people who seemed free to type every flimsy thought or demented impulse that came to them all day long. I was always ready to explore the next thing in this fast-moving world. The Internet was new terrain in my long-march agenda.

I was delighted the first time I saw Mosaic, the first graphic browser, which opened up the amazing World Wide Web. There were some people around the university who saw the Internet as a peripheral and fleeting thing, but I argued that it was important and would soon become mainstream. I argued that the world was becoming connected in a whole new way. I couldn't travel as often once I began full-time teaching, but, on the Web, I had a sense of moving around the world without leaving my office desk. So many things became so easy and instant. As someone who did research in the laborious and time-rested way, it was amazing how so much could be found so quickly once Google came on the scene and became so ubiquitous as to become a verb as well as a noun. There were losses as well as gains. I no longer spent so much time in libraries or bookshops, institutions offering considerable pleasure and discovery, but increasingly displaced for me by Amazon. I scanned many images for possible use in my websites and multimedia slides, and taught myself to do basic video editing for material that I shot or recorded off air. I got a reputation of being very techie for a humanities academic, and even proselytized for creative use of computer technology in academe, politics, and everyday life.

I was conscious, of course, of how unevenly distributed computer resources were. It made me furious to see spoiled first-world kids using the most advanced computers to play Pokemon or Doom on the Internet, while schools and clinics in the third world remained uncomputerized. It was ironic that the games generated by this advanced technology reverted to so much imagery of dungeons and dragons. Much of the bandwidth was taken up by the shallowness and narcissism of celebrity culture, with masses of material about Diana and O.J. Such sophisticated technology squandered on such nonsense. Dotcom euphoria and economic boom multiplied millionaires and even billionaires, which, together with the West-has-won mentality, fueled complacency about first-world privilege and a disregard for the ravages inflicted on the second- and third-worlds.

The 1990s was a decade of denial. In Ireland, the rising tide of prosperity blinded many to the injustices of the world. The epitome of what I most hated about Ireland at this time was the *Sunday Independent,* popularly called the *Sindo,* which was dominated by glib, narcissistic writing that ironically distanced itself from its own stances, so as to say and not-say things at the same time. The worst of this coquettishness was a column called "The Keane Edge," in which Terry Keane both did and didn't reveal her affair with the taoiseach of the time, Charles Haughey, but beyond that projected a society elite who lived the high life for the sake of the "gaiety of the nation," in which we were all supposed to indulge vicariously. With the exception of the progressive columnist Gene Kerrigan, many of the pundits got their platform to opine to the nation through a network of relationships at the center of which were Eoghan and Anne Harris, who had swung from left to right in dramatic fashion. On Monday mornings, I went through the *Sindo* with first-year journalism students, hoping they would develop the critical skills to see through its pretensions. One of them, Cormac Bourke, later became the editor of it.

I engaged with Generation X as best I could. They were individuals and very different from one another, but they had some characteristics in common that made them very different from my generation. What most struck me was that they had grown up in a much less stable and less defined world. There were lots of views and values contending with each other in their world, but they were coming through it without very strong views or values of their own. So many of them seemed so bland and disengaged. They were especially unfocused when it came to anything bigger than themselves. This was one reason why I had such a strong sense of mission about my philosophy classes. The strongest individual identities among my students, both male and female, even those who thought about the national question enough to be nationalist, was what British (primarily English) soccer team they supported. Although I never deliberately engaged in sports discussion with them, I knew who identified with Arsenal, Man United, or Tottenham. Some tried to explain the importance of soccer to me in terms of the meaning of life and their own identities, but I

never did get it. My female students tended toward lipstick feminism. They took it for granted that they were just as good as their
male classmates as students, and could be just as good as journalists, producers, teachers, or politicians, but they still retained
attitudes associated with the traditional division of labor. Where
this revealed itself most starkly was in their assumption that they
might choose to withdraw from the workforce to raise their children, while a man, one they hadn't yet met, would support them
in the lifestyle to which they wanted to become accustomed. I
argued that labor was essential to liberation, but most of them did
not agree. Some very heated class discussions about this ensued
from time to time. These were children of postmodernism, which
they imbibed before reading any exotic French texts, because it
was, as Fredric Jameson so astutely framed it, the cultural logic of
late capitalism.

The popular culture of this time, which I followed more through
television drama than through any other cultural form, was full of
wisecracking irony, even parody, as it commented on the world.
I liked *The Simpsons, The Critic, Seinfeld, Ellen, Frasier, NYPD
Blue, My So-Called Life, Picket Fences, Murphy Brown*, and others.
They were skillfully made, full of intelligence and insight into the
difficulties and dilemmas and crazy contradictions of the times,
although Hollywood would go only so far in exploring the society giving rise to these fault lines in everyday life. My favorite was
Northern Exposure, which was a quirky and savvy orchestration
of a whole array of worldviews of our time, highlighting the ironies, transitions, collisions, confusions. It was often compared
with *Twin Peaks*, which was my least favorite show, although some
people loved both. I hated it for its willful and cynical obscuran-
tism. Another one loved by others, but not by me, was *The X-Files*.
Students loved *Buffy the Vampire Slayer*, but I couldn't see the
point of displacing the need to confront the true dark forces in
the world with fighting the fictional powers of evil vampires and
other such demons. I felt the same about the ever-multiplying
array of superheroes. On the news front, this decade saw the birth

of Fox News, which was the ultimate displacement in featuring the good-versus-evil struggles of the world and the prototype for worse to come. I was working on a social history of US television drama and had written chapters encompassing the 1950s through the 1980s, although other activities prevented me from writing the chapter on the 1990s and finishing the book.

Another research area for me was the science wars of this time, that is, the controversies opened by conflicting theories about the epistemological status of science and the impact of sociohistorical forces upon science. I was becoming increasingly concerned about the anti-science stance of science studies. Many of the ideas swirling around this nexus crystallized in the "Sokol affair" when Alan Sokal of New York University (NYU) wrote a hoax article on quantum gravity, which parodied postmodernist discourse about science. The article went through the peer-review process and was published by the journal *Social Text*. While I had reservations about the ethics of hoax articles, I thought that Sokal was right to expose the nonsense that was passing as theory. I hoped it would serve as a wake-up call for areas of academe and for sections of the intellectual left. I did not believe that the debunking of science in terms of its cognitive capacity was an appropriate activity for the left. It was neither epistemologically sound nor politically progressive. I believed that the left should take its stand with science, albeit a critically reconstructed and socially responsible science. Basically, I found myself on both sides of the so-called science wars, yet wholly on neither. I agreed with those who wanted to defend the cognitive capacity of science against epistemological antirealism, irrationalism, mysticism, conventionalism, especially against anything-goes postmodernism. I also agreed with those who insisted on a strong sociohistorical account of science against a reassertion of scientism that disregarded the epistemological and sociological complexity of science. I argued that a better grounding in what the Marxist tradition had brought to bear on these issues would have illuminated the terrain. When I was invited to speak on this at the New York Marxist School, I was in the company of those who agreed with me, whereas in more mainstream academic enclaves, I had a battle on my hands. Against postmodernists, it was sometimes hard to agree on terms of discourse, because everything was so relative and the ground was so slippery. With scientists inclined to scientism, without even naming it scientism, it was hard to convince them that there was even a problem. At DCU, because I was active in science studies, I thought I could play some kind of role in breaking through the "two cultures" barrier between the humanities and sciences as it played out there, but many scientists were oblivious and reduced it all to "just opinion," irrelevant to actual science.

I was still politically active, although less overtly than in the decades before or after. It wasn't just that my job was so demanding, but more that life on the left was not as demanding. I was a member of a party in government, with which I had a critical, but not oppositional, relationship. Democratic Left had joined the Labour Party in coalition government and subsequently liquidated and joined the Labour Party. The peace process in Northern Ireland brought a ceasefire and the decommissioning of arms. I was happy about this, not only as a citizen, but also as a mother, since my son was caught up with republican politics. In the Republic of Ireland, there was a successful referendum on divorce, and the way was clear for my *de facto* divorce to become a *de jure* one.

I took advantage of the facilities available at DCU, particularly a recording studio, to produce a CD called *Songs of Irish Labour*. The album was set in motion in 1998, after I attended the unveiling of a monument to Jim Connell in Crossakiel in the wilds of County Meath. Connell was the author of the stirring international socialist anthem "The Red Flag." I was glad that the song still lived and I wanted it to continue to live. I created a web page about the event, which included a recording we made at DCU of Jimmy Kelly singing it. After that, I gathered various people who sang at political and trade union functions, including singer-songwriter Martin Whelan, and we made recordings over the following months to come forth with a properly mastered and produced CD.

My protest activity was primarily focused on US foreign policy and demonstrating on the streets against US military interventions, but also contesting Labour Party support for US foreign policy. Our party leader, Dick Spring, who was also foreign minister, played golf amiably with Bill Clinton and never contested any of the Clinton administration's interventions. I was outraged when Spring expressed support for Boris Yeltsin, who presided over blatant and chaotic oligarchic rule and even attacked Russia's elected parliament. By the end of the decade, 75 percent of Russians regretted the demise of the USSR. When Ruairi Quinn became Labour Party leader, I heard him on the radio defending the NATO bombing of Belgrade. I wrote to him immediately and asked by what process could this be party policy. Other leading figures, such as Michael D. Higgins and Proinsias De Rossa, did not support it. Nor did the international affairs committee, of which I was still a member, nor did many activists. I forwarded to him a long letter I had just received from Miloš Nikolić, written in Belgrade as the bombs were falling. One point it made was that the progressive forces that had opposed Milošević from the beginning and supported autonomy for Kosovo now felt utterly disabled, alienated, and isolated. I didn't believe that NATO was the answer to any question worth asking. I was also involved in organizing a teach-in at DCU against this intervention. Clinton was much praised in Ireland for his involvement in the Northern peace process, although in reality this process proceeded much as it would have without him. Many Irish people did point out the contrast between his peace-making efforts in Ireland, in contrast to his bombing of Sudan, Afghanistan, and Serbia. This lifted the discourse a level above the US media's identikit Ken-and-Barbie newscasters who were obsessed with what he did with Monica Lewinsky in the Oval Office but cared little about his deployment of cruise missiles abroad and how they impacted on those living in distant lands.

I still traveled to Eastern Europe, visiting the vanquished and probing the process of political and social upheaval. I went to

Eastern Germany, the Czech Republic, Slovakia, and Bulgaria. In Berlin, my friends, some of whom had been at the apex of academe, now led marginalized lives. In their homes, they had relocated further and further from the center of Berlin where they had previously lived. I was still impressed by the strength and seriousness of their convictions. Some were making ends meet by doing jobs far below their qualifications. I kept my eye on the fortunes of the PDS and *Neues Deutschland* and touched base at the paper's headquarters to hear of their difficulties in this hostile environment. In 1997 I discovered an international conference on the PDS taking place in Reading and attended that. In 1999 I was on RTE for the tenth anniversary of the fall of the Berlin Wall to discuss the end of the GDR. The interviewer came at me like a rottweiler, but I held my ground. As a result, I was asked to come to Trinity to give a lecture on the GDR. I also met up with my students on Erasmus exchanges when I was in Berlin and it was always interesting to hear what they thought about post-GDR Berlin. It was impossible to go to Berlin without encountering the legacy of the GDR, often in an aggressively hostile form, but sometimes in a positive or at least ironic form.

I went several times to Slovakia on university business. In response to the fall of the Berlin Wall, and with the transition to capitalism underway in Eastern Europe, the EU inaugurated its TEMPUS (Trans-European Mobility Scheme for University Studies) program, which struck me as saturated with imperialist West-has-won arrogance. TEMPUS sent Western academics into Eastern universities to show them how "proper" universities were run. On a TEMPUS visit to Slovakia, I was asked to give a guest lecture on a topic of my choice. I said: Marxism. They were surprised, then disconcerted. Nevertheless, they organized it. The room was packed. Marxism had the frisson of forbidden fruit again. I said that the situation was ridiculous. Marxism was *the* philosophy for decades and then it disappeared from the curriculum, as if it had never existed. It was orthodoxy one day and apostasy the next. It was not healthy. Marxism, I argued, was a major intellectual tradition in the history of the world, and things would never be healthy until it found its place vis-á-vis all contenders in the over-all scheme of things. I recalled my own philosophical evolution from Catholicism through existentialism to Marxism. This was the opposite of their trajectory, for they were running from Marxism to Catholicism, to existentialism, phenomenology, etc. People came whispering to me in the following days, saying that they agreed. However, they did not want to join the ranks of those who had declared they were still Marxist and became unemployed or had to find employment outside academe. They told me I should go to a restaurant in the town of Prešov, run by Marxist philoso-phers who had to leave the university.

I had a number of occasions to speak to Eastern European intel-lectuals of different countries, generations, and points of view in these years. There was so much dishonesty and denial. It extended even to the dead. I was profoundly distressed to read obituaries of those I knew as Marxists, whose Marxism was never mentioned. When I asked questions about intellectual orientation and trans-formation, it was sometimes as if I were probing sexual liaisons or spy scandals. Nevertheless, while the topic still generated a con-siderable unease among many, what I found most striking was the surprise of younger intellectuals at hearing someone make a case for Marxism, and their openness to considering it.

In April 1998, there was a big international conference in Paris marking the 150th anniversary of the *Communist Manifesto*. My name was among the international intellectuals from a wide range of countries supporting the conference and the call for papers. It was seen by Roy Johnston, an independent intellectual, who asked me if we could present a joint paper. I said no, because I saw no basis for it. Over the years, I had to rebuff him many times when he tried to draw me into his schemes. He never took no for an answer and continued to harass me about it. He even wrote to Paris to tell the organizer we were submitting a joint paper and I had to countermand that. Despite this bad start, I had a good experi-ence at this event. Eric Hobsbawm gave the keynote address and many luminaries of international Marxism also presented. I had many stimulating encounters. Some of these were in the open air of Paris, making them all the better. I gave a paper remarking on how it was impossible not to be struck by the confidence with which the *Communist Manifesto* conceptualized history, pulsating with vitality, vision, verve. I went on from there to remark on how the positive energy of this bold grand narrative stood in stark contrast to the negative and jaded mentality of our times, which conceived of grand narratives only to tell us that there could be none. I argued otherwise, defending the possibility of grand narratives and asserting that it was only within the Marxist tradition, even in the bloodied state in which it found itself, that we got the really bold and brave thinking that was needed to come to terms with the times. At the closing session of the conference in the Sorbonne, Brazilian comrades struck up the "Internationale" and we all joined in, singing in our own languages, which was a fitting finale.

Another big conference of 1998 offered a more combative arena. This was the World Congress of Philosophy in Boston in August. While registering, I saw a guy wearing a t-shirt stating on the front, "The statement on the back of this shirt is true," and on the back, "The statement on the front of this shirt is false." The opening plenary was dominated by John Silber, chancellor of Boston University, who gave a highly slanted view of the history of philosophy and current trends in philosophy. He lined up Socrates, Plato, Confucius, Kant, and Hegel on his side, versus Nietzsche, Kierkegaard, and Marx on the other side. He contrasted God and reason with secularism and rejection of reason, making God the guarantor of reason and declaring the absence of God the eclipse of reason. He asserted that Marxism was discredited, describing it as the will to power in the interests of ultimate untruth. The common feature of all the philosophies he rejected was relativism, the abandonment of the search for truth in favor of ideology. Marxism was lumped together with postmodernism, ecofeminism, multiculturalism, and deconstruction, as part of the same contemporary assault on reason. Questions of class, race, and gender were treated facilely. There were factually inaccurate assertions about Marie Curie, Frederic Joliot-Curie, and Rosalind Franklin. I was furious. I liked a good polemic, which was preferable to a lot of ceremonial cliché, but there was no possibility of comeback from the floor. I objected to his having such a privileged platform, whereas any answer in the name of an alternative argument was left to more marginal sessions.

One of the sessions that engaged me most was on post-Soviet philosophy. James Scanlon, who had given my book *Marxism and the Philosophy of Science* a great review in *Slavic Review*, outlined four shifts in philosophical focus: 1) a wholesale retreat from Marxism, 2) a new interest in the history of Western thought (more continental than analytical), 3) a rediscovery of pre-Soviet Russian philosophy, 4) a quest for an organic Russian philosophy (primarily in religious orthodoxy). Then Evert van der Zweerde, a Dutch academic whose PhD thesis was on Soviet historiography of philosophy, spoke on how philosophy has always embodied a narrative of its past and how the overthrow of the Soviet narrative of the history of philosophy constituted a new abnormality. Another Western scholar of Eastern European philosophy, Edward Swiderski, also stressed the discontinuity, focusing on the influence of religion and postmodernism and the decline of epistemology and philosophy of science. It was a society at odds with itself, debating whether it even had room for philosophy. He quoted from a letter from a Russian philosopher: "Nothing is happening in Russian philosophy today." Someone from the floor asked what would be something happening in Russian philosophy. I responded that being honest about Marxism would be something happening. The retreat from Marxism was cowardly and dishonest, I charged, considering how many of these philosophers built their careers on it and then turned from it when power shifted. The transition from orthodoxy to apostasy was pathological. In other sessions, there were further discussions on philosophy in Eastern Europe. There was a consensus that philosophy was taken far more seriously under socialism and that it was in disarray now.

Between sessions, I heard accounts of the previous World Congress of Philosophy in 1993 in Moscow. The locus was the site of what was once the International Lenin School, where I had lived and studied. Russian philosophers didn't want to know about Marxism and tried to eliminate sessions of Society for the Philosophical Study of Marxism from the program. However, Marxists stood up for themselves and, as a result of the controversy, their sessions were packed. At this congress, I attended sessions of the Society for the Philosophical Study of Marxism, which drew respectable audiences, but did not attract as much controversy. At the session where I was scheduled to speak, Dale Riepe, a retired professor of philosophy who was chairing it, was gathering bio- graphical background on the speakers. He primarily wanted to know where I went to school and who my teachers were. I was furious. I told him that I was fifty-four years old and a teacher and author myself and did not want to be reduced to someone's stu- dent. When he introduced me, he said, "She won't tell me who her teachers were"—nothing about my own teaching or publications. I gave my paper on Marxism and the science wars. He cut me off before time and did the same with other speakers. Then, when the session was about to open to the floor, he declared it over, despite the fact that it was scheduled to continue for another forty-five minutes. When told this, he said that he was leaving anyway. This was after he had rambled on and on beyond his allotted time the previous day. The session continued without a chair.

In a session on philosophy of science, two speakers talked past each other, taking opposite approaches without engaging in any way. One, from Bulgaria, spoke on the limits of science and veered into mysticism, whereas the other from Germany was aridly ana- lytical. This impasse was symptomatic. There was a session on the relation between analytical and continental philosophy, which attracted such a big crowd that the room divider had to be dis- mantled. This popularity was testimony to the need to break down this conceptualization of contemporary philosophy, but the actual discourse at it was disappointing, much of it obfuscating. As with most conferences, the quality of papers was uneven, but there were too few at this congress that I thought really good. One of the best was by Sandra Rosenthal of Loyola University on pragmatism, articulating a defense of this tradition as naturalistic, processive, contextual, and relational, putting strong emphasis on a participational theory of truth and an ontologically grounded perspectivism. She argued that contemporary philosophy represented a backsliding into spectator theory of knowledge and its rejection. All in all, the congress was not as stimulating an experience as I had hoped, but it was a good opportunity for me to take the pulse of contemporary academic philosophy and to map its positions and confusions.

During this period, I came to the US once a year, combining academic and political activities with visits to family and friends. I had searching talks with colleagues and comrades. I had made peace with my parents, although we still spoke across a gulf of opposing worldviews. I realized that these were probably the last years of their lives. My daughter Clíodna was working in a travel agency in the US for a year, and I showed her around the world of my previous life—from the streets of Manhattan to the convent at Chestnut Hill. It was the first time that I entered my former novitiate or had seen some of my contemporaries since I left. It was vastly changed. I didn't think my daughter could imagine how it once was. Nuns were wearing sneakers and shorts and expressing their own preferences for where they lived and worked. It was a way of life that was dying, even if those within it couldn't quite admit it, even though they saw all the signs. The demographics revealed a dwindling and aged community and few new entrants.

My travels took me to new countries. In Cyprus, we connected with Akel, the communist party, which regularly came in either first or second in the country's elections. A strong Russian presence was evident on the island by this time. Holidays in Turkey and Morocco were my first experiences of Muslim cultures. In those countries, although the hijab was in evidence, there was no pressure on foreigners to cover the head, which was just as well, because I had strong views about veiled women, having been one myself. I found the hustling, the begging, the bargaining over every transaction to be alienating, although some tourists thrived on it. I found ancient Ephesus amazing and I connected with the tradition of pre-Socratic philosophy in Anatolia.

On the domestic front, Sam reached age sixty-five in 1995 and retired from his full-time job as a trade union official, but he continued as secretary of the Dublin Council of Trade Unions and member of the Employment Appeals Tribunal, along with many political activities. My academic salary made it possible to move out of our rented apartment on North Circular Road and into a mortgaged house on Ballymun Road within walking distance of DCU. Cathal and Clíodna were finding their way through various courses, jobs, and travels.

During this time, I noted the deaths of a number of people with whom I had consequential interactions: Marx Wartofsky, Ulrich Röseberg, Wolfgang Harich, Ivan Frolov, Herbert Ushewokunze, Marius Schoon, Paul van Buren, and Cathal Goulding. Several of these were sudden and unexpected. Most of their funerals took place abroad, and I regretted that I couldn't attend. I did attend the funeral of Cathal Goulding, who had been IRA chief of staff, which was memorable for various reasons. The most common site for left funerals is Glasnevin Crematorium, although it is often too small to accommodate the crowd for such public figures. It was full-to-overflowing for Cathal Goulding. There was a large crowd outside who could hear what was happening on loudspeakers. The ceremony clearly articulated his republican, socialist, and secular values. The main oration was given by Sean Garland, who lambasted those who broke away from the Workers Party and formed Democratic Left. I happened to be standing beside Proinsias De Rossa, the leader of WP who became leader of DL. Several WP members came up to him and told him he was unwelcome and even spit on him. I understood their bitterness but was sorry to see it express itself in this way at a funeral.

The main challenge of living through the 1990s was adjusting to the absence of socialist regimes in Europe and coming to terms with the New World Order—or the New World Disorder, as the left called it. The left was in disarray itself for much of the decade or, when not in disarray, in a somewhat subdued state. As the decade was ending, the anti-globalization movement (more accurately called the alter-globalization movement) gathered momentum and signaled fresh perspectives and new mobilizations. The assertion that "Another world is possible" came as a new challenge in this period, when it so often seemed that no other world was possible. It had been difficult for the left to convince others, often even to convince itself, that there was any alternative to capitalism. We came to the end of this decade, which was also the end of the century and the end of the millennium, thinking that the world had stabilized into a state of complacent acquiescence in a global regime that masked its brutal subjugation and extreme exploitation in cunning centrist cant. To those who fell for it, all might have seemed well, but it was not. The ensuing decades would dramatize that, in ways that few could foresee, as the champagne flowed and triumphalist toasts celebrated the dawn of a new decade/century/millennium.

CHAPTER 4

The Dictatorship of Capital

AS THE NEW DECADE, new century, and new millennium began, things continued at first much as they were. The Y2K scare, which predicted global infrastructural catastrophe as computers advanced from 1999 to 2000, causing fears of financial, medical, and transport systems failing, and even visions of planes falling from the sky, did not wreak the predicted havoc, both as a result of exaggerated predictions and multiple task forces preparing fixes.

I did see the year 2000 as a new start for me, because I was granted sabbatical leave for the academic year 2000–2001. I felt that I needed to reorient myself in my job, because I had devoted myself to teaching in a way that took so much of my time that I was not as productive in research and publication as I felt I should be. I was determined to devote myself to research for the year and then come back to my normal job with a better sense of proportion. It was also to be the time when I finally went to Africa.

My major project for the year was to work on a series of papers and lectures, and ultimately a book, titled *The Rise of the Repressed in the History of Knowledge*. I wanted to address the basic processes of the constitution of knowledge, the confrontation of the Western canon with the exclusions of class, race, gender, and geography, and the issues in the contemporary "science wars" and "culture wars" within the context of the epistemological crises of our times. This was the convergence of themes in philosophy of science, sociology of knowledge, cultural studies, and political theory, on which I had been working for a long time. The most important part of my research plan for the year was investigating the intellectual dimensions of the transformation in South Africa, particularly the conceptualization of gender, class, and race in the process of transforming higher education in a scenario where contending forces were at play. A formidable liberation movement had come to power there, but global market trends were prevailing against it.

However, first I went to America, where my adventures included a revivalist mass, an Afrocentrist conference, a brown-bag lunch at *Monthly Review*, and many state-of-the-world, state-of-the-left, state-of-the-universities discussions on campuses and other venues in New York and Philadelphia. I was on the East Coast for the whole month of October and enjoyed walking, talking, and thinking among the beautiful autumn leaves. Returning to the places where I began and where I took my first steps from home, school, and church into the wider world provoked much reflection about the vast distance between the world as it seemed then and now. I couldn't walk through Philadelphia city center or the campuses of Penn or Temple without bittersweet memories of huge antiwar demos, resistance dinners, block parties, teach-ins, communes, all suffused with hope that we could change the world, while realizing how much the public space had thinned out in the interval.

In New York, I ran into Irish writer and broadcaster Nuala O'Faolain, whom I knew from Dublin. She was bowled over by America, seeing it as having everything that Ireland lacked. I was glad that she was so happy, but thought it was a much-romanticized view of America. While I was there, the 2000 presidential election was underway, filling the airwaves and everyday conversations. The mind-numbing debates between George W. Bush and

Al Gore were on all channels, even pushing primetime drama off the air. During one of these debates, the candidates were asked about morality and the presidency. Bush spoke of how much he loved his wife and admitted that his opponent also loved *his* wife. I found the mainstream discourse about the election myopic and often ridiculous, assuming so much that should not be assumed. I realized how superior European political discourse was on the whole, especially as it expressed itself in the mainstream media. Of course, among my left friends, it was different and their commentary was progressive and critical. David Kairys, now a law professor, was supporting Ralph Nader's candidacy, but others on the left were critical of that, either because they didn't consider him radical enough or because they didn't think that third-party candidates had a chance. I engaged with the election, but it made me realize more strongly that this wasn't my country anymore.

I had more contact with Catholicism than I intended. When I arrived, the big news was the canonization of Mother Katherine Drexel, scion of the wealthy Philadelphia Drexel family, who founded a religious order. Then my parents prevailed upon me to attend a revivalist mass. They had been involved in the charismatic movement since the 1960s. I was reluctant to go, but I did have an anthropological curiosity about it, which was enhanced by their insistence that the inspiring priest, named Vince Walsh, whom people came miles to see, was someone I had once dated. Parts of the mass were as alienating as I imagined: the rosary, the homily, speaking in tongues, and other odd behavior. One man kept running around inside the church. One woman had the "gift of laughter" and kept cackling at odd times. Some went down in "dormition," seeming to fall asleep suddenly At one stage, the priest went through the congregation of two hundred, shouting odd syllables at them, which sounded to me as "she-she-she-she-she." While he was doing this, a nun (supposedly with the Holy Spirit speaking through her) was saying to me, "Be simple. Don't be sophisticated. Don't try to understand it." Although such statements of irrationalism normally set me off, I sat still and observed.

This was a cult. It was their scene; not mine, and I was there on sufferance. The sound of singing in tongues was fascinating. I never heard anything like it. It was a group accustomed to doing this together, and it had an amazing harmony. They even did it during the consecration. The body language between the main priest, truly the guru, and the immediate acolytes, and then the layers of believers, was also interesting. Twice, someone (first an older woman and later a young nun) laid their hands on me and prayed over me. My mother said that those who went around and prayed over the people had to be anointed by the priest, because otherwise "it could be the devil." The homily was the uncritical Catholicism of the 1950s. Although I interpreted it all in a materialist manner, I thought it was an interesting manifestation of community, of longing for transcendence. Parts of it made me wish that I had something comparable, i.e., some such way of ritually celebrating my whole worldview, some way of articulating my deepest hopes and anxieties, some sense of belonging to such a strong community of believers. It also turned out that the priest wasn't the Vince Walsh whom I dated, but a cousin of the same name.

Another event, where I was also an outsider, was billed as an academic conference titled "The Afrocentric Study of African Phenomena: Challenging the Traditions." The presiding presence was Professor Molefi Kete Asante of Temple University, who was born Arthur Lee Smith in Georgia and also known as Nana Okru Asante Peasah, since he was enstooled as a king in Ghana. In that role, he arrived at the conference venue, the Airport Hilton, draped in kente cloth with matching sandals, wearing a gold crown and carrying a gold scepter. The conference opened with a libation ceremony in Twi, a dialect of the Akan language, spoken widely in Ghana. Many speakers opened their presentations with incantations by invoking the creator (not the Christian God or Islamic Allah but the Kemetic Ra) and the ancestors. When speakers were at their rabblerousing best (often), others would shout out revivalist responses. Many African-American participants were dressed in colorful African ceremonial attire. In case anyone came unprepared for this couture, there were vendors selling clothes and other Africana paraphernalia. The first presenter declared: "We are the descendants of ancient Kemet [Egypt] . . . we can be like them . . . we are pharaohs . . . we are nobles . . . we are aristocrats." He also said that they needed to learn how to use computers and make money. Then Asante ascended the podium in his royal regalia. The conference was no longer sponsored by Temple, "because of politics," but they were now a movement against Western triumphalism, against Eurocentrist scholarship, against the entire paradigm that falsified the history of the world. Next up was an Ossirian priest of Amen Ra Seminary in California, a center of Nubian-Kemetic spirituality, who asserted that Ra was the life force in existence before existence. Although the dominant line on religion was return to the religion of the ancestors, it was clear that some of the audience adhered to Christianity or Islam, but this was never confronted. After this session, when Asante asked me what I thought, I said that I was wondering why the discussion seemed to assume that the choice was between alternative theologies rather than alternative philosophies; why there was no secular philosophy in the frame. He said that I should raise such questions at the conference, but there was no opportunity to do that.

There was much denunciation of foreign ideologies in Africa. The articulation of a pure African worldview was based on a characterization of Africa as synonymous with wisdom, spirituality, holism, community, religion, nature. In contrast, the "West" was logic, abstraction, materialism, fragmentation, secularism, individualism, survival of the fittest. Marxism was lumped together with the ideologies of the colonizers. Some seemed implicitly out of sync with the rest, but this was never made explicit. A Portuguese postgraduate gave a paper on Mozambican literature, which made positive references to Marxism and Frelimo. A Zimbabwean professor addressed the problems of contemporary Africa, focusing on neoliberalism and structural adjustment policies, political corruption, economic and political inequality, alienation of leaders from the masses, while quoting white Marxists, such as Basil Davidson and Colin Leys, affirmatively. One speaker, when denouncing Marxism, asked, "Any Marxists in the house?" I raised my hand, probably the only one to do so, although I couldn't see behind me. Feminism also came in for strong denunciation. Clenora Hudson-Weems, a professor of Africana studies, declared Black women to be warrior queens, and white feminists to be destroyers of homes.

In terms of my research agenda, I saw this event as an example of how the return of the repressed could take many forms. These were the descendants of perhaps the most oppressed people in the history of the world standing up and demanding their place on the stage of history, but blatantly falsifying that history. Why this claim to descend from pharaohs rather than from their servants and slaves? Why, after all that vast oppression, did they rush to identify with the oppressor rather than the oppressed? It was a static, ahistorical fantasy of Africa of "kings, superheroes, and bucolic bliss" in the words of Stephen Howe, a British professor whose book on Afrocentrism was under fire at the conference. It was an Africa without slavery, corruption, poverty, or capitalism. The lack of class analysis was evident in many manifestations, such as the Asante & Associates pilgrimages to Ghana and Kemet in air-conditioned buses and five-star hotels, including a visit to court where a king would "sit in state and receive homage," as if this would reconnect the diasporic Black bourgeoisie with the lives of their impoverished ancestors. Two days later was the Million Family March in Washington, which I watched on cable television for most of the day. One African-American speaker said: "We are not the descendants of slaves, but the descendants of kings and queens....We respect the values of kingship." There were also tones and themes of earlier radicalism, especially that of the civil rights and Black Power movements. On contemporary issues, there were repeated condemnations of the blockades of Cuba and Iraq, even more general denunciations of imperialism and US foreign policy. Once and future Nicaraguan president Daniel Ortega was among the speakers. However, and even stronger, were constant invocations of God, the family, and even monarchism. I found this alienated Africanism much in contrast with my experience of actual Africa.

Before Africa, I went to Cuba. I attended a world solidarity conference in Havana, which was interesting and inspiring in many ways, but also wearying in that there were far too many clichéd and repetitive speeches. Fidel Castro, of course, was the speaker everyone most wanted to hear. His scheduled speech was hours late starting and continued for many hours before I collapsed in exhaustion after midnight. It was chaotic in its structure. It leaped from political arguments to economic statistics to jokes to reminiscences. Some of it was fascinating, while some of it was like a grocery list. I later bought a collection of his speeches, which had obviously been heavily edited, and from this I learned much. This reflected my sensibility as an academic, I guess, because the rambling oral discourse seemed to win with the masses. A few days later I heard him speak again at a massive outdoor anti-imperialist rally in Havana. At this, there was lots of flag-waving and singing as well as speeches in the scorching sun. I tried to spend as much time as possible talking with ordinary Cubans and with other participants in the congress. I was especially happy to meet South Africans and to begin relationships that would continue when I traveled there.

My most productive conversations were with Cuban intellectuals to whom I could ask probing questions and get honest answers. I made a point of visiting the faculty at the University of Havana's Philosophy Department, where students were dancing in the foyer when I arrived, which conveyed an atmosphere of routine fun. I wanted to probe the position of Marxism vis-à-vis other philosophies, particularly to gauge how much freedom there was to uphold other philosophies, and therefore how much adherence to Marxism was genuine. I received impressive answers, assuring me that many perspectives could be aired. I also visited schools and local communities and found the people, especially the children, bubbling with energy. I had a digital camera and took many photos of children, which I showed them instantly, to their amazement.

The level of technological development, including Internet access, was behind world standards. Their health service, conversely, was far above world standards. The whole experience was both inspiring and troubling, and not always in the ways I expected. There was a constant hustling for dollars, and even fleecing of foreigners there for a solidarity conference, that left a bad taste. It wasn't so much the annoyance of being hassled or even ripped off, but it was wondering about the scale of it and the erosion of socialist morality that it represented. Shortly after, my son Cathal went there on a work brigade and came back full of enthusiasm, despite some dubious experiences.

Then it was home for Christmas before going off to Africa in the new year. One of my first tasks of 2001 was to write a final letter to Dave Gracie, who was dying, which was particularly difficult because we had such different positions on ultimate matters, such as deity and life after death. He had been an important influence for me in my early days on the left.

After that, I flew to South Africa, where I was based at the University of Cape Town and reached out from there to South African life in many forms. I stayed for three months and found it hard to settle back when I returned to Ireland. I came back with an altered sense of the world after looking at it from Africa. It came into nearly every conversation and lecture for quite a while. I went back four more times during the decade and once more in the decade after that. My experiences and reflections from those trips demand an entire chapter.

During this sabbatical, my research agenda was disrupted by a request to write a book other than the one I had intended. It was an offer I found difficult to refuse, and I agreed to write a sequel to my history of Irish television drama for a series called *Broadcasting and Irish Society*. This project took my time during the summer and into the next academic year. I had a number of tussles with the series editor, who said that class analysis might have to do with my own political commitment but had nothing to do with television drama. I faced him down on this.

In September 2001, I was interviewing Bob Collins, the direc-
tor-general of RTE, who came to DCU for this and other business
on the day. During the interview, his mobile rang several times.
He looked at it and saw the calls were from RTE, but continued
the interview. Then RTE rang my phone and I intuited that they
wanted to reach him and that it must be important. It was news
that a plane had flown into one of the Twin Towers of New York
City's World Trade Center. It was 9-11. He departed for RTE, and I
got to a computer and then to a television. I contacted philosopher
and editor Andrew Nash, who was on his way to work at *Monthly
Review* and saw people on the street exclaiming and pointing to a
huge column of smoke, and then saw a plane hit the second tower.
Later in the day, he wrote back with critical analysis of the immediate US media response, which was comparing New Yorkers
walking across the Brooklyn Bridge to refugees in Yugoslavia or
Rwanda, and complaining that the rest of the world was not grateful for all that the US did. Most Americans did not see the extent
to which America was the problem. Paradoxically, all the policies
that had been justified to make the US safer actually did the opposite. Bush was the puppet of forces that he barely comprehended,
forces pursuing the project of full-spectrum domination at the
expense of the majority of the world's population.

I got a call from RTE on 9-11 asking me to appear on a current affairs show in the morning. When I was asked what my first
thought was on hearing the news, I replied that I thought it would
make the US even more dangerous in the world than it already was.
I was attacked in one newspaper column and several blogs. There
was a really chilling editorial in the *Sunday Independent* saying that
the Irish media were partly to blame for what happened in the US,
because they helped create a global atmosphere in which criticism
of US foreign policy could flourish, and promising there would be
retribution for this. It made me even more determined not to be
cowed. In the weeks that followed, there were more articles along
such lines, several singling out DCU as if it were a hotbed of radicalism, which it definitely wasn't. As I took in more detail, heard

the professional commentary and vox pops and beheld what came after, I knew I was right. In the "war on terror" launched by Bush, proclaiming, "Either you are with us or you are with the terrorists," many of us refused the choice. DCU started an official book of condolences at the top level of the university website, and staff and students poured out their sympathy for the victims of 9-11. When the US attacked Afghanistan, we formed an antiwar group at DCU, using the staff email list to solicit support, bringing a wave of support as well as a barrage of emails defending the US, the war, and capitalism, and attacking us, Marxism, and socialism. We organized a series of teach-ins. I created a multimedia presentation with images of the war with antiwar songs on the soundtrack. When we later proposed that DCU produce a book of condolences for the victims of the wars in Afghanistan and Iraq, the proposal was rejected. We did it nevertheless, although we could not get it on to the top level of the university website.

I was back in the classroom and adjusting to a more demanding rhythm of life than when on research leave. My energy was up to the challenge of combining teaching, research, and antiwar organizing, but the endless memos and meetings around the constantly changing procedures of DCU often left me frustrated and exhausted by the end of the day. I also had several spam attacks at points of peak stress, where I got thousands of identical emails that took ages to delete. I had recurring bouts of chest pain. Nevertheless, I kept up a reasonable pace. In a typical semester, I taught three courses, presented six papers, did a dozen media gigs. At one point, I spoke in London three weekends in a row. Sometimes, just when I thought I finally had it cracked, unexpected events ambushed me. My daughter was assaulted on the streets of Dublin in an attempted gang rape. Then my mother suffered a severe heart attack and seemed to be dying on another continent. She stabilized, but I got to the US as soon as term ended for what would be my last visit while both of my parents were still alive.

I was back in the US several times in the aftermath of 9-11.

My family were caught up in it in various ways and felt personally attacked. My cousin had been in the Pentagon when it was
hit, and pulled bodies out of the wreckage. My brother served in
US Central Command and later in both Iraq and Afghanistan. I
stayed in the family home, in a room with a "George W. Bush for
President" poster on the wall. I listened to media commentators
discussing 9-11 and retribution in terms of military tactics, weapons, and timing, focused only on when and how, but not if and
why. I went for a walk around Springfield. One house had a lawn
with a hundred US flags. When I was photographing it, the guy
came out to talk to me. I asked him why so many flags. He said,
"This is America. My country. It's been good to me. I got a corner
property and people come and take pictures of it." I felt like ranting about global distribution of wealth, terms of trade, imperial
wars. Because I had been to Africa since I last came here, I felt
overwhelmed by the amount of living space, the number of big
cars, the so-muchness of consumer stuff. The opulence seemed
obscene. This wasn't even close to being the poshest area, either.
I passed gated communities where the houses were the size of
hotels. When I left there, I stayed in Harlem, a place that struck
fear in the people of this suburb and in my relations. I thought a
lot about 9-11, but as a minor theme, a part of something longer,
bigger, deeper, darker.

I was back a few months later for the funeral of my father. The
funeral was religious and military. It was in the church where I
made my confirmation and attended thousands of masses as a
believer. The coffin had a US flag on it. The Army was officially
represented and presented the flag to my brother (in full marine-
officer uniform) who presented it to my mother, "On behalf of the
President of the United States, all members of the armed forces,
past and present, from a grateful nation." Navigating my way
through all this, I felt acutely my alienation from this world from
which I had come. My father requested that all his sons and daugh-
ters carry his coffin. So I did that, but I didn't genuflect, kneel,
answer prayers, or salute the flag. However, that was not enough

for some of my family. The world was at war and I was not on their side. Eleven months later, my mother died and I again arranged cover for my lectures and crossed the Atlantic for her funeral. My brothers, sisters, and I were all dealing with the primal experience of the death of parents, but with the tensions of doing so within conflicting worldviews. In between the two funerals in 2002 and 2003 came the US attack on Iraq. I was organizing protests against it while my brother was on duty at US Central Command. I was with my own family, but also behind enemy lines. I heard the television news assuming the right of the US to do whatever it saw fit to do in Iraq or anywhere else. Blood ties flowed through all this, but there were forces that were deeper. While in the US, I also met with comrades who were doing their best to resist these wars in difficult conditions.

Back in Dublin, there was a huge response to the attack on Iraq. On February 15, 2003, there were millions of people, all over the world mobilizing to say, "Not in our name" and "No blood for oil." Among these were more than 100,000 on the streets of Dublin, which was massive for a city of its size. The day was bitterly cold but bright. There was a carnival atmosphere. There was something new and hopeful in this coming together, especially for those who were protesting for the first time. They were accustomed to feeling powerless, but felt they were exercising some kind of power in asserting that those who spoke in the name of the "international community" were not speaking for them. These protesters were saying that they were the international community, and that the devastation of an already devastated society was not being done in their name. They did not come because of any self-interest narrowly defined, but to protest against global structures of power, but it was also about themselves and the sort of world in which they wanted to live. The experience of the march itself was an alternative way of being in the world and coming together with others. Sadly, Sean O Cionnaith, Workers Party activist, came home from the march and died, unexpectedly and alone in the open door of his flat in Ballymun.

In the days before this protest, I wrote an email, and a number of colleagues signed it, asking our students and colleagues to come out and to march behind a DCU banner. Many did, although the streets were so packed not everyone who came could find it. I wrote another one prior to "Day-X," which was an initiative to walk out of all classrooms and workplaces on noon of the day the attack came, which turned out to be March 20. There was a lot of ferment around DCU about the war and controversy with staff and students objecting to the use of academic email for non-academic purposes. I responded with questions about the relationship of the university to the world and asked specifically if we should organize our lives and plan our work as if we were not watching a doomed population hopelessly stacking their sandbags against weapons of mass destruction. It was the US and not Iraq who had the real weapons of mass destruction. I also argued that it was necessary for a university to address the assaults on logic, on standards of evidence, on norms of morality and on structures of legality. While I was at it, I asked how many objections to non-academic use of academic email from such quarters came in response to sales of concert tickets, invitations to parties, lost items, lame jokes, and dubious views on date rape. I wondered why, with so much to be angry about in the world, were university staff and students so incensed about an antiwar movement on campus, why they were so driven to side with the powerful against the powerless. Stories about the controversy ran in the university newspaper and radio station. I was asked to participate in a debate to confront my student-critics. I had trouble in the classroom too, especially in a big first-year class on critical analysis of the news agenda, where students complained about me being "anti-American." Nevertheless, there was wide participation in our antiwar activities, and some of our teach-ins were packed, especially those to do with the media and the war. The younger generation, who had been inclined to be critical but to feel powerless, began to get a rising sense of their own power, power to at least say something to the world, even if not confident of power to bring an alternative into the world.

Opposition to the war was strong throughout Irish society. We continued the protests week after week with massive numbers on the streets. One day we had a "die-in," when thousands lay down in the City Centre to represent those who had died. For the first time in a while, I felt the wind at my back. Through these months, I had a sense the "we"—the millions who took to the streets—were playing our part in shaping the new world order that was emerging from all this trauma. At the same time, I had a strong sense of other forces, those against which we were protesting, being able to carry on and wreak such havoc on the world, no matter what we did. We expected the death and injury, but the looting of hospitals, schools, museums went beyond that. To hear those waging this war call this "liberation" was terrible. When Bush came to Ireland in June 2004, we had a DCU banner among the many others unwelcoming him on a march through Dublin.

I was thinking a lot about death—the deaths on 9-11 and the wars that followed, as well as the deaths of my parents, but there was also new life. During this time, my daughter Clíodna gave birth to my granddaugher Saoirse. I hadn't been pining away to become a grandmother in the abstract, but once there was an actual little person, I was delighted. Babies had been off my radar for a while, but suddenly I found them fascinating again. It put me in touch with the beginning of the life cycle all over again. Meanwhile, Cathal graduated from university and became a teacher. He didn't land a secure position immediately, but became part of the precariat, getting jobs covering maternity leave and having to look for another job each year. One of the schools where he worked as a teacher was one from which he was suspended as a pupil. He was quite preoccupied with discipline, now seeing it all from the other side, becoming a poacher turned gamekeeper. Clíodna was working in the civil service, first in international aid and then in social welfare.

At DCU, I was embattled on several fronts. I even had to fight for what had already been won. There was a round of cuts to options offered to our students, and my history of ideas module was on the list. It was highly regarded, and growing numbers were opting for it. I refused to accept it being cut without a fight, especially when I saw modules that were badly conceived and badly taught being kept because those who taught them couldn't be moved to anything else. I wrote megabytes of email, argued with the head of school, mobilized students, appealed to the president of the university and external examiners, and finally won. I was contacted by the media about the controversy and connected it to global trends moving toward an ever-more commercialized agenda for universities. Soon the financial pressures of the early part of the decade eased, and we were into boom-time expansion again. Room could be found in the curriculum for modules on puppetry, flash poetry, animation, and all sorts of fluff, but I had to keep fighting for modules with more intellectual heft.

In 2006, our faculty was organizing a humanities festival. I suggested a debate on whether the increasing commercialization of universities was a threat to the humanities. On the day of the debate, I went head-to-head with the university president, Ferdinand von Prondzynski. The auditorium was packed. I argued that universities had always been subjected to conflicting agendas and demands, not only by internal factors, but also most characteristically by forces within the wider society. In our own time, the rate of change had become so dizzying that many academics did not know what was happening. I referred to the ferment in universities in the 1960s and the debates between conflicting paradigms that it engendered. I noted that the energy of this engagement had subsided, because a new orthodoxy had taken command, not so much by winning arguments, but by wielding systemic power on a global scale. I was not opposing any commercialization whatsoever, but the dominance of a culture of commercialization and its effect on the idea of the university, the curriculum of the university, the ethos of the university. I was opposing the downgrading of epistemological and ethical norms and their displacement by market norms, the undervaluing of teaching and the overvaluing of inconsequential research, driven by questionable priorities. I gave many examples of how this was shaping teaching and research agendas, leading to a waning of philosophical and historical consciousness, an erosion of public service ethos, and sometimes utter nonsense.

As an example of the lowering of intellectual standards, I cited the appointment of Edward De Bono as adjunct professor, lauded on the DCU website as "the father of thinking about thinking." De Bono gave an inaugural lecture in the big hall of the Helix where he talked megalomaniacal nonsense, characterizing the history of philosophy as being "Socrates, Plato, Aristotle, and De Bono," and making many spurious claims about how his methods had solved problems, spurred innovation, reduced conflict, and stopped wars. After that, HR was organizing six-colored hats workshops, which academic and administrative staff were encouraged to attend and think about thinking in terms of yellow for positivity, green for creativity, red for emotion, and more such nonsense. The phrase "McDonaldization of universities" was being used in some quarters, but we actually had a McDonald's-funded PhD on "managing an intercultural workplace." I asked if DCU's research capacity was for sale to anyone who offered funding, if we had any criteria regarding sources or terms of funding, if we might accept funding from Haliburton for studies of the political economy of oil or the reconstruction of Iraq. After I spoke, von Prondzynski responded, although it is hard for anyone to remember what he said. To his credit, he welcomed the debate and pitched up for it. He showed respect for the concerns I was articulating, but reassured the audience that this was the way universities were going and it would be all right. Although I didn't expect it, a vote was taken at the end, and it was overwhelmingly in support of the proposition that the humanities were threatened by the increasing commercialization of the university. I won the debate, but he won the university. DCU's agenda continued as it was going. The fact that so many came and endorsed my position testified to the degree of interest and concern, but that was still a long way from resistance.

I was defending the humanities, but much that was happening

in the humanities was difficult to defend. De Bono wasn't the only celebrity speaker at DCU to wind me up and make me rail against the prevailing lack of knowledge of intellectual history. Sociologist Steve Fuller declared himself to be the "founder of social epistemology," which was manifestly untrue. Philosopher Marx Wartofsky and others had used the term before him, and others, including most Marxists, had practiced it earlier and better than Fuller. In a "Making Waves" series of lectures, Fuller was invited to address the question "What is science?" as part of an attempt to bring the two cultures of DCU together, but did more to set that back. His lecture was full of non sequiturs, contradictions, and conceptual chaos, and the scientists had no idea what he was saying. Similarly, linguist Ruth Wodak came to speak on critical discourse theory and gave the impression that she and close associates in her academic bubble invented the critical analysis of discourse. I pointed out that it had been around far longer and in far more coherent form before they appeared on the scene. She gave another lecture on her "ethnographic work," consisting of following one MEP around the European Parliament for one day, which came to no clear conclusions about anything, but it was highly funded. To me, it was a waste of public resources. I saw these events as symptomatic of the hollowness and confusion at the heart of the intellectual life of these times.

I don't know if colleagues dreaded seeing me show up when they hosted guest speakers or if they were glad to see a bit of energy generated around them. I attended a business school lecture on macro-marketing by Clifford Schultz of Arizona State University. He clearly saw himself as one of the good guys, exuding missionary fervor talking about foreign direct investment in Cambodia. He was the happy face of exploitation and dismissive of any concept of cultural imperialism. I told him that he portrayed the people of Cambodia as utterly helpless to organize a society without foreign capital to do it for them. His dream projects turned people into slaves of foreign tourists. He replied that foreign direct investment was the only model there was and *Kum ba ya* wouldn't cut it. He said that only the local mafia was against this path. On other occasions, when I raised questions about global distribution of wealth, I got a whole spectrum of responses. One colleague, a lecturer in company law and owner of a property company, replied to a forwarded article on the email list about 1 percent owning 40 percent of wealth: "Dear Helena, Thanks for this piece of excellent news. It is good to see that wealth is distributed into the hands of an elite that can appreciate it, like ourselves. It would be wrong for the majority to enjoy minority pleasures. It would spoil them. I think we should plan a trip to the opera together to celebrate this!"

As DCU celebrated its twenty-fifth anniversary and published its strategic plan, which was all about innovation, networking, entrepreneurship. Many initiatives were presented in inflated language. The "leadership roadshow" was actually only the president and deputy-president walking a few meters from one building to another to visit various units. The "metric dashboard" merely displayed some statistics. The "wisdom of crowds" was no more than organizing a survey. We put much effort into performance management and quality review processes, but I wondered how much came out of them in relation to all the effort that went into them. There was one initiative called "full economic costing," producing an acronym of FEC. We were to measure what percentage of our time went into the different aspects of the job. One absurdity of it was that someone who worked sixty hours, and another who worked six, could come out with the same score. Another absurdity emerged when a colleague asked the finance officer what the cost of the exercise was and he couldn't answer.

I was all for measures to enhance accountability. I proposed, in the interests of mutual accountability, that the annual reports that had to be submitted to the university vertically also be distributed horizontally, because there was much resentment about inequity of workload. While it was good to see the honest achievements of some colleagues listed, those of us who worked scowled over the bloated and false claims and empty fields of others. As I gained in seniority, I was among the gatekeepers on the academic promotions committee and employment interview panels. I joked about being a poacher turned gamekeeper. I was often on my own, opposing stronger weight to be given to external funding, patents, and commercialization projects, and arguing for greater emphasis to be on books, teaching, and service. I didn't like the fast-tracking of yuppies into puppy-professors. One candidate whose promotion I opposed was promoted because he brought in external funding, but bought out (sub-contracted) teaching, and listed nothing under service except showing US Homeland Security operatives around the campus.

What mattered in advancing up the promotion ladder was research, not so much the quality of it, but the quantity of it. Some of this research was interesting and valuable, but much of it was bland, trivial, useless. Many studies were short and shallow, driven by market demand and fast-track careerism. So much of what I heard, read, and reviewed was so half-baked. Conceptualization was weak and confused. Contextualization was thin and random. Conclusions were banal and shallow. Writing was pretentious, clumpy, uninspired, and uninspiring. It was being driven by external funding agenda, metric dashboards, and promotion prospects, and not by curiosity, exploration, and conviction. Theory was not thriving in this milieu. Much of what passed as theory was obfuscating, postmodernist nonsense. There were powerful pressures disincentivizing, eroding, marginalizing critical thinking, creative thinking, systemic thinking—especially systemic thinking. There was an unraveling of powerful explanatory concepts into a confused dissipation of explanatory energy. So much of what was published did nothing to clarify our common condition, but only added to the clutter and confusion.

I saw a new type of academic emerging, one that thrived on bringing in external funding, without being much good at anything else. Once these academics scratched their way to a certain level of seniority, they could collect high salaries and subcontract all their actual work. With this funding, they "bought out" their teaching to do research, and hired researchers to do the actual research and write applications for future funding. Some did genuinely lead research teams and write articles, but others parasited on the labor of others to a degree I never imagined possible. Their citation indices rocketed as their names appeared on papers in which they hadn't written a word. One colleague proposed a formal rule making it compulsory for every publication written by a doctoral or post-doctoral researcher to include the supervisor's name as co-author. I was so opposed to this that the only time I co-published a paper with one of my PhD students, I wrote 70 percent of it.

The rituals around research became more rigid, but not more rigorous. In supervising PhDs, my first advice was to write a book that would advance knowledge and not to imitate clumpy writing, superfluous citation, or overstated and underdigested methodolgism. However, doctoral students were subjected to mixed signals and contradictory advice, because others insisted otherwise. During the progression exam for one of my PhDs, a colleague asserted that he had to identify his key theorists to give himself "ballast" or "cover." He even used the term "crutch." He was saying that he couldn't say anything without referencing someone who said it already. It was not a matter of being less erudite or intellectually rigorous, but a matter of writing in a more lucid, accessible, and graceful way. I received a manuscript from a university press, based on a PhD from their university awarded to a member of the faculty of that university, that they wanted to publish as a book. The cover was already designed and its publication was announced on Amazon prior to peer review. It was suitable neither as a thesis nor a book. The work was riddled with technical problems, factual errors, conceptual confusion, and gross plagiarism. I wrote a report, stating that both intellectual and ethical considerations put it beyond any possibility of publication. Whereas I thought this should raise questions about the author's doctorate and her job, the university press instead gave this report to the author and asked her to resubmit for publication. At the same time, I saw people with good PhDs, serious publications, and strong moral commitments fail to achieve university positions, which made me furious.

Walking around campus, I was constantly confronted by a visual assault on my idea of what a university should be: posters for the annual fashion show, hype about who would be named DCU's top model, the window of the campus bookshop displaying cookery books, children's books, popular novels, but no historical or theoretical works. Watching a film called *Six Semesters*, made by our students, which was all about the pairing and triangulating of their relationships with each other, I wondered where their studies fit into all this, or was the university just a state-subsidized dating service with all this effort at teaching just a thin veneer. I did all in my power to make it otherwise, but I had moments of despair when I came up against a mentality that was pervasive in the wider culture. I was constantly taken aback by the degree of casual irrationality, even in very bright students, when I had to defend basic logic, including the principle of non-contradiction. Their views displayed a kind of intellectual promiscuity, an epistemological recklessness. They seem to believe that simply stating that they wanted to believe something was justification enough for believing it. When I criticized their work for superficiality or confusion, they asserted their right to be superficial or confused. A graduate wrote to me asking if I was still "inspiring and scaring students in equal measures"! While I felt myself at odds with so much going on around me, I had strong rapport with certain colleagues and students, especially my PhD students, and could blow off steam when I was seething with anger or verging on despair.

All this took place against the canvas of the wider world and my sense of the responsibilities of universities to it. I was glad I had a broader platform to make my arguments. I still had many invitations to public lectures and media appearances. One RTE producer referred to a long interview with me as being about "the loneliness of the long-distance Marxist." While some media interviewers took a hostile and hectoring tone with me, most treated my Marxist convictions with curiosity and indulgence, even respect, but I wanted them to see how those convictions gave me clarity and purpose that eluded others. I was invited to speak in a debate at another university on the topic "This house resolves that socialism is a spent force." I expected a rough ride, with the champions of the overdog out in force, but there were a lot of voices on my side. When the vote was taken at the end, the house divided evenly on the motion.

I still got much email from abroad. Of course, I got the usual spam promising me untold riches, whiter teeth, weight loss, stock tips, and extensions to organs I didn't even have. On top of that, there were a variety of responses to my published work. On the same day I got an email telling me not to lose hope, because there would soon be a global armed uprising, and another telling me to grow up because communism was gone forever and good riddance. One informed me that he was impressed with my writings and asked me to keep his contact info so I could let him know when I returned to the church. There were emails taking an imperious tone and making inappropriate demands: "I require lecture notes on theories of science." An art student on another continent informed me that the theme of her "term garment" was existentialism and that she expected help from my side. One asked if an interview I did answered certain questions (which it did, which she would know if she read it), but if it didn't, she suggested that I do the interview again to answer the questions for her assignment. Eventually, as more academics became Internet-accessible, the burden spread, but I still got a disproportionate amount of this. However, many emails I received meant a lot to me. One young man told me that he was a broken man, considering ending his life. Somehow he came upon my history of ideas website and read through the lecture notes and student diaries and began to cry. He wrote, "You and your class are the reason I can see the sun coming up today. I thought I should at least say thank you."

I kept my resolve to manage the teaching-research balance better and I kept the flow of publications going. One task I was given was to write the introduction to Nikolai Bukharin's *Philosophical*

Arabesques, which was one of four book-length manuscripts Bukharin wrote between the time of his arrest and execution. The manuscripts had been buried deep in Stalin's personal archive and only came to light in late glasnost days, when they were published in Russian in the 1990s. It was a heavy experience to have Bukharin's voice from the dead come to me, reaching over time, to have these words handwritten deep in the Lubyanka in 1937 appear in forty-two email attachments sent from New York to Dublin in 2001. I wondered what depths of despair he must have experienced intermittently amid the surges of fervor for the future of Marxism that gave him the energy to write these manuscripts. There was also an autobiographical novel, *How It All Began*. The last thing Bukharin wrote, it was an amazing affirmation of life from one who knew that he was about to die, and in the most abysmal way. It really gave me a jolt even knowing that it was coming, when the text broke off abruptly, knowing that was when he was brought out to be shot. In the course of writing this, I met Stephen Cohen, Bukharin's biographer, who played a major role in recovering these manuscripts and was very helpful to me in my task.

Although I wrote several papers and gave many presentations pushing ahead in my most ambitious project on contemporary universities in the context of the historical struggle over the constitution knowledge, I didn't write the book I intended, because I kept being pulled away in other directions. One problem for authors is continually being requested to speak and write in the area of previous publications. In mid-decade, I got a rash of invitations to speak on Marxism and science. I wrote a new paper sweeping through decades of the impact of Marxism on science studies. I presented it initially in response to an invitation from Princeton University to speak at a symposium marking the fiftieth anniversary of the International History of Science Congress in 1931, where a Soviet delegation led by Bukharin dramatically appeared and put Marxism on the agenda. I arrived at Princeton on a beautiful spring day and walked around the campus, among the halls of ivy, many of them like cathedrals. This was a very memorable conference for me, because it brought me into intense interaction with several authors whose work converged with mine. The opening presentation was by Chris Chilvers, who had recently completed an Oxford PhD on the Soviet delegation at the 1931 congress and their subsequent fates.

I spoke at the second session. I struck a highly engaged, even passionate tone and got a warm and vigorous response from some, while drawing some indications of skepticism or hints of hostility from others. Of course, I had to answer the usual questions about Lysenkoism and to deal with the charge that totalizing thinking inevitably led to totalitarianism. A highlight of the conference was a remarkable paper by Gary Werskey, who had written *The Visible College*, a book about British Marxist scientists of the 1930s, but had been out of academe for the past thirty years. His presentation was as sweeping and passionate as mine. He sketched a history of Marxism and science in terms of a symphony in three movements. Another stimulating speech came from Philip Kitcher, a professor of philosophy at Columbia, who argued that analytic philosophy had completely degenerated and run out of steam. He claimed that the disavowal of politics distorted both philosophy and science studies. On the second day, there were some flaky papers, coming at Marxism in terms of crude antimodernism or quasi-mysticism. There was a final session where everyone, including the Princeton PhD students, articulated their concluding thoughts, which encompassed a very wide range of positions. My interactions with other speakers and audience were intense, especially with Loren Graham of MIT, an eminent historian of Soviet science, with whom I had a number of sharp but good-natured exchanges, stemming from the convergences and contrasts in our positions. He agreed with dialectical materialism as a philosophy of science but disagreed with radical left politics.

On another occasion devoted to the fiftieth anniversary of the 1931 congress, this time on the site of that congress in London, I gave a variation of the same presentation to the British Society for the History of Science. The session where I spoke was packed.

I got some interesting responses, many of them contesting my position on grand narratives, either from positivist or postmodernist positions. Later at the social, I had an interesting encounter with some young historians, who took a teasing tone with me, one saying that my presentation was "rip-roarin'" and another declaring that it made him feel suicidal. My scathing critique of the contemporary academic culture made them think the prospects for their generation were bleak. I did my best to incite them to challenge what stood in their way. I came at this topic in various ways, in response to invitations from other venues in London and Paris, from as far away as Kolkata, and as near as Limerick. The University of Limerick was devoting a conference to an evaluation of the Irish scientist J. D. Bernal. It was driven primarily by the fact that a local man had achieved such prominence on the international stage. Present at this conference was Andrew Brown, who had just published a massive and impressive biography of Bernal, which was being widely and favorably reviewed. I took quite a polemical tone against the Brown biography and the reviews of it. Basically, Brown was admiring of Bernal's science and war effort, bemused by his sexuality and hostile to his philosophy and politics. I therefore took it as my task to come to the defense of Bernal's philosophy and politics. The chair asked Brown to respond, which he did in good grace, recognizing my defense as an honest position that some Marxist was bound to take. Also present was Martin Bernal, J. D. Bernal's son, whose work was equally controversial and also came into my lectures, when I dealt with Eurocentrism and Afrocentrism in the history of ideas.

Then there was an international philosophy of science conference in Dubrovnik. This was held annually at the Inter-University Center for Postgraduate Studies. I had participated in it in 1981 and now discovered what a difference twenty-six years makes. In the past, it had been a stimulating interaction between Marxist and non-Marxist views. This time it was dominated by mathematical logicians who saw Platonism as a defense of scientific realism. I listened to their papers, but it still didn't make much sense to me. Once you accepted certain premises, you could spin off in all sorts of directions, but I really didn't see the point of these thought experiments and possible worlds. It seemed so decontextualized, dehistoricized, and ungrounded in empirical reality. I felt quite alienated from the whole thing, although I found the participants quite friendly and pleasant. They knew my book *Marxism and the Philosophy of Science* and welcomed me warmly. My paper was utterly out of sync with everything else going on, yet it was received in a positive way. The younger participants were curious about Marxism, while the older ones were well-informed and well-disposed toward Marxism, although it had no effect on how they pursued philosophy. They asked me for an expanded version of the paper for the journal *International Studies in Philosophy of Science*, where it was published.

Among the older generation of Eastern European philosophers there, I thought that a particular kind of dishonesty about Marxism prevailed. It extended even to the dead. I spoke at a memorial meeting for Polish philosopher of science Wladislaw Krajewski and also spoke of others, such as Croatian philosopher of science Srdan Lelas, who had died since I was last there. I knew both Krajewski and Lelas as Marxists, but I was the only one to mention that Marxism was ever a part of their lives. I read obituaries of them where it was not mentioned either. I spoke to a younger Croatian philosopher of science, an empiricist in philosophy of physics but a quite credulous Catholic, who was a student of Lelas and never thought of him as a Marxist. A young Bulgarian woman observed that, previously in Bulgaria, those who weren't Marxist dressed up what they had to say with certain phrases to make it seem that they were Marxist. Now it was the opposite. A young Hungarian guy said that it was much the same in Hungary, but it varied with disciplines. When Croatians in the conversation were asked about the position of Marxism in Croatia, they said: zero. It was not taught anymore in schools or universities. I asked if there were any who did research and made arguments from a Marxist point of view. Yes, but only if they were very old and very brave.

The Russians agreed there was a huge retreat from Marxism, a silence about it, but there were still those who believed in it quietly.

Dubrovnik was still a beautiful place, but it felt so different to me than when it was part of Yugoslavia. I did not find ethnically cleansed Catholic Croatia so attractive. I hadn't seen so many nuns wearing habits in decades. In the hotel where I was staying, there was a conference on weapons of mass destruction. All badges had US or Croatian flags on them. It was a threat management course where the USA was instructing Croatia on playing its part in their war on terror. I went to a concert of contemporary Croatian music with a choir and symphony orchestra. I thought it sounded great, but found it hard to judge its meaning. For all I knew, they could have been singing praise to the glorious Ustashe or saying that Franjo Trudjman was the greatest leader in a thousand years. I was struggling with questions about how those I knew had managed the transition to this Croatia. I was especially troubled by the fact that Srdan Lelas had become deputy minister of higher education in the Trudjman government. Whenever I was inquiring about such matters, I sometimes felt as if I were riffling through people's underwear drawers or reading their intimate correspondence, that it was somehow obscene to mention Marxism.

I later investigated what became of the Tito Political School in Kumrovec and discovered that this fantastic purpose-built building became a military training facility, then a refugee center, and then was abandoned. Books from the library and the shelves were looted or left to rot. Stipe Mesic, when president of Croatia, suggested seeking private investors to make it an elite golf club. I processed the geopolitical tragedy over a period of time, but sometimes discovering the details made me want to weep about it all again.

I continued to follow developments in this part of the world, from national elections to the transformation of everyday life. I was appalled when the former king became prime minister in Bulgaria from 2001 to 2005. What was most upsetting was to see so many lives deteriorating in so many ways. People were flailing about, not knowing what to believe or what to do. Berlin was a city where I kept tracking the transformations. At times, I felt overwhelmed by how the space of what had been the GDR was being swamped by market forces. The traces of the GDR were either disappearing or being marketed as kitsch. The authentic traces were harder to find, but still there, and I found them in my visits to Marxists who continued to believe and band together, despite their reduced circumstances.

I liked walking alone around foreign cities, thinking of how history had flowed through them. In Paris, I walked along the Left Bank of the Seine and thought about Peter Abelard lecturing at Notre Dame. It was a city rich in evoking the centuries in the history of ideas. It was all so visually there: medieval Christianity, modern rationalism, monarchy, empire, enlightenment, bourgeois revolution, Marxism, existentialism, new left, and postmodernism. As I went to speak at a symposium on Marxist historiography of science, I even came across a square named after Paul Langevin and a school named after Frédéric Joliot-Curie. The streets were named after saints, kings, scientists, communists. I thought, too, of those who came from abroad and the impact the place had on them, especially the British Marxist writer Christopher Caudwell, who came here in the 1930s, during the high tide of the Popular Front and crossed here again on his way to death in Spain. I had several occasions to travel to London to speak about him for the centenary of his birth. During holidays in Italy, Spain, and Greece, I absorbed all I could about their history and culture, especially about the life of the left. The Historical Materialism conferences built up during this first decade of the twenty-first century attracted nearly a thousand activist intellectuals across a broad left spectrum from all over the world each year to London. I participated every few years and was happy to see the conferences expand beyond Britain to other continents.

The left in Ireland struggled to make its case, despite the thinned-out political milieu of the time. Fianna Fail, which had transformed itself from a party of Irish republicanism to a party of integration into neoliberal globalization, was in government for the whole of the decade, although elections yielded an ever more diverse opposition. They gave free rein to market forces and ran the public sector in the interests of the private sector. They did not support the US war on terror, but didn't oppose it, either. They turned a blind eye to use of Shannon Airport to transport US troops to Afghanistan and Iraq, and even prisoners for "extraordinary rendition." Election debates between Fianna Fail and Fine Gael in 2002 and 2007 were excruciating exercises in competitive accountancy with all the excitement of slightly contrasting spreadsheets. The left did our best to expose and oppose this. When I was invited to speak on a panel about the aftermath of the 2007 election, I engaged in a polemic against too narrow a definition of the political, and for the need to address political questions in a more global and zeitgeisty way. I was delighted when the other speakers also addressed the question in this way, although the chair was caught on the hop and puzzled by it all.

Ireland was steadily secularizing. The Church had been losing its grip over decades. Revelations of clerical paedophilia accelerated this process. The Church still had considerable control over the school system, though. One day, Saoirse was at my house and asked about pictures of Marx and Engels on the wall. Who were they, she wanted to know. I said that they were men who lived in the nineteenth century, who thought that nobody should be rich or poor. She asked if they were in heaven with God. I asked why she thought there was a God and a heaven. She just knew it, she said, though it was obvious that she was taught it in school. I had little to do with the Church, but it still kept popping into my life. I was asked to be external examiner for philosophy at Milltown Institute, a Jesuit institution, and I was very impressed with the commitment of those who taught there. I got to know the chair of the department, Kevin O'Higgins, a Jesuit priest. One night I was in his apartment in the Ballymun towers until all hours, asking him questions about his belief in God, afterlife, and being a priest today. The old answers were truly gone, but the new liberation theology responses didn't work for me either. Kevin was involved in a project to bridge the gap between the disadvantaged subculture of Ballymun and the universities, running courses to bring their confidence and study skills to a university entrance level.

This was a time of prosperity in Irish society. Wages soared. I was astonished when my own salary pushed over the line of €100,000 for the last years of my working life. House prices soared too, especially in Dublin, but I was fortunate enough to buy my house just before that. Colleagues at DCU were buying houses farther and farther from Dublin, where many new housing estates were being built. They had nicer and newer houses, but very long commuting times, but I was happy living within walking distance of work. Not everyone was so fortunate. Although there was not as much good Irish television drama as there had been in previous periods, one series called *Prosperity* captured the growing disparity, showing the new housing estates, high-rise office blocks, and glossy malls from the perspectives of those excluded from them or entered them only to clean them. Even during this boom, our public health system was in crisis. Despite more money than ever coming in taxes, the country conformed to the global trend to privatize public assets and services, to underfund public services, and to run the public sector in the interests of the private sector. The situation in accident and emergency departments of our public hospitals was the stuff of many talk shows and wringing of hands, but it didn't improve. The left highlighted all this, but the center got its way.

The "Celtic Tiger" was the cause of much international attention and approbation, which was the source of dangerous hubris. At the same time, there was an undercurrent of discomfort and disaffection that manifested itself in two referenda on EU treaties. The treaties of Nice in 2001 and Lisbon in 2008 were both supported by all major political parties as well as business and trade union bodies. Nevertheless, there were vigorous "No" campaigns run by the radical left and traditional right, combining all sorts of arguments: opposition to neoliberal hegemony, decision-making structures moving further from people, militarization of Europe, enlargement of the EU, worries about abortion being legalized. In both referenda, against all expectations, the No side won, the treaties were rejected, and the political establishment went into overdrive to frighten the electorate into reversing the decisions during the following years when the treaties were ratified.

Such disaffection with neoliberal globalization was global. It expressed itself most visibly in the World Social Forum, which met annually, all over the world, formed to be the polar opposite of the World Economic Forum meetings in Davos every year. I was no longer free to go wherever the action was: Porto Alegre, Mumbai, Caracas, Bamako, Nairobi, Genoa, but I related to it as best I could. The World Social Forum was a movement of civil society organizations, not political parties, which was both its strength and weakness. It was opening new space and recognizing a new scenario where fewer felt they could fit into political parties, but tended to be too hostile to what political parties could achieve. It developed much in the way of good critical analysis and alternative proposals, but emphasis on horizontalism, localism, direct democracy, small-is-beautiful downscaling, and "changing the world without taking power" limited its challenge to existing structures of economic, political, and social power. It was good to build alternatives from below, but still necessary to take on the power exercised from above. Not that we really knew how to do that anymore, but we had to think about how to expropriate the expropriators in this era of financialized globalized capitalism.

The dictatorship of capital was the primary plot of this period. It was the title of a song by Alistair Hulett whose albums *In the Back Streets of Paradise* and *Dance of the Underclass* gave engaging expression to the milieu in which the left had to make its case. I corresponded with Hulett for a while. He even took on postmodernism in his songs, which I told him I appreciated. He thought that what Trotsky said about anarchism applied to postmodernism. It was like an umbrella with holes, which was fine until it started to rain. Even if postmodernism saw itself as oppositional to capital, it was, as Fredric Jameson asserted in the subtitle of his book on the subject, "The Cultural Logic of Late Capitalism." I was conscious of how capital not only dominated economies but also colonized minds. I could see it in academe, where various forms of neopositivism and postmodernism prevailed. Although these two phenomena seemed to be opposite, they were both the rhythms through which capitalism, the most totalizing system the world had ever known, paralyzed totalizing thinking. All the mania for metrics, the surveys of the surface, the exotica of deconstruction, the conclusions of inconclusiveness blindsided any drive toward unifying vision. This was how capitalism characteristically functioned as a system disabling systemic thinking and therefore systemic opposition. Year after year, I saw students falling under the spell of these ideas, and colleagues narrowing their horizons to conform to the latest trends and methods. I was reviewing an edited collection on television studies that was nothing more than a series of bitty postmodernist celebrations of pleasure as resistance, and failed to look at any interesting questions raised more broadly by the television of this period. I was asked about the US series *Nip/Tuck* on one occasion and I observed that it pushed out the boat in various ways. It dramatized decadence, but I alternated between wondering if it was a critique of decadence and thinking that it was just decadent. For some academics, the concept of decadence was out of order.

US presidential elections, as ever, received saturation coverage in Ireland and the rest of the world. I thought it was ludicrous for the person elected to be regarded as "the leader of the free world." Still, in 2004, I wanted the Bush administration to be defeated. I thought they ruled ruthlessly and recklessly, representing a tiny elite of the world's elite, not only against the interests of the working people of the world, but even against the interests of the mainstream elite. Of course, I would also oppose a Kerry administration, which would serve the interests of this elite better, as a more sophisticated and multilateral form of capitalism, dominating-profiteering-privatizing the world all the more effectively. I remembered John Kerry from Vietnam Veterans Against the War in 1971 and was disappointed that he did not offer anything more critical or radical now. Whatever problems there were in the world, the US armed forces were not the answer to any of them. I especially hated the way the US, no matter which party won, usurped the role of the UN in dealing with international conflicts. I hated it on *The West Wing*, which gave dramatic expression to the fictional liberal alternative administration. Although the series was sophisticated, intelligent, ironic, well-written, and well-made, it was overbearingly myopic and arrogant. The characters, supposedly the brightest and the best, graduates of Ivy League universities, spoke as if they made the day dawn and the planets revolve. The White House was seen as the center of the universe, and the presidency was approached with regal awe. It accepted without question that, as a *West Wing* character said: "America stands today as the one truly indispensable nation," which justified imperial domination as humanitarian intervention. The series debated a number of vital issues and aired real ideological tensions at a remarkably high level for television drama, but it did so within the parameters of US mainstream political discourse and was oblivious to the richer political discourse of the wider world. Its conception of America made me feel very European. US exchange students made me feel European, too. One wrote in her course diary that she thought that Bush was doing a great job, because he made her feel safe. I asked her if he made Iraqis feel safe. Because of "Operation Iraqi Freedom," a hundred thousand Iraqis were dead and not free to live another day of their lives. Although he did not make most Americans safer either, Bush won the 2004 election. There was also the question of the class interests of many of those who voted for Bush. It was voting as if rich, while living poor. It was clear that you could fool a lot of the people a lot of the time.

It was the same choice that was on offer in the 2008 election, although it was hard not to be seduced by Barack Obama. He was handsome, intelligent, sophisticated. He promised to stand up for Main Street against Wall Street. He was critical of wars in Afghanistan and Iraq. He had written a fine book, *Dreams of My Father*, which was graceful, reflective, and progressive. I dared to hope, although not for much, just something more social democratic and less imperial. Watching Pete Seeger and Bruce Springsteen singing "This Land Is Your Land" at the inaugural concert, I found myself in tears. However, Obama fell below my low threshold of expectation even before the Inauguration, when he summoned Larry Summers and Tim Geithner to his economic team, signaling from the start that he would stand with Wall Street against Main Street and not vice versa. He also continued US wars. In some ways, he was even worse than Bush, because he knew better, or at least he once did. Although the US election was fascinating, not least for the comic ignorance that Republican vice-presidential candidate Sarah Palin brought to it, the coverage of it was so disproportionate. All sorts of things happening else-where, even elections, were barely noticed. For example, elections in Nepal brought communists to power and led to the abolition of monarchy.

By this time, the global economic crisis had transformed the whole political atmosphere. The US subprime mortgage crisis led to an international banking crisis, which led to global recession. Even with my critique of capitalism, carried for decades now with constant revelations of its distortions and injustices, I was still stunned by capitalism's process of socialization of losses while still protecting the privatization of profits. In 2008, the Irish government announced a blanket guarantee on the six main banks, making the public sector liable for billions of private losses, result-ing in monumental public debt and cuts to public funding for health, education, salaries, pensions, welfare. The public reaction was furious. I had never seen so many people in Ireland so angry. This anger came into every encounter and dominated every con-versation. Every day brought new financial scandals and a dawning realization by many, who thought they lived in a democracy, that they actually lived in an oligarchy. In 2009, more than one hundred thousand, organized by the Irish Congress of Trade Unions, protested on the streets of Dublin against financial corruption, public-sector wage cuts, and rising unemployment. Earlier that week, we had a packed union meeting at DCU, which fully supported this protest and called for a public sector strike. On the day, many workers marched in uniform—doctors, nurses, firefighters, even police. Cathal was out that week performing in street theater, where he was wearing a Brian Cowan (Irish prime minister) mask and shaking a can collecting money for the banks.

Every day we woke up to more gloomy news: a story about university pension funds being transferred into the exchequer to cover the current deficit, an embargo on recruitment and promotion in public service, the creation of a bad bank to use government bonds to acquire distressed loans created by the property bubble, and constant new levies, new taxes, new cuts. We had little time to recover from one attack before steeling ourselves for the next one. These assaults on the working class were being administered on behalf of those who had already overaccumulated at our expense. The class nature of our society had never been so clear to so many. The rollercoaster ride from boom to gloom was at least bringing a degree of illumination to the land.

Meanwhile, I took my Internet use to a new level and joined Facebook and Twitter. Among the many aspects of these new social media was the articulation of our common experience of this crisis and the facilitation of our struggle against it. It also gave me a way to reconnect with people with whom I had lost contact, to communicate with many people all at once instead of writing individual emails, to read many articles and blogs I would not have found otherwise. I also became connected to many people I did not know previously: people who read my books or agreed with my comments on a particular thread or found me by one circuitous route or another.

The years were whizzing by. One of the most difficult aspects of advancing age was seeing so many people who walked some of the way with me passing from life. I was sad to learn of the deaths of Monty Johnstone, Adam Schaff, Paul Sweezy, Harry Magdoff, George Labica, Mihailo Markovic, Svetozar Stojanovic, Milos Nikolic, Nuala O Faolain, Michael O'Riordan. I was able to attend the funerals only of those in Ireland. Nuala's funeral was full of contradictions, not least in that it was in a church. She was neither a believer nor someone who had resolved her relationship to such belief. Mick's funeral was otherwise. It was secular and communist. There was a procession full of red flags marching into the cemetery in Glasnevin. He was an iconically significant person in the country, and his passing got a lot of national media attention. Around the same time, Charles Haughey, ex-taoiseach, received a pompous state funeral, although he was corrupt, deceitful, hypocritical, vainglorious, and reactionary. The public discourse was mixed, but dominated by an avalanche of nauseating, dishonest commentary.

At work, I was on the last stretch of this road, but kept busy processing postgrad applications, formulating learning outcomes, planning policies and structures for the future—a future without me! I was being treated as if indispensable, just before becoming dispensable. I took none of my allowed holidays. As the clock ticked toward September 30, 2009, my retirement date determined by the end of the academic year in which I turned sixty-five, I was sorting out my files and office, and seeing the traces of me disappearing from it, as I moved books and other objects to my home. Every time I gave a lecture for the last time, I had this sense that it was such a waste, having to put such an abrupt end to my teaching, after spending so many years fine-tuning my capacity to do it and still being so passionate about it. I thought a lot about retirement as a rite of passage. So many of the clichés about it didn't work for me: "You're only as old as you feel" or "This is ME time." It represented the possibilities of life closing down and being that much nearer to death, but it also opened up more time to write, to protest, and to travel. It was the writing that would last, and that was the only kind of afterlife for which I could hope. So I was positive about my plans for the next phase of life. As always, although there was a plan, there would be quite a few surprises and unanticipated turns as well.

CHAPTER 5

Under African Skies

AFRICA LIVED A LONG TIME in my imagination before ever I set foot there. My images of Africa, my connections to Africa, went through many stages over the decades. My fascination with Africa started when I was a child, peering at the globe and seeing a huge, distant continent, where nobody I knew had ever been, a vast and distant land where people supposedly lived a more primitive way of life. In the 1950s, there were collections in our Catholic classrooms to save "pagan babies." For every five dollars the class collected, a baby in Africa could be baptized and we could choose their names, which were always names like ours: Joseph, John, Mary, Margaret. We admired the work of missionaries, who wore long white habits and moved among the native masses, bringing them health and truth. It was so glamorous. I thought I might do that. My city, Philadelphia, was inhabited by the descendants of Africans. Those around me saw them as dark and dangerous. They lived in ghettoes. If you went there, you would be mugged or murdered. I wasn't so sure. When I was a teenager, I went to these neighborhoods and formed relationships there.

My ideas about the world advanced as I did. The civil rights movement of the 1960s stirred me to my depths. I loved singing

"We Shall Overcome" and seeing my light hands interlaced with dark ones. The harmony of this movement gave way to the disharmonies of radical feminism and Black Power. I was hurt by Black rhetoric denouncing all whites, just as progressive men were by feminist condemnations of the male of the species. Whatever Black Power activists said in public, activists of all hues could still talk and work together. As our movements increasingly saw ourselves linked to international movements, we cheered on national liberation movements everywhere, delighting in the decolonization of Africa and decrying the assassinations and coups bringing down regimes headed by Lumumba, Nkrumah, and Sankara.

I was a member of the Irish anti-apartheid movement in the 1970s and 1980s. At first, it was just one of many organizations to which a left activist was expected to belong. Kader and Louise Asmal and a core group around them ran it, while the rest of us attended protests against apartheid in South Africa, in between those against the US war in Vietnam and the Pinochet regime in Chile. We were busy with many causes. We marched down O'Connell Street so many times, protested outside Dail Eireann or the Department of Foreign Affairs or the US Embassy over so many issues. We picketed Dunnes Stores in support of suspended and striking workers, when cashiers heeded the UN boycott of South African goods and refused to sell Outspan oranges. At the many protests and public meetings, I heard so much about South Africa from visiting South African speakers. Sharpeville, Soweto, Group Areas Act, ANC, UDF—I listened and learned.

During my stint at the International Lenin School in Moscow in 1978 I met many comrades from many countries but became especially attached to those in the South African Communist Party. We had social events where people sang political songs from their own countries. The first time I heard the South African Communist Party (SACP) group sing "Give a Thought to Africa," I felt my relation to Africa intensify. Through the 1980s, I met many Africans in Europe. I sought more and more occasions to do so. I went through periods when I was obsessed with Africa and read many African novels as well as histories, biographies, literary criticism, almost anything I could get. I found some of these easily in paperback editions in Irish bookstores, but others I ordered from obscure African publishers by post and eagerly awaited parcels from distant places like Gweru. I frequented the Development Studies Library of UCD, where I was teaching. I grasped at any source. I was suspicious of *Africa Confidential* but found it compelling all the same. I subscribed to *The African Communist* and then started receiving *Umsembenzi.* aimed at underground activists. The latter was full of instructions about how to check that you weren't being followed and how to use dead-letter boxes. It was not exactly information I needed, but I was somehow chuffed to be receiving it. In Yugoslavia, in 1989, I had met a government minister from Zimbabwe, who asked me if I would come and give lectures at the ZANU-PF political school. I was honored to be asked and agreed to do it, but somehow it never happened.

The 1990s saw South African exiles, including a number I knew, returning to South Africa. I wondered about the lives they were living there. Sketchy correspondence answered some of my questions, but South Africa was still exotic and mysterious to me. I thought that the time would come when I could go and see for myself. I didn't want to go too soon, though. It meant too much to me to go only for a quick visit or holiday. I wanted to go in a way that would be meaningful, that would allow me to penetrate and participate in some way. From afar, I watched the big events that made world news: the release of Nelson Mandela, the masses queuing in the sun to vote in South Africa's first democratic elections, the victory of the African National Congress (ANC), inauguration of Mandela as president of South Africa. I had gone to Dublin's Merrion Square, to the statue of Mandela there, to celebrate with others on the day of his release. I had stood in Kildare Street when he was given the Freedom of the City of Dublin awarded to him in 1988 and presented in 1990. I had my reservations about the emphasis put on the role of Mandela, because I did not accept the Great Man theory of history. Even less did I believe in the idea or reality of "the Mother of the Nation" who stood by his side. I watched the inauguration on live television. I felt elation at some moments, but a massive disappointment when the first words Mandela spoke as president of the new South Africa were "Your royal highnesses." In the years that followed, I winced when he honored royalty, posed with princesses and Spice Girls, wined and dined with the global rich and powerful, when he pronounced patriarchally that neoliberal economic policy was nonnegotiable. I knew that he was a great man in his way, but there was a tendency to talk of him as a god.

I wanted to know what the new South Africa meant for those who were not Nelson Mandela. I wanted to know what happened after the world's media had packed up and gone elsewhere, what happened when a liberation movement came to power. I was curious about the texture of everyday life, about the long march through all the institutions of society, about the transformation of media, schools, universities, townships, trade unions, everything. When the time came for my sabbatical in 2000–2001, I prepared to go. I was interested in investigating the intellectual dimensions of the transformation in South Africa, particularly the conceptualization of class, race, and gender in the process of transforming higher education. I wanted to probe the extent to which academic disciplines were being reconceptualized in this process. I planned to write a book, "The Rise of the Repressed in the History of Knowledge."

I consulted Kader Asmal, who had become minister for education. He advised me to go to the University of Cape Town (UCT) and gave me my initial contacts there. After that, I sent megabytes of email, making further academic and political contacts. Although my first flight was delayed and I ran like the wind, wondering if I would arrive to a missed connecting flight or a cardiac emergency, I got the flight in London and arrived in Cape Town, even if my luggage did not. I found the physical actuality of a place I had for so long only imagined nearly overwhelming at first. The UCT campus was strikingly beautiful. Built on a mountain, there were vistas of Devil's Peak above and a panoramic view of the Cape Town suburbs and townships below. By day or night, I thrived on sitting on the steps of the upper campus and processing my experiences from there. The buildings were of various styles. The central Jameson Hall looked like it had been transplanted from classical Greece. I liked best the structures built on multilevels in a modernist African style, with the interior décor featuring African motifs and art celebrating national liberation movements. The campus was a melange of mixed signals, of unreflective juxtapositions and unresolved contradictions, of ragbag eclecticism, as well as considered syntheses. The names of buildings honored oppressors and oppressed alike. You could walk from the Steve Biko building across the Cissie Gool Plaza to the Oppenheimer Library to the Otto Beit Building. You could see a mural celebrating education for women in Africa and a series of paintings depicting UCT in struggle. You could attend a lecture on poverty in the Nedbank Room and study environmental science in the Shell Building. These were not just names and symbols, of course, but a reflection of real forces in motion in unresolved contradictions in the university and society.

Presiding over it all in a commanding position on the upper campus was the statue of Cecil John Rhodes with an inscription evoking his dream of empire from Cape to Cairo. Every time I passed it, I cringed. Rhodes was a symbol of white supremacy, colonial conquest, capitalist expropriation, ruthless class rule. One day I heard a UCT student showing incoming students around campus, stopping at the Rhodes statue and explaining, "We honor him for giving us all this." I wanted to scream that it was not his to give and ask how she could be so blinded by false consciousness. I constantly raised the question of Rhodes with various colleagues at UCT and even comrades in the SACP, none of whom seemed so agitated about it as I was. They agreed with my critique of Rhodes, but said it was only a statue and it didn't matter so much. I thought of what I would like to see happen to it. Options of smashing it or putting it in a museum had their merits, but what I thought would be a good idea would be to con-textualize it, to build around it a representation of the whole class structure of the Cape Colony over which he so oppressively pre-sided. Nobody seemed very interested in the idea. At the same time, the statue of Rhodes featured in a series of paintings on campus surrounded by demonstrators demanding "people's edu-cation." In one, Mandela was on a platform in doctoral robes with fist clenched beneath the statue of Rhodes with the masses below. Eventually, the Rhodes Must Fall movement came along, but it took another fourteen years for all the questions swirling around this statue to burst forth in high drama.

I resided in All Africa House (AAH). It was situated on the UCT middle campus, where it housed international academics like me, doing research on Africa, and African postgrads doing research in all areas. There were individual rooms with beds and desks and communal kitchens in different clusters. There were also commu-nal rooms for computers, television, celebrations, and lectures. In the middle was a courtyard, where there were sometimes big *braais* (barbecues) and small tête-à-têtes. The atmosphere was harmo-nious on the whole, but there were tensions to do with deciding what channel to watch on television, stealing food (where the poorest were not the culprits), a patriarchal male trying to domi-nate discussions, an aggressive female intruding on conversations and demanding other people's contacts, and miscellaneous minor irritations. I got on well with most residents and enjoyed the atmo-sphere of the place.

There were lively discussions and debates surrounding news, current affairs, and even drama in the television room. When I first arrived, there was a news item about a pageant for the annual opening of parliament, depicting the parliament's history of strug-gle. The opposition were complaining that it was necessary to get past all this, because it created divisions. On the news another night, President Thabo Mbeki was on a state visit to Britain, where he bowed to the queen and his wife curtsied to her. I thought it was deeply dis-edifying for the president of a republic to bow to royalty, whereas others said it was protocol and didn't really matter much. Another night there was an item about Mandela visiting a rural community and telling them that the multinational companies investing in South Africa cared about them and their poverty. I launched into a critique of GEAR, the neoliberal economic policy that Mandela had imposed. Africans were defensive about Mandela and were a bit shocked to hear anyone speak negatively of him. However, when any matter of US foreign policy came on the news, the tide was well against it. AAH ran a lecture series with outside guests, followed by a catered dinner. The night I gave a lecture in this series, the discussion was lively and went on for many hours, as members of the local SACP branch mingled with UCT academics. After a while, AAH residents told me I was still conducting the seminar and they wanted me to dance. So I danced.

Some mornings the discussion and debates began at breakfast. One day I asked what would be happening for International Women's Day and then it was off. The African patriarch announced that feminism had gone too far, and a bunch of feisty African feminists were tumbling over each other to take him on. Sometimes I would read out loud stories from the morning papers that I thought were particularly scandalous but others thought unproblematic. I was incensed by a report that Sir Anthony O'Reilly, head of the Independent group that owned many SA newspapers, invited two hundred of the rich and famous of the world, including "the cream of Anglo-Irish society," which included Kader and Louise Asmal, to celebrate his knighthood at a banquet at Cape Town Castle. What bothered me that day, as on many subsequent days, was glancing at the social columns and seeing people, who came to power through a liberation movement, mixing so intimately with global oligarchs.

I spent much of each day on the upper campus, where most lectures took place. I was based in the Centre for Higher Education Development (CHED), where I had a desk and computer and UCT email account. There was a start-of-term reception and everyone was very welcoming. Many of them told me they had been to my website and read my work. Linda Cooper gave me a paper she wrote on trade union education in South Africa, characterizing it as a shift from a liberation movement's collectivist ideological struggle for knowledge to a technocratic path to individual social mobility. I was also attached to the Graduate School of the Humanities, where I also received a warm welcome.

There was a societies fair on the plaza. There were lots of stands to do with religion, finance, and sport, but initially no politics. One Christian publication I was given said that UCT was once called "Moscow on the hill," but these days, even though there were still "a few pinko profs" around, it was different. Later I saw a SACP table and made contact with the students and former students running that. The ex-students, some graduates and some expelled, were still hanging around campus with no work, no income, no home, but surviving by sleeping in other people's rooms and eating in residences.

The move away from politics wasn't just reflected in extracurricular activity but in curricular choices, as well. One academic after another told me that students were voting with their feet, away from politics to business, more generally away from humanities into commerce, law, media studies. One political issue that a substantial number of students did care about was the financing of higher education. On television news, I saw a number of demonstrations at various universities at the beginning of term about "financial exclusion," or students not being able to register because of not paying fees. The next day, it was happening at UCT too. I caught sounds of liberation songs on campus and investigated. Students were marching through campus, and cleaners were joining in the singing and toyi-toyi-ing. I spoke with students and they told me of their struggles to get into university and to keep going financially once there. Moreover, they explained that they felt alienated from the culture of UCT, with accusations ranging from racism on the part of lecturers and administrators, to Eurocentrism in the curriculum, to neoliberalism in government education policy. A few weeks later, I saw one of the leaders of the student demonstrations all bandaged up and I asked him what had happened to him. He said that he was stabbed, because students who were poor and stood up to authority were systematically victimized.

On another day, during orientation week, Jameson Hall was packed with students for Pieter-Dirk Uys, a stand-up comic and AIDS activist, giving a serious but satirical speech about AIDS. He spoke of the debacle of the ministry of health issuing millions of free condoms with instructions on how to use them in eleven languages, which they then stapled to the packs, effectively meaning death sentences in many cases. He said that every woman should carry condoms and ask the man to use them if being raped. Most shockingly (to me, at least), he said that they should make condoms the right size for eight-year-old boys.

I spent much time talking to UCT academics and probing them about the process of academic transformation as they saw it. I started with Martin Hall, the dean of CHED, where I was based. His field was the archaeology of Cape Town. He took me to the waterfront for a walk and talk and spoke of the original inhabitants of this area, San hunter-gatherers, whose forced labor built the breakwater. He told me that my UCT residence was built over a burial ground for slaves. He communicated many fascinating and disturbing facts to me, but always within a well-conceived theoretical framework, talking about the materiality of culture and the grounding of ideas in economic, social, and political realities. He moved between past and present in such a way that the one resonated with the other, coming to contemporary problems of academic transformation, nation-building, and globalization as experienced from below.

In my one-to-one meetings on campus, some conversations flowed more easily than others, but all were instructive in their way. One of the people who had the biggest impact on me was among the first I met. Neville Alexander was a political activist as well as a professor. He had spent ten years on Robben Island and then five years under house arrest. His office was tastefully decorated with

African art. I briefly told him what I was investigating and after that I hardly had to ask any questions. He addressed the question of how to Africanize the curriculum, how to overcome the disabling effects of Eurocentrism. Basically, for him, it was a matter of seeing European and African intellectual traditions as interdependent rather than as Manichean opposites. Afrocentrism was the colonized mind trying to free itself, but in the wrong way. He thought the transformation process at UCT left a lot to be desired, but there were things happening. White South African scholars had begun to change, to position themselves in Africa, and to look at the world from there. He thought that Afrikaners who changed tended to liberate themselves more profoundly and to scrutinize and even satirize their previous selves. In some ways, he thought, the germ of revival was there, even more so than with English-speaking liberals or even Blacks. This surprised me and I had many experiences confirming this to some extent.

I regularly visited the Centre for African Studies. The look of CAS was bright, modern, attractive, and African in its decor. There were murals and sculptures all around and a good use of space. There was an open invitation to tea every Friday at 10:00 a.m. The first day I attended, it was mostly foreigners around the table, with each of us asked to introduce ourselves and our research projects. Then I had a long talk with Brenda Cooper, the CAS director, who was warmly welcoming. She was a once-Marxist. She admitted that many intellectuals had lost their bearings, becoming decentered with the dominance of postmodernism and the decline in political engagement. She was still a progressive intellectual but she had lost clarity and focus at the level of rock-bottom philosophical assumptions. The courses put forward by CAS were really interesting: problematizing the study of Africa, images of Africa, debates in African studies. Their posters and leaflets were well designed, visually and textually. There was a small restaurant there on campus called Afrikwizeen, where I became a regular and came to be called "Mama."

CAS also ran events. One of the first that I attended featured a

musician and poet from the Cape Flats, an area of densely populated townships southeast of Cape Town, performing original
work. I had never seen poetry so fully performed and not just read
or recited. There was hardly any audience. I stayed until the end
and talked to the performers. The poet lived in a squatter camp
"where no mail comes." He said that he could have been either
a gang leader or a village idiot. He chose the latter. He claimed
descent from the Khoi, the indigenous inhabitants of the area,
and much of the poetry was about recovering continuity with that
past. Others were about life in Manenberg, where crime, drugs,
and AIDS were part of the new South Africa. I recorded a lot of
ihis performance on video. He said, "You will take me away with
you. That's beautiful." Another CAS event attracted a large audience, a guest lecture by a visiting professor, John Hope Franklin,
described as the "doyen of African American historians," who
spoke on "slavery, race, and reconciliation." It would have been
fine if he had been speaking to a class of US first- or second-
graders, but for a university audience it was baby-talk. The Cape
Flats performers were scheduled to give another performance at
the same time, but they were put out of their space to accommodate the overflow audience for the visiting professor. I watched
them walking away. I felt sad and angry at the contrast between
the reception given to local guys striving to come up from under,
to say something thick and textured, who were vulnerable, being
treated so carelessly, with that given to the foreign visitor, who was
so empty and inflated, being obsequiously honored. That evening,
I asked the Nigerian patriarch what he thought of the lecture. "The
issue of slavery will resonate," he orated. "I didn't ask you what you
thought about slavery," I said, "I asked you about the lecture." He
then remarked that the guy was old, as if that explained everything.

   I attended lots of departmental seminars and guest lectures on
campus. Being a philosopher, I naturally made contact with the
philosophy department. They were very welcoming, but I found the
atmosphere, nevertheless, alienating due to the same issue I found
in many other philosophy departments in the Anglo-American

world. Although I was well familiar with the discourse of analytical philosophy, I was not on the same wavelength. There was one seminar on the concept of "agency" that was mind-numbingly tedious in a stiflingly hot room. I did my best to persist to be polite, but eventually I had to leave, because I was afraid I would pass out. The head of the department followed me out and asked if I was all right. I said I was faint. He asked if it wasn't that I was bored. I had to admit that it was that, too. Another day the seminar was about economic justice, which seemed more promising. However, I argued, the speaker tended to use relatively benign examples of variable distribution of resources, which seemed to make the limited range of options discussed seem reasonable. I cited examples of how people were living at the top and bottom ends of life in South Africa, the massive, unearned wealth juxtaposed with the grim, unremitting poverty. One day I presented a talk titled "The History of Philosophy: Questions About Class, Race, and Gender." I explained that I was sketching on a big canvas and would be skimming over things about which there was much more to be said, but that I would rather say too little about too much than too much about too little—which was what most philosophy seminars in my life had done. It was received politely, but there was no real meeting of minds. I also presented in CHED on global trends in higher education, and what an agenda on academic transformation might be. This was well received and led to a lively discussion and subsequent talks and emails about it. Salma Ismail came to see me to discuss these ideas, saying that I had raised questions that many people thought they had dealt with, but had actually left unresolved. My talk had reminded them of what they had forgotten.

Another day I went to a lecture on economics organized by the UCT Communist Society. It was given by economist and ANC-MP (and later government minister) Rob Davies. He outlined some of the ways in which the banks had to be forced to serve the needs of the people. An audience member, an old guy, who spoke when the floor was opened, declared that he had taken a course in banking years ago, and could assure everybody that it was very complex and you couldn't have people's banking. It would be a mess. His tone implied that he was the most important person there and that what he had to say was the most important thing to be said: a vivid example of class, race, and gender arrogance. I spoke to Jason Myers, a politics lecturer, who told me that, despite the agenda of transformation, it was difficult to raise issues of class and capitalism. Some students were quick to call all sorts of things Eurocentric, but had no conception of the possibility that there might be something other than racism keeping people in squatter camps. Myers was intending to leave his job at UCT to return to the US, because he found it hard to be a foreigner in South Africa and was not earning enough to repay his student loans. I was sorry to hear that, because he seemed to have a lot to offer. Other students seemed oblivious to any of the battles of class or race. One lecturer told me of a student who missed an exam because she was "shopping in London." When the lecturer failed her, the student appealed and won. Other lecturers carried on teaching and researching as if they were anywhere, more oriented to international conferences and journals than to the contexts and needs of Africa.

As time went on, I started taking a harder look at white liberals, feeling less inclined to take them on their own terms. UCT at its higher echelons was so white, despite having a Black chancellor and vice chancellor. They seemed so cozy and comfortable, with their well-chosen and safe progressive gestures. I was uneasy with those claiming to be left without ever skipping a beat on the promotional ladder. Even if being left didn't land a person in prison, political activism took time. One told me that white, vaguely left academics at UCT were now rather tired, incestuous, hit hard by poorly thought-out structural changes and funding formulae, and dissipated by postmodern angst about identity. I expressed my lack of sympathy. I thought that they should get out of the way and stop monopolizing scarce resources, only to indulge themselves and sow confusion in others. In my research, I read an essay by

Colin Bundy, a Marxist historian, in a volume called *Transgressing the Boundaries*, which argued that ex-Marxists had conceded too much too soon, insisting that it was necessary to be wary of post-modernist relativism, which denied critical thought any political or ethical point of vantage, and to be prepared to defend the "total-izing" powers of Marxist analysis. I wanted to meet him.

Early in my sabbatical, I had an opportunity to observe a wide crosssection of South African educators at a most interesting national conference on "Values, Education and Democracy in the 21st Century." It was convened by Kader Asmal as minister of edu-cation, which was how I was fortunate enough to be invited. It got off to a good start for me, because I got a lift to Kirstenbosch with Martin Hall, and conversations with him were always so rich that I wanted to take notes, even when I couldn't do so. After that, it had its ups and downs, as all conferences do. When we arrived, Jacob Zuma, South Africa's deputy president, was reading a speech that someone else had obviously written, and droning on with no rhythm, no intonation, no comprehension. Nevertheless, Kader, who was presiding, gushed with appreciation of Zuma's vast humanism and wisdom, which I assumed was less about truth than power. After that, there was a sit-down dinner and chance to meet Mandela. There was a great sense of occasion as the par-ticipants moved out of the hall and through the courtyard with music and anticipation. I wanted to stay, not so much for Mandela, but for the ambience, the ritual, and the opportunity to mix with participants. However, I had accepted an invitation to come to the local SACP branch, so I did that.

The next day was packed with presentations, conversations, impressions. One of the most striking features of the discourse was that participants addressed each other as "comrade." I liked that, but I wondered how long it would last. In a plenary session, Kate O'Regan, a justice in the constitutional court, who reminded me of Mary Robinson, spoke about South Africa's constitution and human rights in a solid but not stimulating way. However, she spoke one sentence that stayed with me as a concise articulation

of the state of the nation: the constitution foreclosed on race and
gender but not on class, and this had to be fought out in the political arena. In parallel sessions, I chose one on history and was not
sorry. Luli Callinicos reminisced wistfully of the excitement of
being a historian in the past, of the power of Marxist critiques, of
the modifying influence of feminism, of adding dimensions of the
oral and experiential. Eddy Maloka regretted that South African
liberation coincided with the collapse of the Pan-African project,
the hegemony of the Washington consensus, students' disinter-
est in history and their preference for marketing, the celebration
of greed, the retreat of the state, the ideological sophistication of
contemporary racism, and its integration into the discourses of
geopolitical power. Next Jeff Guy complained of how history was
being rubbished in the dominant discourse. The discussion from
the floor was quite rich. It reflected a contrast between the ANC
and the Black consciousness tradition, between a concept of history as contested terrain versus common nationhood, white versus
Black history, patriarchal versus feminist history. There was also
discussion of the need to examine the history of historiography, to
ask such questions as whether Shaka Zulu was an imperialist, to
explore how history could be made attractive to the postmodern
generation. Colin Bundy was excellent in summing up the types
of questions that emerged, and said that there was a deep-seated
and systemic crisis of history and historical studies. In contrast, a
keynote speech on affirmative action from John Powell, an African-
American professor of law, was liberal, legalistic, and bland.

The following day, South African author Nadine Gordimer gave
an elaborate introduction to Palestinian-American scholar Edward
Said, all about the examined life and literature as political memoir.
I tried to keep my cool as I beheld the biggest, hairiest spider I had
ever seen creeping along within an inch from my sandaled feet.
Said's talk was about the epistemology and existential texture of
reading, and how reading was the basis for critical thinking. He
stressed how important it was to cultivate alertness to lazy rhetoric, dead clichés, distorted ideological discourses, especially to do

with the free market. The lecture was very evocative of the libraries of the past, with their card catalogues and shelves and skepticism (but not rejection) about the Internet and digital technologies. I think that he was overdoing the dependence of reading and thinking on the physical paper book and overstating the discontinuity between the book and newer, electronic media. I had my hand up to say so, but only a few got to speak. Some in the audience just made speeches flattering Said and talking about the Palestinian struggle, instead of engaging with his presentation. Elinor Sisulu declared that cyberspace was the junk food of intellectual discourse, a statement, which to me, exemplified the junk food of conference commentary. At a session on technology, I spoke about the positive possibilities of the Internet in education. At a session on gender in a small, packed hot room without air conditioning, a feminist shocked me when she defended *lobola* (bride price), but nobody took it up. The final plenary session was addressed by Njabulo Ndebele, the UCT vice chancellor. I had occasion to attend other lectures he gave over time. He always sounded impressive, but it was often hard to say afterward what he said. On this occasion, he was asking: "What does it mean to be South African?" To be honest, I am not sure how he answered his question. He did say, as I heard many other people say, that apartheid and the struggle against it bound people together, but now he heard only silence. I read in a newspaper the next day something by attorney and activist Albie Sachs saying that they had expended the whole of their passion to create a society that was boring. Sachs was among the many luminaries of the liberation movement with whom I spoke in the social time between sessions. I was honored to be in this environment, to hear the nation's intelligentsia discussing the state of the nation and its educational system.

During this period, the television drama *Yizo Yizo* was creating much controversy in the parliament, school system, and wider society. It was set in a township school and showed the realities of gangs, drugs, sex, and poor teaching. Various bodies within the ANC condemned it, and there was even a motion in parliament, but Kader Asmal defended it at this conference and elsewhere, insisting that human rights were being violated every day in the schools. Every form of abuse, including sexual abuse, was taking place between students and teachers. Teachers in township schools told me they discussed the series with their pupils, who said that it told the truth about their lives, but they also complained about the minister sowing disrespect for teachers.

The SACP meeting I chose to attend instead of the conference dinner was the first of many such meetings for me. Ed Wethli, whom I had met in Cuba, collected me at Kirstenbosch and brought me to the Alternative Information and Development Centre (AIDC) offices in Mowbray, where the meeting was held. The membership consisted of older whites, several of them MPs, and young Blacks, lots of them, mostly males. The younger ones talked in a way that was like books and documents much of the time, but with a lot of energy. The agenda started with a discussion of the role of SACP in government, of the perils of their situation in winning power when the enemy was not on the ground, of the emergence of a bureaucratic bourgeoisie, who used the power of the state in a parasitic way. The question was whether SACP members who were also ANC government ministers could be subjected to party discipline. Rob Davies referenced speculation about whether SACP ministers were selling out or had put forward more progressive positions in the cabinet and lost. However, this was the terrain they were in and letting the alliance collapse would mean letting the right take power. The discussion didn't come to a point of resolution but probed the role of parliament, tailism, the class composition of the post-1994 period, and differences within the branch itself on privatization. They referred to the dictatorship of the proletariat as "the dop." Then there was a report on the recruitment campaign at UCT. There were six applications in two days. Why only six? Why had the applications and money collected gone missing? That was left unresolved. Next, there was the national campaign on transformation of the financial sector, as well as a party campaign to elicit fifty thousand debit orders to give the party a monthly income of R500,000. Finally, Rob Davies gave an analysis of the budget, which was moderately more expansionary. Pluses were measures on skills and training and no abolition of company tax. Minuses included an increase in arms expenditure. In a broader analysis, investment had not been forthcoming and 3½ percent growth would not transform the economy. He predicted that the country was entering an extremely rocky road in relation to global capitalism.

Among the questions on the application form for party membership was: "Do you live in a: 1) backyard shack; 2) informal settlement; 3) own home; 4) rented house; 5) hostel. Some comrades had none of the above. They were couch and floor surfers. I got to know certain comrades quite well as time went on. Ed Wethli was especially kind to me. He often invited me to meetings and events, and transported me to them. When I first arrived, he took me for a drive, where we told our condensed life stories while beholding spectacular mountain and sea vistas. He held degrees in psychology and agriculture (to PhD level) and had lived in various countries and worked at all sorts of jobs, from poultry farming to Umkhonto we Sizwe (MK) operations. He was modest, sincere, and committed. In the evening, we went to his house in Woodstock to see a documentary on a sustained MK operation, which involved setting up a company to run safaris, which smuggled arms into South Africa. Some of the people involved were interviewed, including a top female operative called Major Muff, who was in charge of organizing the hiding and distributing of these arms in SA. The best person she recruited, she said, was a guy who always came through, took enormous risks, and had no contact with anyone else. They interviewed him. After the program, Jeff Guy phoned Ed Wethli from Durban and said he had known the guy for years and thought he was politically uncommitted. Apparently, this "guy who always came through" had not gone around talking about arms smuggling, even when it was not only safe, but advantageous, to do so. I also spent many hours with Sheila Barsel, a feminist comrade, a strong personality, who was my age, on the party central committee, and always forthcoming in exploring the problems of the party and wider movement. Another comrade was Norman Levy, a professor of government, who joined the party in 1944, was arrested for treason in 1956, imprisoned, banned, and then went into exile in Britain. He brought me to the University of the Western Cape (UWC) one day and we explored what had happened to UWC, an institution for coloreds under apartheid, once called "the home of the left." He told me that many of those who gave UWC its edge had gone, many to government. There was no longer a philosophy department. I asked if I was correct that all of the intellectual buzz in the universities, and in South African life generally, was in the earlier days, that once the liberation movement came to power, that energy dissipated. He and others said it was so. We attended a seminar on global trends in higher education. The tone was discernibly left, although a bit bewildered.

Another of my cherished comrades was Brian Bunting, a stalwart of the party and movement, who was a surprise to me. I had heard of him for many years and somehow formed an impression of him as a rigid, assertive, dogmatic hardliner. When I got to know him, I found a quiet, gentle, courteous, open, thoughtful man. I looked forward to those times when he would open his gate to me at Burgh Road or come to collect me at UCT. Conversations with him were very rewarding, but I had to make an effort to make it so. He was more inclined to listen than to talk and I had to draw him out consciously and constantly. When I did, he was always forthcoming and to the point with his replies, but usually brief. I had to ask many supplementary questions to explore his thinking on a topic. When attending a play or film or meeting with him, or when discussing a book we had both read, he was always first to ask what I thought. When I asked what *he* thought, he was always razor sharp. If our views diverged, he considered other angles and even contrary opinions and either conceded some considerations or came back and argued his position. We never did agree about J. M. Coetzee's novel *Disgrace* or Gillian Slovo's autobiography *Every Secret Thing*. Some conversations were on difficult terrain.

We spoke on a number of occasions about the history and legacy of the Soviet Union. When I was working on an introduction to a manuscript by Bukharin that had been buried deep in Kremlin archives until glasnost, I spoke to Brian of the terrible injustice done to Bukharin and to many honest communists in the purges and Moscow trials. When I wrote up my research and reflections, I sent it to him. He said that it was an eye-opener, that it told him much that he didn't know. He faced many difficult truths, including daily revelations about life in the new South Africa, which was often far from what he envisioned in the days of struggle. He always arrived on time for party meetings, even though he knew that they were unlikely to start on time. Whenever he gave me a lift, we were always first to arrive. Usually, he said nothing about it or just remarked on it quietly but firmly. Once, however, after a very long delay, he lost his temper and told younger comrades that they were betraying the liberation movement by their undisciplined behavior. Despite all revelations and disappointments, he never gave up on the movement. In the last years, he lived a difficult life, feeling acutely the daily absence of his wonderful wife and comrade, Sonia, who had died during my first months in South Africa. I had met Sonia in London many years earlier. She was still alive when I arrived, but died during my first months there. He also missed his children and grandchildren, who lived far away. Although he faced the incapacities of aging with candor and fortitude, he still held himself to difficult standards. He wrote me that he envied my productive activity and did not feel that he was a very productive member of society. He was surely the only one who thought that.

Sonia's funeral was a moving experience. Comrades were toyi-toyi-ing as we entered Maitland Crematorium. The coffin was covered with the party banner. The event, chaired by anti-apartheid activist, author, and government minister Ronnie Kasrils, began with the national anthem led by a choir from Khayelithsa Township. Then Brian spoke of Sonia, the outlines of her life and characteristics of her personality, mentioning that she cared even for spiders. He said that she thought that socialism was the answer—then stopped somewhat abruptly. Into the silence came spontaneous song. It was in isiXhosa, but I could detect Sonia's name in the lyrics. Then cabinet minister and ANC National Executive Committee member Pallo Jordan spoke on behalf of the ANC, about how much behind-the-scenes work she did, how much danger she faced, how brave she was, how much she loved the Soviet Union. Then party chair and government minister Charles Nqakula spoke for the SACP. As he was leaving his seat and walking to the front to speak, he began to sing, as others added their voices. He emphasized Sonia's steadfast commitment to the party to the very end. Then her son, Stephen, showed photographs of her last days, using a projector. Many people were crying. Finally, the choir led the "Internationale." Outside there was more toyi-toyi-ing, milling around, and talking.

Topping my list of those I was keen to meet was Jeremy Cronin. He was a member of the local party branch, deputy general secretary of the party, member of parliament, and respected author of poetry as well as political tracts. He had been a philosophy lecturer at UCT, active in the SACP underground, for which he served seven years in prison. I had read much of what he wrote and recognized a sensibility akin to my own. When I wrote to him before coming, he responded warmly and came to my residence and drove me higher up the mountain, to a café, where we could have tea and talk. The café was at the Rhodes Memorial, which seemed an odd venue for communists to meet, but the views were striking and the conversation was great. We did the whole condensed life-story thing, declared our positions on a wide range of topics, discussed what party work I might do, as well as the modus operandi of the SACP as a party within a party, especially a party in power. He asked me to write a polemical response to an article on the global left published that week in the *Mail and Guardian*, which I did and got a lot of responses to it. Informally, we continued our interactions on other occasions, but more formally in a long interview that I conducted with him and published on my website. It took the form of an intellectual autobiography as well as a potted history of the SA left and SA culture and academe. It was intelligent, insightful, and stimulating. After two hours, we ran out of time and we both felt there was more to say, so we continued the interview some months later. I did one with Brian too, but Jeremy was much more comfortable with a first-person, personal-as-political mode, sketching out the terrain of the times with the thick texture of personal experience.

I also got to know a number of younger members of the party and tried to help them with some of their practical problems. I was glad to do this, but I began to feel a bit overwhelmed by their needs, especially their financial needs. There were also intricacies of intercultural communication, which could be a lot trickier than they seemed at first. After some weeks, I was presented with a party card and felt freer to be critical than I did at first, but I knew I had to be careful about it, always aware of being white and foreign. I undertook tasks, such as presenting a document on party work in universities, advising on upgrading the party's website, designing posters for party events. I was glad to do these and other things, but got increasingly annoyed with comrades who were not so dependable about what they undertook to do. Of the younger comrades, Sikelela Mkabele stood out as upright and disciplined. He was a young engineer, who did what he said he would do and also explained many things to me, including the residues of tribalism as they played out, even in the party branch.

I received invitations to attend other branches on special occasions. One in Elsies River was to commemorate the death of Chris Hani, SACP general secretary, who was assassinated in 1993. The commemoration began with singing "Solidarity Forever." Then a group called the Khoi Konnexion performed poetry. I had met Jethro Louw, the "ghetto poet," earlier at UCT. There was an address by Jeremy Cronin, who told the life story of Chris Hani. It was a human story told in a very human way, in which political points were well made: how he had to deal with disturbing experiences in his own organization, how important it was to know people's

names and their stories, how he was resisting going into government, and the perks of power. Then there was more local poetry
and finally the singing of the "Internationale," which was a bit
botched, as there was a sheet with a translation that no one really
knew. Before, after, and in between, there was much spontaneous
singing and toyi-toyi-ing. I also attended another Chris Hani commemoration in Philippi. When we arrived, we discovered there
had just been an intra-ANC shooting, which killed an ANC coun-
cilor and his bodyguard. The atmosphere was very menacing, and
the event was hours late starting. During those hours, I got a vivid
sense of the poverty and terror of life in Cape Flats townships. I
walked along dirt paths through shacks cobbled together from
anything and everything. There was much inspiring speaking and
singing and toyi-toyi-ing at the event itself, but a dark cloud of
violence and assassination hung heavily over it.

I also attended ANC meetings. My residence was between the
areas of two branches and I attended both of them. It was interesting to note the difference between them in membership and
atmosphere. I was invited to the one in Rondebosch by Louise
Asmal. It was in a big and bare church hall. There were wide rows of
uncomfortable, stackable chairs. The racial profile was about two-
thirds white. There were very few people younger than me. There
was one MP there, Sue van der Merwe, who had a New Labour
way about her. The chairperson dressed like a woman and sounded
like a man. There was an isiXhosa interpreter. There were reports
from the ANC provincial council, the parliament, the city council.
There was a long report on the division of the new unicity into
subcouncils, and then an item on zoning of Newlands Stadium for
multipurpose use. There were apparently class and race issues tied
to rugby versus soccer. Then there was the big issue of the night,
where tempers flared. On Human Rights Day, Kader Asmal was
addressing a rally in Langa and referred off-the-cuff to a Christian
rally in Newlands as "sectarian" and "divisive." Bill and Judy Sewell
led the charge and others came in huffing and puffing about irrep-
arable harm. At the very most, Kader was mildly indiscreet, but I

thought it was much fuss over very little, while little or nothing was said about things that I thought should be upsetting ANC members, such as neoliberal economic policies. The meeting wasn't exactly inspiring. I was also surprised that no one mentioned the death of Sonia, who was a member of that branch. I found the whole discourse about human rights on Human Rights Day noteworthy in that it took for granted that human rights included clean water, food, health care. It was material conditions, not bourgeois legalities, that constituted the baseline.

I also attended the Woodstock branch in Salt River, a suburb of Cape Town. The meeting was late starting, so there was much milling around, gathering mass, because there had to be 70 percent to have a quorum for the Annual General Meeting (AGM). It was quite different from the other ANC branch. There was a wider mix of people in terms of age and race, and more whom I knew from SACP meetings. It had a better vibe. The meeting began with a moment of silence for Sonia. The meeting was addressed by Ebrahim Rasool, ANC leader in the Western Cape, who said not to be afraid to confront the difficult questions that people were asking about arms spending, AIDS, corruption. The ANC, in its ideas and ideology, had a moral authority lacking in other parties, which had to pay US consultants millions to brand them. The ANC had to go beyond its defensive strategy to an offensive one, beyond its comfort zone into new territory. There were cultural items in the program, which I generally liked at these meetings, but one was a group of very young, imitation Spice Girls, which I thought dubious for the occasion. I got a lift home with Rob Davies and had a good talk about his life as an MP and then about the changes in the ANC over time. I asked if the culture of criticism was closing down. He said that there was still scope, but it depended on how you did it. You could articulate a strong critique of the GEAR policy to a university audience, for example, as long as you didn't name people and use terms like "traitor."

GEAR (Growth, Employment, and Redistribution) was the macroeconomic policy adopted by the ANC in 1996 to replace

RDP (Reconstruction and Development Program). The left called the shift "the 1996 class project," a neoliberal capitulation to the agenda of global capitalism. It was brought in under Mandela, who was convinced by the masters of the universe at Davos that there was no alternative, and pursued under Thabo Mbeki. The collapse of the socialist alternative in Eastern Europe had also undermined the ANC's confidence in an alternative. The opposition to GEAR came not only from the left outside the ANC but inside it as well, with SACP figures, such as Cronin, playing a leading role, building up much tension within the ANC. The discourse around GEAR from its proponents sometimes made the structures of economic power seem so impenetrable as to render all the other imperatives that flowed from it, such as privatization of public services, seem inevitable. I got the strangest sense of it one night around a dinner table in Cape Town. It was at the home of Martin Hall and Brenda Cooper. Dave Kaplan, an economic advisor to the government, once a Marxist—an Althusserian one—was dealing with the privatization of telecommunications. He just kept saying, "It is very complex . . ." I didn't think that he was deliberately obfuscating, but it was as if the world had clouded up and it was impossible to see anything clearly and it was hard to know how to break through the clouds. At one point, he said that he was a socialist trying to make capitalism work. The conversation reminded me of an article in the *Irish Times* about SA politician Alec Erwin and his visit to Ireland under the heading "Communist Trade Minister Wins Praise from the IMF," quoting him as arguing that the move from RDP to GEAR and privatization was made "in open and public debate" and justified by "Marxist dialectical thought processes." Patrick Bond captured the contradictions of this discourse in his book titled *Talk Left, Walk Right*.

I went to a people's budget meeting in Mowbray, another suburb of Cape Town. The hall was packed. There were lots of people from townships. The isiXhosa interpreter did his job in a most lively manner. The event began with a youth choir singing and swaying and there were at various times in the meeting a cacophony of *amandlas* and *vivas*. The trade union speaker from the Congress of South African Trade Unions (COSATU) was, to my surprise, a New Yorker named Neva Maketla. She argued that government fiscal policy was schizoid. The next speaker was activist Mercia Andrews, with earthy ways of relating high policy to people's lives and dreams. The most interesting exchanges centered around the question of the relationship between COSATU and the ANC government. Why, if this critique was COSATU policy, how did it support the ANC government? The answer given was: Because the ANC is our party and we are not going to hand this country over to the opposition. However, the tensions in the ANC-COSATU-SACP alliance were building. Ed Wethli said that the meeting felt like the old days, when they were the opposition. There was, at this conjuncture, a sense of a force that was in power and opposition at the same time. This contrast was dramatized in the march to the parliament organized for the next day: a march for a people's budget. I went to that too and felt oddly connected both to those in parliament and outside it.

I went into the parliament building on several occasions, as well as attending protests outside it. One time, I went to see Jeremy Cronin. He showed me around with a brief history of the parliament, pointing out where Hendrik Verwoerd, the architect of apartheid, was assassinated. He pointed out the old and new coat of arms of South Africa. The old one was in Latin, meaning "Out of Unity Strength." The new one was in San, an extinct language, meaning the same thing, although, he added, there was an alternative translation meaning "people urinate." He introduced me to his secretary, who was a sangoma (traditional healer). On another occasion, I was invited to a meeting that my branch had set up to brainstorm with MPs Rob Davies and Langa Zita about setting up cooperatives. I stayed silent, because I had no expertise to offer and wondered why I had been invited. The comrades proposed grandiose schemes that I knew by then were utterly beyond their organizational capacity. After the meeting was over, I walked along many corridors with Rob as the bell summoned MPs to session. I took my place in the gallery and started taking in the scene. I got a buzz, watching the MPs and trying to see how many I could name. After a moment of "silent prayer," the session came to order. It was question time. Jacob Zuma, deputy president, was up. He stumbled over prepared answers and mispronounced words. There was a supplementary question referring to Kader's speech in Langa, as if it constituted a grave threat to freedom of religious expression and assembly. The form of address between ANC members was "comrade deputy president," "comrade minister," etc., whereas, among the opposition and between government and opposition, it was "honorable member." There was high attendance but much meandering. Winnie Mandela made one of her rare appearances in parliament. She never stopped walking around and talking to people until she left. Some, such as Kader Asmal, brought a huge pile of paperwork and made their way through it, while occasionally looking up when there were heated exchanges. Sometimes it was really rowdy.

I attended all sorts of meetings and found the discourse and rituals involved fascinating. At the AGM of the New Women's Movement, groups from the various townships each made an entrance singing and toyi-toyi-ing. Each session had a chairperson, but also a "mama" presiding in elaborate traditional dress. Visitors from abroad were welcomed and asked to come to the top table. Throughout the proceedings, there was much singing and speaking in isiXhosa. Speeches focused on various issues: domestic violence, housing, social security, unemployment, health (strong emphasis on HIV/AIDS). At one stage of the proceedings, an executive of a local welfare office was a guest speaker and did he ever get a hard time. Whenever he tried to evade responsibility, he was told that he either had to take responsibility or add his voice to theirs in support of improved delivery of public services. They were assertive but not nasty. He left, to all sorts of audience hoots and gestures, but it wasn't ugly or threatening. The mama said, "Our government is there because of us," which was followed by all sorts of stamping and clapping and swaying. At lunch break, she

proceeded to tell me the facts of life in her township of Gugulethu:
the poverty, unemployment, crime, hunger, hopelessness, suicide,
rape. She talked in detail about one house where, because the parents died and the children had nothing, she cooked for them and
another house where the mother drank too much and let the children run wild. It was grim. A number of times she said, "You must
help me, my sister." I asked what she wanted me to do. I gave her
money, as she requested. There was a fierce dignity to her. She was
poor, overweight, wore tatty clothes, had several front teeth missing, but she held her head up and had her place in her community
and in her own scheme of things. This New Women's Movement
offered a very different gender agenda from many women's meetings I had attended over the decades, being much more rooted in
issues of material survival than nuances of personal identity.

There were lots of struggles over personal identity, too. One day
I received an unexpected call on my mobile. It was someone with
a male voice and female name. Sally Gross heard I was giving a
lecture at UCT on class, race, and gender, and wondered if I was
dealing with intersexuality. No, I said, and she proceeded to give
me all sorts of research findings on intersexuality. It dawned on me
that I had heard the voice before, so I asked if she had chaired an
ANC branch meeting the other night. Yes. She asked if we could
meet, so we met at a restaurant in Rondebosch. She told me her
story. She was born Selwyn Gross nearby, in Wynberg. Although
of indeterminate sexuality, s/he was classified as male and grew
up vaguely aware of the indeterminacy, but not overly bothered
by it. S/he didn't feel any sexual drive at puberty and after. S/he
got involved with religion, became Orthodox Jewish, and started
studying to be a rabbi, but became disturbed by Jewish emphasis on reproduction, so turned to Catholicism for its emphasis on
celibacy. S/he became a Dominican and was ordained a priest after
moving to Britain. Eventually, s/he decided to have counseling and
a testosterone test, at which point s/he discovered that his/her testosterone level was midway through the female end of the scale,
and decided to live as a woman. The Dominicans were not too

pleased to be told that they had ordained a woman. She moved then from Catholicism to Quakerism and Buddhism. She worked in the Land Claims Commission of South Africa. She was only in her forties at the time, but had various health and mobility issues typical of a much older person. She was into makeup and hair dye and other traditional markers of femininity that I had renounced. It was quite a story. I met her on subsequent occasions. We talked about philosophy and politics too, but it always came back to gender. She founded Intersex South Africa, but found it difficult to get traction in townships, which was her ambition.

I met so many different people in so many different settings. I moved from talking to academics on university campuses to activists at political meetings, to people struggling for survival in squatter camps. I was shocked by the conditions of life in these "informal settlements." People lived in shacks made of corrugated iron, cardboard, rubbish bags, almost any discarded material imaginable. Children died when they were bitten by rats, or tripped over pirated electricity cables, or when paraffin stoves went up in flames. People of all ages were terrorized by gangs. The whole discourse about crime in South Africa was transformed for me, as I learned about the conditions of life on the Cape Flats. I heard so many news items, so many anecdotal stories, so many warnings, about crime in Cape Town. Don't do this; don't do that. I received much conflicting advice about what I could and couldn't do. If I listened to all of it, I would have never ventured out of my room, because some told me I couldn't even walk around campus on my own. I did walk around on my own in many places, although I was wary. I traveled in the communal taxis, the only white person packed tightly into vehicles with shattered windscreens, upholstery in tatters, doors held in place by coat hangers. Even in bed at night, when I had my window open, I thought of a story on the news of a man pole-vaulting through a window and robbing and raping a mother and daughter. I went to the bank one day in Rondebosch and got R5,000 after going through elaborate security. I walked along leafy streets, past houses with huge locked gates, electrified fences, guard dogs, security alarms, and warnings about instant armed response. Private security personnel outnumbered public police by four to one. I rarely saw police, but around shops, banks, wherever there was substantial property to protect, there was private security. However, poor people and ordinary working people were so unprotected. They were the real victims of crime. The poor were not only living in poverty, but in fear. A young doctor in my residence came back one day after being carjacked. While shaken, he looked at the wider picture and spoke of what it must be like to live in that township and what should be done.

A teacher invited me to visit the school where he taught in the township of Manenberg. It was surrounded by the usual dilapidated housing. The school was bleak and ill-equipped and walled-in behind electrified fences. The library had very few books and even those were relatively old. This teacher brought me into a union meeting, which was already underway. The members were angry about Kader Asmal undermining teachers and about inequalities in resources and conditions between schools. There were schools where there was never enough funding for basics. Walking around the area, there was a row of shops that had been burned out. I visited various social centers, where there were nurseries, gyms, meeting rooms, training schemes. The discourse was about giving the place a positive image, an alternative to gangs and drugs and crime. I stood in waste ground that was between the territory of two gangs called the Clever Kids and the Hard Livings. Sometimes they shot it out there. My teacher friend told me that some of his eleventh-grade students were in those gangs. The adjoining township of Heideveld also had two warring gangs called the Americans and the Junky Funky Kids, which made it necessary for a primary school to be closed down during the week to prevent the kidnapping of children related to rival gangs. The police in Cape Flats were complaining about the withdrawal of a small danger allowance. I wondered what percentage of these kids would be likely to go on to university. About 5 percent, he said. I asked him about the *Yizo Yizo* controversy. He told me he discussed it in class. Kids said that it showed the realities of their lives, whether their parents liked it or not. On the way back, we drove through the school grounds of Newlands, where my teacher friend's son went to school. It was like Eton in Africa.

Book launches were also good occasions for mixing with different people and hearing of their experiences and ideas. Ed Wethli brought me to an event launching a book by his ex-wife, Helena Dolny. She had been shafted from her position as CEO of the Land Bank and wrote her account of it in *Banking on Change*. I liked meeting her. We had a good chance to talk at a dinner after the launch. She had also been married to Joe Slovo and told me that he was reading my pamphlet *Has the Red Flag Fallen?* in 1990, while writing his pamphlet *Has Socialism Failed?* I was very pleased to hear that. I read her book and learned much about agricultural economics. She had presided over the transformation of the Land Bank, from an inefficient, racist institution to a multicultural, capitalist one. I had reservations about some of her role-playing methods and management techniques and about arguments for market norms in management salaries in the public sector, especially where so many people were so poor. She was not forced out over any of these issues, as far as I could tell; it likely had more to do with the Mbeki presidency clearing the decks. At this event, I also met Ed's cousin, Jeff Rudin, who told me he was shafted from his job as a parliamentary researcher for trade union activity, which seemed crazy, considering the ANC's relationship with the trade union movement.

In my research on academic transformation, I had found interesting texts by Marxist historian Colin Bundy, who had gone into university administration and had resigned his position as vice chancellor of Wits University to take up a position as director of SOAS at the University of London. Accompanying him was Eve Bertelsen, a UCT academic who had also written a few biting pieces, arguing that marketization was the real transformation. Before they left, Colin invited me around to his flat near UCT. I was glad to meet and talk with both of them and was sorry they were going. I told them I would be quoting both of them in what I was writing. Colin laughed and asked if I would be quoting them against each other. No, in their quotable texts they both spoke the same line, but Colin, in his practice as an administrator, was being accused of acting along very different lines. We pursued this a bit, but not too far, as the arrival of two other guests—one an academic wife—giving rise to four hours of frustration, in which she with the least to say talked more than everybody else put together. If Colin asked me a question, or vice versa, she would cut in, talking-talking-talking. Eve barely said a word. Sometimes it was all about the couple's multiple properties. At one stage, because I had also met her at Sonia's funeral, this woman commented that Sonia wasn't a communist at all, that she went along with whatever her husband believed, and all she wanted to be was a wife and mother and grandmother, that she didn't want to come back to South Africa, that she wanted religion in the end, and Brian wouldn't allow it. I was angry. To each assertion, I said firmly "I don't think so." The woman's husband, when I met him on his own after that, was a thoughtful and interesting man, but whenever I ran into them together, she dominated the conversation with objectionable nonsense. I found it hard to fathom the dynamic of that relationship.

I got to know UCT staff who worked in many jobs around campus, and not just academics, especially the cleaners in AAH. They lived in Cape Flats townships, such as Gugelethu or Phillipi, arose at 4:00 a.m., took two trains in dangerous conditions to arrive at work at 7:00, and received very low wages (R1,129 a month), on which they had to support huge extended families. One day I got new eyeglasses and paid R3,000, which was more than they earned in two months. What happened if *they* needed glasses, I wondered. Another day a comrade contacted me about someone in MK who died and there wasn't money for the funeral, so I contributed to that. I heard stories about corpses being unclaimed, because there was no money to bury them. As time went on, I got an increasing number of requests, some of which made me uneasy, especially after I found out that a few were less than honest. I started to plunge into feeling that I could drown in other people's needs. Poverty was so bitter in so many ways, and not just in the obvious ways. It was degrading. It muddied relationships. I thought a lot about the psychology of poverty, both the effect on me and on them. Everything I gave made me feel worse about what I was not giving. I wanted to give without counting the cost, but I did count the cost. Before I left, I felt as if I was being squeezed for whatever could be extracted from me, but my academic salary was not adequate to be an alternative social welfare system. I asked advice, sometimes somewhat obliquely, from comrades, who urged caution. The poor were often defiant and impressive and deserving of a better world, but also dangerous, deceitful, manipulative, murderous. The poor were both criminals and victims of crime.

I stayed clear of the tourist trail most of the time, but thought I should do the Robben Island trip before I left. I went with a few of the younger comrades, who had never been there or able to afford it. They got into arguments with the tour guides. One was going on about the role of Helen Suzman, liberal MP, in a way that overshadowed the role of the mass movement in the country and abroad. The guide didn't get our arguments about personalities and forces of history. Another guide, an ex-inmate, spoke narrowly about prison conditions and put exaggerated emphasis on Nelson Mandela and his cell. We put up a bit of resistance again to the agenda, but the guy said he wasn't going to have a political argument or change the story. After that, we had more freedom and it was possible to walk around the cells. On the wall of each cell was a photo and the story and possessions of the person who had been incarcerated there. There was also a box on the walls where, if you pressed a button, you could hear the person speak about prison life. In one recording, a guy sang a liberation song and my comrades joined in the singing while toyi-toyi-ing.

My time in South Africa was coming to an end and I was preoccupied with summing it all up for myself. It was such a rich collage of customs, perceptions, ideas, choices, hopes, terrors that

I needed to focus and synthesize. I had been living among a new set of life stories and had become politically engaged in a new way. I had been seeing the world from a different place and leading an alternative life. When I reflected by day or dreamed at night, it was on new terrain, about new problems and possibilities, amid a new cast of characters. I had formed meaningful and enduring relationships. I had learned a lot about the history, politics, and the everyday life of this place. I got to live briefly in a place where my side had won. At least they had won state power. Even with all the limitations of state power, I did not think they were doing all that could be done with it. Those at the top had taken a wrong turn. They had succumbed to the deceptions and seductions of the times. The world in which they had anticipated coming to power was one where the USSR and other socialist countries stood, but now it was a world of the high-tide capitalist triumphalism where they found it difficult to forge, or even imagine, an alternative. We all had to ask hard questions in this period about what was the alternative to capitulating to the global orthodoxy, about how to expropriate the expropriators in this era, about how to achieve radical redistribution of resources in every sense.

I was finding it hard to pull away. I was really moved by the speeches at the farewell party that the SACP branch gave for me, and by comrades coming to the airport to see me off. I found it hard to adjust when I arrived in Ireland and talked about South Africa constantly. I plotted to return as soon as possible. I was back to teaching through the autumn, but I got all my grade-marking done over the Christmas holidays, so I could spend January 2002 back in South Africa before teaching began again in February. I arrived after three connecting flights and went right down to the AAH common room, anxious to see the television news as a reintroduction to the world from Africa again—only to find the television monopolized by wrestling. Not a good start. It was a good trip, though, although it lacked the same sense of discovery as the first time. You can only discover a place for the first time, once. However, there was still so much to discover. I renewed old contacts and made some new ones. I advanced my research agenda.

Being January, it was the peak of the tourist season. People were phoning into the talk shows, saying how they would love to bump into Britney Spears or Brad Pitt. I hated this version of South Africa, a playground for the rich and famous to come and rub shoulders with Mandela, investing their conspicuous consumption with a vague aura of a liberation movement, while those who were supposed to be liberated were still so poor (and unfamous) and languished in squalor in squatter camps. I read on an Irish news site that Mary Harney, tanaiste (deputy prime minister) and right-wing politician, was here on honeymoon.

It was the 90th anniversary of the ANC. There was a rally in the harbor town of Hout Bay. I went with comrades from the party branch. Along the scenic ride, I reflected on my ambivalence about the ANC, but I still believed that there was much in those ninety years that deserved to be celebrated. The hall was full, mostly with people from the townships. Pallo Jordan gave the main speech and sang in the middle of it. Jeremy Cronin also spoke. He was wearing a t-shirt with a picture of Thabo Mbeki on it, which I found surprising, given the bad vibes between them. There was lots of singing and toyi-toyi-ing, lots of *amandlas* and *vivas*, lots of affirmations of unity and leaving the disunity for another day.

I attended all-day strategy sessions of two SACP branches. The session for the Jack Simons branch, my own branch, in the Community House in Salt River, was late starting. Then there were so many words to say so little from the branch officers. Such grandiose discourse for no activity and unfocused strategies. The other session was the Fred Carneson branch meeting in Hout Bay, where branch officers were more mature and focused. It started with the question: What does it mean to be a communist? Then there was a lecture on the history of the SACP. The introduction to it, which I feared would be a list of dates and documents and legislation, focused on certain themes and gave rise to a lot of searching discussion. One comrade was shocked by my revelation that Dialego, an anonymous author who had written an underground pamphlet in the 1970s on dialectical materialism, was no longer a Marxist. I got a lift back to my residence with Lucky Montana, a UCT graduate who worked in government and drove a posh BMW, which was quite a contrast to the cars of both academic colleagues and political comrades who gave me lifts.

Moving into another milieu, I participated in a three-day conference of the Philosophical Society of Southern Africa at Stellenbosch University. Traversing the forty-five kilometers each day from Rondebosch to Stellenbosch and passing by thousands of horrendous shacks, I wondered what chance did some little girl running around Khayelitsha Township that morning have to become a philosopher, as opposed to a boy growing up in Stellenbosch. There were so many barriers of class and race and gender. I raised this question when I spoke at the conference. My presentation focused on deeper questions about the foundations of knowledge as shaped by class, race, and gender, as well as the overwhelming obstacles to access. I spoke extempore from a visually elaborate PowerPoint, which looked impressive, shown from a high-res projector on a huge screen. My presentation went well. There was lots of affirmative body language, interesting questions and comments from the floor. I was surprised at how white the conference was. As so many conferences were, this was mostly people reading their papers past each other, with little real engagement. I attended the AGM of the PSSA and I found the discourse about the current state of the profession in South Africa quite interesting, especially a debate about paying large subscriptions to international bodies, as opposed to scholarships for young academics to attend conferences. I had a good series of conversations with Andre Du Toit, philosopher and head of political studies at UCT, in transit, covering the various periods of development of philosophy as a discipline in South Africa and current global trends in higher education.

I walked around Stellenbosch, both the university and the town, which was such a bastion of privilege. I had my camera with me, but there was little that I felt an impulse to photograph. It was very plush land with lots of vineyards, but visually very bare, very Protestant. I picked up a book in Stellenbosch, an autobiography of Wilhelm Verwoerd, whom I'd met in Dublin, where his wife, Melanie, had become SA ambassador to Ireland. I got much more out of reading *My Winds of Change* than I would have if I had not gone to Stellenbosch. The cover showed him at an ANC rally, smiling and clenching his fist against the background of the mass movement. The symbolism of having a Verwoerd, grandson of the architect of apartheid, in the ANC was important to the ANC at that stage. During this time, there was a month-long strike at the SA Embassy in Dublin. Since 1998, the Irish employees there had been in dispute over trade union recognition and failure to pay nationally negotiated wage increases. The embassy was claiming diplomatic immunity from laws regulating trade unions and national wage agreements. The strike was reflecting badly on South Africa in the Irish media and trade union movement, led as it was by the same union that famously went on strike against Dunnes Stores in support of the anti-apartheid movement.

Another autobiography I read at this time was Raymond Suttner's *Inside Apartheid's Prison*. Suttner was in prison for writing and distributing anti-apartheid pamphlets, where he was interrogated and tortured. After release, he became active in the movement again and was detained again for over two years without trial, and then put under house arrest. I was interested in reading his story because, due to my work on the Bukharin manuscripts, I was thinking about the psychology of prison. I found the intricacies of coping with prison intriguing and well conveyed in Suttner's book, but I found the last chapter on the years since his release frustrating, sensing that there was more in between the lines than in the lines. Since 1990, Suttner had been head of political education of the ANC, then MP, then ambassador to Sweden. Now he was back in South Africa working on a PhD. I wrote him an email about his book and got an immediate response. From there, we had a flourishing correspondence for a while, covering many themes, such as the psychological dimension of political activity, Stalinism, and the SACP (he was a member). I was also conducting an active email correspondence with Andrew Nash, a philosopher away from South Africa and working in New York, telling him about the PSSA conference, and launching from there into a discussion of whether philosophy was doomed. We both thought that much of academic philosophy deserved to be doomed, as it was going on and on in well-worn grooves of mediocrity, but we hoped that the philosophical impulse to probe the foundations of knowledge would survive.

I had agreed to do a presentation in Ireland on culture and transformation in South Africa, encompassing novels, plays, biographies, news, talk radio, music, murals, museums, monuments, rallies, funerals, so I was constantly making notes and taking photos for that. I watched the SA "soapies" as often as I could. There were a lot of them and in many of the languages of South Africa. One called *Isidingo* was set in a mine, and dealt with a lot of the political and social nuances of life in South Africa. Some of the others seemed quite yuppified, dealing in the drama of those benefiting from the Black economic empowerment agenda without worrying too much about the millions left outside it. I was also interested in museums as sites of contestation and reconstruction of SA history, from the early Stone Age to the present. When I went to the South African Museum, I wished that I had gone there before a controversial diorama was closed. The exhibit, on display from 1960 to 2001, was a reconstruction of a hunter-gatherer encampment in the Karoo, which the Khoisan community claimed depicted the bushmen as natural history specimens. There were other such reconstructions of primitive lives still in the museum, but problematized with provocative questions and contemporary images, challenging the assumptions underlying the original exhibits. Traditional Sotho, Xhosa, or Zulu living in straw huts and wearing skins were side-by-side with photos of contemporary Sotho, Xhosa, or Zulu living in modern houses and wearing modern clothes, making the point that cultures were not static

and Africans were not frozen in the past. There were also reconstructions of traditional tribal rituals in exotic garb juxtaposed
with photos of Catholic bishops in full liturgical regalia, raising
questions of what was considered exotic. I found the displays and
commentaries quite stimulating. When I went back to see them
again years later, they were all gone. Much of the problem was
that the original conception of this natural history museum was
to display indigenous African lives alongside animal species while
another museum, the South African Cultural History Museum,
assumed that culture only arrived with European colonization.

A highlight of my trip was the continuation of my discussions
with Jeremy Cronin. I spent nearly five hours with him one day, of
which three hours were recorded as a formal interview on digital
video. This one concentrated more on the current conjuncture. I
asked him to address international critiques of the ANC from the
left, especially John Pilger's documentary film *Apartheid Did Not
Die* and John Saul's *Monthly Review* article "Cry for the Beloved
Country." I also put to him other expressions of dissatisfaction,
inside and outside the ANC, in South Africa. He agreed with much
of the critiques and made a sharp critique of his own of the ANC
under Mbeki, especially about how communists were being marginalized, despite the fact that Mbeki had been a leading member
of the party before 1990. Nevertheless, he argued that the contestation was still in play, although there were many tactical difficulties.
I said that he should look at his interview when transcribed and
that he could delete anything he didn't want published, but he said
that he wouldn't want to delete. I insisted that he should go over it
and gave him an opportunity to do so, but he didn't, so I posted it
to my website and sent the link to Jeremy, the SACP, and various
international left lists. He asked if it was too late for him to write
a reply to the Saul article in *Monthly Review*. I said that I would
pursue that, which I did, and it was subsequently published.

The trip back to Ireland was exhausting enough, but then, when
an announcement about the third flight diverting to Shannon was
made just near the end, I felt as if I would collapse. However, the

airline made an attempt to land, despite strong gales that had blown another flight off the runway. I was glad they did, even though it was tense. Upon landing, I received news that my mother had had a heart attack. I had to plunge right into my work at DCU, while trying to gauge what to do about the fact that my mother might be dying on another continent. My sister, a nurse, told me she might pull through, although she would not live for long. I got home to see her before heading back to South Africa again.

I received an invitation to come to the SACP congress in July 2002. In the run-up to the congress, there was a lot of media attention on the SACP, with an explosion of controversy over my interviews with Jeremy Cronin as the focal point of the tensions within the ANC. The *Sunday Times* in SA ran an article on July 14, citing Cronin's description of the left as being marginalized by the ANC leadership and the danger of "Zanufication" of the ANC. By this time, Zimbabwe, as governed by ZANU under Robert Mugabe, had become a negative example for South Africa. The next day at the ANC press briefing, ANC head of communications Smuts Ngonyama accused Cronin of being unfaithful and spreading lies. After that, the story was in almost every paper every day and spread to the talk shows, too. It was even in the international media, including the *Irish Times*. The SACP put out a statement saying that the interviews were not intended for publication, but also asking for those commenting to look at the full text and context of the interviews. The ANC replied that the full text fully confirmed their position. Dumisani Makhaye of the ANC wrote an explosive article in *The Sowetan* headed "We Do Not Need a White Messiah to Succeed." Makhaye claimed that other commentators had been mistaken in concentrating on the second interview, because the first interview revealed who Jeremy Cronin really was: "a factory fault," a petit bourgeois, an ultra-left white. He then preached Marxism to Cronin, because he did not have the opportunity to go to Eastern Europe to learn it (without mentioning that Jeremy was in prison when Makhaye and others were being treated to vodka and caviar along with the dialectical and historical materialism).

General secretary of COSATU Zwelinzima Vavi called Makhaye's article racist, as did others. Journalists were calling me at DCU, looking for my response to the controversy. I replied that the ANC couldn't say that it fostered a culture of robust debate and then say that Jeremy Cronin shouldn't speak in the way that he had. I explained that the interviews were aimed at an international left audience and defended the ANC against a left critique. I insisted that the interviews were intended for publication and I had emails to document that.

Amid all this turmoil, I flew to South Africa. In my stress, I left my Filofax in my office with my credit card, SA SIM card, and all my contact information. When I arrived in the airport in Johannesburg, where international delegates were to meet, the person in charge seemed surprised to see me, which surprised me, as I had been invited. What I did not know until later was that they had decided to disinvite me, to take the heat out of the controversy. However, the person in the party who was to inform me, Mazibuko Jara, wanted me to come and did not disinvite me. In transit to Rustenburg, where the congress was to take place, I engaged in conversations with other visitors, especially those from Greece, Cyprus, and Brazil. I woke up early in the Orion Safari Lodge, turned on the television, and the conversation in the South African Broadcasting Corporation (SABC) studio was about Cronin, the congress, and the interviews. There were various logistical mix-ups about transporting international delegates to the congress venue. A Greek communist MEP, who was not impressed by the fact that I was ex-CPI, lashed out at me about undisciplined behavior of intellectuals who couldn't deal with party discipline, as if I were somehow responsible. During registration, I was mistakenly given media credentials, which alerted the media to my presence. They had all read the interviews carefully, and remarked that they were well done and broke new ground. Party members had a lot to say to me about them, too. Occasionally, I got a negative reaction, accusing me of making internal matters public and delivering the party into the hands of hostile media, but many more said that, despite the bad atmosphere now, these matters had to be aired. I had to struggle all the time to keep things in perspective. At times I got overwrought. I reminded myself that this melee was a battle of ideas and a struggle for power, that others were in the eye of the storm, and I was just caught up in the surrounding swirling winds. It was not about me, I knew, but I was sensitive to being scapegoated. I watched Jeremy Cronin throughout this congress. Under extreme pressure, under attack from various sides, he performed all his functions at the congress with remarkable lucidity, composure, and commitment.

When the opening session of the congress finally started, the hall was full of delegates, visitors, and media. The delegates were a sea of red, as the registration pack included t-shirts and hats, with which most adorned themselves immediately. There were also condoms, although it was less obvious how these were deployed. There was tension in the air. There was as much more happening under the surface than on the surface. The "Internationale" and *Nkosi Sikielel' iAfrica* were sung vigorously. The first session was devoted to speeches of solidarity from alliance organizations. There was singing and toyi-toyi-ing before and after every speech. The South African National Civic Organization (SANCO) speech didn't really take hold. The speaker seemed to be arguing that there shouldn't be right and left positions, but everyone should be pulling in the same direction. The speech just wasn't dealing with the issues or problems. Then came Zwelinzima Vavi, speaking for COSATU, who was the opposite. Before he spoke, he sang and the delegates sang back and forth in call-and-response. The rhythm and vitality of it was bracing. Vavi's speech was spikey and strong. There was a big (positive) reaction from the floor to his opposition to privatization. He was critical of party members in the cabinet. He detailed the rise in unemployment, the problems of the informal sector, the poverty. He used the phrase "Irish coffee syndrome" to describe the composition of the SA society. The body of it black with white foam on the top with black flecks scattered through it.

He also emphasized educational strategies and the formation of a Chris Hani Institute.

Much of the tense atmosphere was created by the last-minute announcement that Mbeki would not speak as scheduled. The official statement said that he had to attend a cabinet meeting, which no one took at face value. Unofficially, it was said that he didn't want to subject himself to being booed and hassled. Mosiuoa Lekota, defense minister who came in his place, gave a very conciliatory speech, obviously with the aim of damping down the sparks, about debate in the alliance and the art of managing contradictions. However, before he could speak, he had to wait while delegates sang, in African languages: "Let us fight because Mbeki does not want to talk," and after Lekota spoke: "Those who will be hit will be hit and those who will be removed will be removed," and then something else about the ANC wanting to purge itself of the SACP. At breakfast the next day, there were discussions among delegates and diplomats about the first day of the congress and accounts of it in the morning papers. It centered on the alliance tensions, the Mbeki cancellation, the Lekota speech, and its reception. When I arrived at the venue, several journalists asked me to comment on the congress and the draft program, which saw socialism as something to be fought for and evolved within capitalism, which I defended. The session started with tributes to communists who had died since the last congress. Naturally, I was most moved by Jeremy's tribute to Sonia, as I knew them both. That was followed by the "Red Flag." Again, there was more singing, both scheduled and spontaneous, all through the congress, before and after (and sometimes during) every speech. Then there was the political report of general secretary of the party Blade Nzimande, who elicited a positive vibe from the floor before he even began. Delegates sang and waved their copies of the report. In an obvious reference to Makhaye's "white messiah" article, he emphasized that Marx and Engels were white, middle class, highly educated, and got a big affirmation from the (mostly non-white) delegates. He spoke of the dangers of careerism, bureaucratism, and demobilization, the problem of accountability of SACP ministers in an ANC government, the necessity of balancing the short-term interests of the working class with long-term vision. Following that, Jeremy Cronin delivered the organizational report. There were various speeches of international solidarity from international visitors, which repeated formulas I had heard many times, which dissipated focus and energy, but delegates responded with many *vivas*.

On the second day, the congress was in closed session for the financial report, while international visitors went off to a game reserve. I got caught up with my email and took time to walk and think. That night there was a social event in Sun City, a place I never expected to be. It was a luxury resort and casino created under apartheid in the eye of the storm during the UN cultural boycott. However, all had changed and I had recently seen Paul Simon in a television studio with Dali Tambo, who had led the charge against Simon's breaking of the cultural boycott with the *Graceland* album in 1986, in a reconciliatory encounter. The SACP event was a fundraising function, where R300,000 was raised from the sale of tickets and auction. The auction was a bizarre mini-drama of incongruity. Presiding was Ronnie Kasrils, a government minister and stalwart of the struggle, whom I admired before and after, but not during this period, as he flogged golf caps signed by Thabo Mbeki and Jacob Zuma. I tasted impala for the first time and had some good conversations, but the event did not gel for me.

On the third day, most of the internationals went off to Soweto, while I stayed around for party commissions. I went to one on the international context that took place in the hot winter sun, a phrase I never had occasion to use before. I was impressed with the level of discussion regarding globalization and the growing movement challenging the form it was taking. The following plenary session was concerned with constitutional amendments followed by a cultural event that went on until late. On the last day, results of elections to the central committee were announced. Several MPs, two of them ministers, were defeated, which was seen as a victory for the left of the party. Overall, I thought the quality of the documents and discussion quite high and the rituals and conversations running through it intellectually stimulating and emotionally moving. However, I couldn't romanticize it anymore. I knew that, for many, there was a gap between speaking/ singing/toyi-toyi-ing and doing what they promised they would do. I read the Sunday papers, which were full of the congress and fallout from the interviews.

After that, it was on to Johannesburg and the next phase of my trip. I stayed in a residence at the University of the Witwatersrand (known as Wits). Omano Edigheji, a Nigerian academic at Wits, gave me a lift from the congress, helped me settle, and invited me to his home, where his wife's extended family were visiting, and I heard much of interest about their lives and jobs. One told of a training exercise at the bank where she worked, which involved spending a day in Khayelitsha with only twenty rand and no cell phone, and going into people's houses and finding out how they lived. The family offered many observations about the differences between different subcultures on the Cape Flats. They kindly presented me with a cake for my fifty-eighth birthday. I spent the next weeks exploring Wits and Joburg and meeting as many people as I could. There was much security on campus (where it wasn't possible to enter without an access card) and elsewhere in the city. It was more difficult to make my way around Joburg than Cape Town. I found walking through the Braamfontein and Hillbrow areas alone after dark somewhat scary, but I did it when I needed to do it. The place names seemed much in need of renaming: Jan Smuts Avenue, Empire Road, Queen Elizabeth Drive, Oppenheimer Building.

Eddie Webster, a professor of sociology at Wits, helped me with library and internet access. We discussed global trends in twenty-first century universities, both the positive and negative sides. He traced the trajectory of the project of transformation in South Africa through the past few decades. There was an atmosphere of critical debate and engagement with social movements. There was also a sense of ungovernability at Wits in the 1980s and early 1990s. The management lacked legitimacy, because of its collusion with apartheid. Students could disrupt but could not put forward coherent alternatives much of the time. In looking at the discipline of sociology, Marxism was a powerful influence, perhaps the dominant influence. Marxism had now been replaced by a growing pluralism, leading to fragmentation and non-engagement. There was no agreement as to core or canon. There was a demobilization of civil society and a shift to commissioned research and policy. Transformation as a developmental project had been displaced by the market and a management discourse assuming that universities were businesses like any other. Universities had not been transformed. Instead, there was a conservative restoration underway. Webster gave me a copy of a report he wrote on the state of the discipline of sociology for the National Research Foundation in May 2000, which was useful for my research. I also spoke at length to his wife, Luli Callinicos, a historian who sat on many boards dealing with heritage projects and history teaching. She felt that there needed to be redress, not only in jobs, housing, etc., but in identity, in the inner self. She thought that the ritual burial of Sara Baartman was an important gesture of symbolic reparation.

I was fascinated by the ritual of the burial of Sara Baartman that happened when I was there. She was a Khoi woman, who was taken by white colonists to Europe, where she was displayed as the "Hottentot Venus" in freak shows and museums in Britain, Ireland, and France in the nineteenth century. In 2002, her remains were repatriated to South Africa from the Museum of Man in Paris, and her burial took place on August 9, Women's Day, an SA national holiday. Campus was quiet, much in contrast to other days. I watched the ritual live on television. Although some of my colleagues and comrades were cynical about all the attention and money spent on the burial, rather than alleviating poverty, building houses, dealing with water and electricity cut-offs, evictions, etc., I felt that it was positive and progressive to give symbolic respect to the disrespected. This was part of a profound postcolonial discourse about colonialism, race, gender. However, there were other aspects that were less positive and progressive: the confused politics of who represented the Khoisan, the place given to royalty (even if Khoi or Xhosa), the romanticization of the primitive (wearing skins, "appeasing ancestors"). There were a succession of speakers: government ministers, provincial leaders, tribal elders. Each of them went through the tedious protocol at the beginning: "President Mbeki, Mrs. Mbeki, your royal highnesses," etc. Thabo Mbeki, to his credit, began by addressing the assembled simply as "Fellow South Africans." Some of the discourse and the unthinking recycling of clichés was ridiculous to the point of referring to Sara Baartmann as a role model.

Another Wits professor I met was Patrick Bond, an economist and prolific author. We went to a documentary and discussion of Zimbabwe and then to his house for dinner. We had corresponded for a few years, so it was good to meet. There was so much to discuss that we moved too quickly from one thing to another. Another of my correspondents I met face-to-face was Raymond Suttner. We circled around various topics we had discussed more fluently by email, but conversation did not flow. His wife, Nomboniso Gasa, was with him, and she was clearly hostile to me. She questioned whether the Cronin interviews were supposed to be recorded, transcribed, and published verbatim. She said that Jeremy had been walking a tightrope and that I had knocked him off it, that I had destroyed his modus operandi, that I was having an effect on the politics of a place where I didn't live and take responsibility. I reiterated the facts, which could be verified, but let the rest of it pass. Yet another correspondent I met was Dale McKinley, who had been expelled from the SACP with Jeremy Cronin playing a leading role in it. The conversation here flowed better. McKinley thought that Jeremy was getting a taste of his own medicine. Another person I knew from previous contact was Fritz Schoon, who had been a child when he came to Ireland with his father Marius, after his mother and sister had been blown up by a parcel bomb before his eyes in Angola in 1984. Marius died in 1999 and Fritz was now a student at Wits. He was studying philosophy, politics, and law. Fritz was very articulate and confident and very anti-ANC. He thought that the best thing that could happen would be for the ANC to lose an election, and the opposition to win. He didn't seem interested in the critique of the ANC from the left and thought other parties more promising. He didn't want to play on being the child of martyred struggle icons. His attitude seemed to be: that was then, this is now. I had lots of time alone to walk and reflect, to read and write, watch television, burrow into the library and generally extend and deepen my knowledge of South Africa.

I was asked to come to a meeting of the SACP branch in Pretoria to discuss the congress. When I arrived, I discovered that I was the main speaker. I had nothing prepared, but I improvised. The discussion was lively and interesting. The whole ideological spectrum in the party was evident here. Two party members especially stood out—one a University of South Africa (UNISA) academic was pulling to the left, while another, working in government, was pulling to the right and defending the government. The latter spoke of how her view changed when she moved from university to government, of how hard people in government were working. Another comrade said that they were really hard at work at doing the wrong things. One day I walked to COSATU House, where the SACP had their head office, to meet Mazibuko Jara, the press spokesman for the party. We discussed the congress and the interviews. I told him I was unhappy with the party statement about the Cronin interviews not being intended for publication. He apologized for that. We had previously corresponded when I put the interviews on my website. He wrote to me saying that this was the kind of thing they should have on the party's website. He had read both interviews and had them photocopied and circulated around the party. He especially liked the first interview and said that it made his wife want to come back to the party. He thought that the effect of the interviews and events surrounding it had been to move the congress to the left and he was happy about that. We agreed to meet again for dinner before I left to discuss future work, which we did in his home.

Jeremy called me and we had a long discussion on the phone. We had spoken at the congress, but there wasn't time to do so in any depth during those days. I asked him if he believed that everything that I had done was aboveboard. He said yes, that he believed that what I did was out of commitment to the movement and out of respect for him. He admitted that he had not been sufficiently responsive to my emails advising him to check the texts before publication. He said that things were difficult, that some comrades were angry with him. He thought the interviews had been discovered earlier by those close to Mbeki and saved up to have an impact on the congress and to undermine his position in the party. That backfired and he got strong support at the congress. However, there was still an ANC process coming.

That was not long in happening. There was a meeting of the ANC national executive committee where the interviews were discussed for a day and a half. At no time were the substantive issues engaged, but there were accusations of a dark conspiracy involving him as well as others in SACP and COSATU against the ANC. He was given three choices by the ANC: to apologize for the interviews; to be expelled and lose his seat in parliament; or to face a disciplinary tribunal. He apologized. There was another wave of publicity. I was back in Ireland by then, but being contacted by comrades, colleagues, and journalists for comment. I was very upset by this outcome. I did not think he should have apologized. A journalist from *The Sowetan* called and told me that Blade had indicated that the interviews were done as background research for a biography of Jeremy I was writing and asked me to confirm this. I told her this was not true. Moreover, Jeremy had repeated the "not intended for publication" formula in several interviews. I was disappointed in the apology and felt angry and betrayed by this account of the circumstances of publication. To my surprise, *The Sowetan* made my response to the apology and these allegations a front-page story. "Dr Helena Sheehan, the Irish academic who conducted the controversial interviews with Mr Jeremy Cronin, yesterday expressed her disappointment at the public apology by the deputy general secretary of the SA Communist Party and stopped short of calling her subject a liar and a coward."

After this, there was a difficult correspondence between Jeremy and me. The subject heading on my email to him was "On loyalties and lies." He came back and insisted that what he meant by "not intended for publication in their present form" was that he was remiss in not checking the transcripts, as I had asked him to do. I insisted that others took it to mean that I had done something underhanded and published what wasn't meant to be published. We at all times agreed on the facts in conversation and correspondence between us in every nuance, but what went out in public seemed to me to be slanderous. It was a sly maneuver that allowed others to conclude one thing, while he told me that he meant something else. He also insisted that he did not apologize for the substantive positions he took in the interviews but for indiscretions in referring to people and incidents, some of which broke norms of confidentiality. He also admitted that the apology was not his preferred option. If there had been a disciplinary process, the charges would have to be specific, but, as it was, there was a muddling of disciplinary matters and ideological questions.

Back in Cape Town, members of the party branch wanted to discuss it, since it was not only national news but also involved two members of their own branch. The central committee members (more than in any other branch) took the position that the apology was made and the case was closed, but the younger members insisted. One wrote to me saying that Jeremy sounded like a *sangoma* (Zulu word for shaman or healer). Ironically, although the intent of the interviews was to defend the transformational possibilities within the ANC against those who had come to believe that the place of the left was outside it, even in opposition to it, the interviews set in motion a process undermining that position. The reaction to the interviews on the part of the ANC indicated that the space for those in the left who wanted deep transformation, even the space for anyone who wanted to speak honestly about it, was narrowing. That was deeply disappointing for those of us who supported transformation for so long from afar, but it was tragic for the masses of the poor who still placed their hopes and their fates in the hands of the ANC.

Also in the month of August 2002, South Africa hosted the World Summit for Sustainable Development. Many international leftists were present for that and mixed with the left inside South Africa. There were various sessions and events where the ANC came under criticism from the left. There were turbulent street protests outside the summit, highlighting the ANC's failures to deliver on its promises, which were met by tear gas, rubber bullets, arrests, and government denunciation. There was a march planned to go from the impoverished township of Alexandra to the upscale financial district of Sandton, to highlight the gap between poor and rich. It turned into two marches: one led by the ANC, COSATU, and SACP and the other by a range of social movements critical of the ANC. The first attracted five thousand people whereas the second mobilized more than twenty thousand. Into this fractious scenario, exacerbated by the interviews, the congress, and the protests, Thabo Mbeki gave a speech attacking the "ultra-left" in and out of the ANC as acting in the interests of the right. Then a document issued by the ANC's political education unit for internal consumption came into the public domain. It employed clumsy Marxist terminology and produced a convoluted argument that the anti-neoliberal alliance opposing the ANC as neoliberal were on the side of the real neoliberals. Others came in on both sides, either condemning an ultra-leftist conspiracy in the country with shady international allies or asking those on the right of the ANC to have the courage of their convictions and defend capitalism instead of muddying their position with pseudo-Marxist mumbo-jumbo. Jeremy wrote a not-for-publication reply to the ANC document that somehow got published, but at least I wasn't in the frame for it this time. In December 2002, the ANC conference took place in Stellenbosch. Mbeki hit out at his internal and external critics and prevailed against them, insofar as he was reelected party leader (and consequently national president). His allies were elected to the top six posts, although many leftists were elected to the national executive committee, including Blade Nzimande and Jeremy Cronin. Resentment seethed and these issues were far from settled.

In January 2005, I returned for a month in South Africa, based once again at UCT. This time I was able to get a direct flight from Dublin to Cape Town. The flight was full of golf clubs (in both senses) and I was hoping there would be no emergencies, because I wouldn't want to end my life in such company. They watched US movies or read *Hello* magazine or had what they thought was mighty craic, while I tried to orient myself to the transition from the north of Europe to the south of Africa. I read an entire novel, Damon Galgut's *The Good Doctor,* set in a desolate hospital in a desolate ex-Bantustan, which was grim but good. I got a late-night taxi to AAH. The taxi driver was an industrial biochemist, recently downsized by Bayer, and we had a good conversation about poverty and injustice. I ran into Kader and Louise Asmal when out shopping the next morning, and then Salma Ismail when I went to swim. As with many conversations to come, the Cronin interviews and their impact came up quite quickly.

My cluster of AAH was full of African-American students on a school trip. They made a lot of noise, drank the juice meant for other people, and left the kitchen in a mess, despite notices about one-bottle-per-person-per-day and cleaning up. Another American moved in next door to me. He was a postgrad and publisher of a journal called *Safundi*. He was taking a course in isiXhosa and gave me a lesson on the clicks in the language. In the ongoing tug-of-war over the television, it was nearly always the Europeans and Americans who wanted to see the African programs, and Africans who wanted to see the American ones, but they did get into the African ones, too. One night, a current affairs program called *The Round Table* was followed by a highly animated discussion of what should happen in the way of land reform in South Africa. I was keen to check out a police drama called *Interrogation Room* and a series set in a newspaper called *Scandal*. There was a drama called *Molo Fish*, which the listings described as about a character who heard that Chris Hani of the SACP had been assassinated, so I negotiated with a Zambian guy watching a US show to change the channel to SABC. Sure, he said, but then talked to me the whole time, so I missed the drama. There were a number of African academics in AAH working on an international diploma in research ethics. An Ethiopian professor told me that he was a Marxist in the past, but found Marxism depressing, so he became a Christian and believed that he was saved now, so he was happy.

As usual, I listened to as much talk radio as I could. One host posed the question: "Was the ANC statement on the need for transformation of the judiciary a threat to the independence of the judiciary?" Jeremy Cronin defended the ANC position and criticized the media representation of it. Then a guy phoned in and ranted: "Why are you listening to this guy? He's a communist. The Communist Party is dead in Russia and China. Why are communists so popular here?" He went on and on. There was also a lot of discussion of whether Margaret Thatcher's son, Mark Thatcher, was getting off too easily in receiving only a fine and suspended sentence for involvement in a coup in Equatorial Guinea. Most callers thought Yes. Another story that had people talking was the revelation that Mandela's son Makgatho, who had just died of AIDS, had had an affair with a seventeen-year-old girl, now twenty-four and pregnant, and infected by him with HIV. Another debate was about monarchy. Despite being a republic, South Africa still sustained a number of monarchies at considerable public expense. One side argued that the Zulu kingdom shouldn't even exist, while other sides defended royal traditions. There was discussion of the fate of twelve thousand left homeless by a raging fire in the Joe Slovo informal settlement in Langa, set off by a child at an unattended paraffin stove. There were complaints about couples having sex in the open, of women being afraid to undress, wash, or sleep for fear of being harassed or raped. There was also lots of talk about water:

how to save water, who was wasting water, what should be done to secure it. Another big topic was who would succeed Thabo Mbeki as president, a topic that would gather steam in the times ahead.

I was invited to a *Safundi* gathering on the upper campus in the African Studies library. I was talking to Chris Saunders, a professor of historical studies, who asked if I was the one who did the Cronin interviews and what was my own political position. We arranged to meet again in his office. I asked him about the state of historical studies in South Africa. He thought that a major issue was the absence of Black graduates who could then become academics. There were too many other attractions that paid better for the brighter students, who didn't want to be spending time in archives. There was much ferment in the 1970s and 1980s, when Marxism played a big role. Most transformation of curricula had taken place before 1994. Saunders's approach was liberal, empiricist, and pluralist, which was criticized by those who were more radical. Still, he regretted the absence of such debate now, as well as the decline of interest in history. There was a course in African liberation, but it was mostly American students who wanted to take it. I read a thesis by Jade Davenport that Saunders supervised in 2004 titled "Moscow on the Hill," on student anti-apartheid activism at UCT from 1976 to 1983. The National Union of South African Students (NUSAS), in response to the Black consciousness movement, adopted an Africanization policy, inciting white students to relinquish a worldview imported from Europe and to identify with Africa, to break from egoistic individualism and to see their future as contributing to South Africa. I had another good meeting with Martin Hall, now deputy vice chancellor. He said that there was no particular reconceptualization of the world going on, but in the meantime there were tasks being tackled. He clarified a lot of things about the positioning of UCT in terms of the dynamics of South Africa and forces of globalization. I also met with Ian Glenn, the director of the Centre for Film and Media Studies. He said that there has been a market-driven change of what mattered. A lot of older disciplines and activities, such as literature, were drying up, he thought, while media studies was a big growth area. There was brand mania. Rhetorics such as Marxism, class struggle, trade unionism had no resonance anymore, Glenn believed. South Africa, he contended, was in escapism mode. After the TRC, people felt enough already. He added that the Independent Newspaper Group had been a disaster for South Africa and was doing more harm than apartheid ever did.

There was a murder at UCT while I was there. A professor of mathematics was assaulted in his office by his former PhD student, who was upset at not being appointed to a permanent academic position. The professor was battered with an umbrella and died several days later. Various issues swirled around this—personal relations, mental health, academic standards, racial tensions. My friend Salma Ismail was chair of the transformation committee in CHED. She reported that some wanted to take a soft approach to transformation and not deal with the hard issues. It was very hard to be a nonwhite academic at UCT, she said. Others said so, too. I got to know Lungisile Ntsebeza on this trip, who was tackling transformation issues in the university and pushing ahead in his crucial field of land reform. Back at AAH, I had breakfast one day with two African ethnomusicologists, one from Zambia and the other from Nigeria. One was a professor in Pretoria. I asked him about transformation. There was none, he stated emphatically. Those in charge were charlatans. He added that capitalism was evil and that Americans were the real terrorists.

I also met with comrades in the party branch. We had long talks in cafés, in their homes, walking along the sea and up in the mountains. When visiting Sheila Barsel in Observatory and Ed Wethli in Woodstock, I noticed added security in those areas with many more signs warning possible intruders of instant armed response. We passed a house that Sheila suspected of being inhabited by a coven. I often visited Brian in Rondebosch by day and had late-night visits at my residence from Sikelela Mkabele. These conversations were wide-ranging, but much preoccupied with the state of the party and struggle within the ANC. There was a debate about whether the party should contest elections in its own right or within the ANC. One night, I went to a café with Sikelela and his friends, and we talked for over three hours about religion and politics and epistemology. We had a lively debate about monarchy, with much of it focused on Zulu and Swazi kings and chiefs in rural areas. I still argued a strong line against inherited position, even if only symbolic and ceremonial. A Swazi guy, an engineer, argued for monarchy.

People were asking me if I would be seeing Jeremy and wondered how it would go if we did meet. We met and talked for two hours in a café in Rondebosch. He asked about my life, my job, my projects, my take on South Africa. I outlined my readings, discussions, observations, reflections, and turned the questions on him. Eventually, we came to the interviews saga. He had discovered further details about how it was orchestrated and played into tactics surrounding the congresses of the SACP and ANC where the Africanist and technocratic elements had allied against the socialist forces in the ANC. He argued that the struggle was still in play. Deep transformation was being blocked, but progress was nevertheless being made in reforms in the financial sector and land. He spoke of alternative paths of accumulation that built on the structures of rural and township societies that could be built into sustainability. He cited the position of Bukharin on the NEP in the USSR and said that he read what I had written on him and agreed with it. Later that day, I was reading an essay of his in *Voices of the Transition*, where he quoted Joe Slovo saying that many were prepared to die for the struggle, but asking how many were willing to kill for it. In this time, Cronin went on, it was important to speak truth to power, but it was also necessary to go the next step and take up the challenge of actually wielding power, of making the truth powerful and power truthful. The rapport we had had come under strain, but it was still there.

Jeff Rudin asked me to speak to a group called Socialist Initiative on the topic "Socialist Re-Alignment: Challenges and Prospects in SA and Internationally." I didn't feel well, but somehow I got through it. The group wanted to find a way to relate constructively to the ANC and SACP, while staying independent from them. I spoke about the historic role of communist parties, as a force on the left that dared to exercise power. Although they did so monumentally and tragically much of the time, I argued that there was more to defend than to denounce. Everyone on the left should have an understanding of that, I contended. The discussion was quite wide-ranging.

Back at my DCU job, I did my best to follow events in Africa. I went on a Make Poverty History march in Dublin in 2005, but I was very critical of this campaign. There were many positive aspects of this coalition addressing issues of aid, trade, debt, poverty, and justice, but the negative dimensions did much to undermine any positive impact. The prominence of global superstars (the worst of whom were the Irish ones, Bono and Bob Geldof), the dominance of a liberal discourse, and the marginalization of African voices did more to obfuscate than to clarify the problems of Africa. As I watched the televised Live 8 concert, harking back to the 1985 Live Aid concert raising money for famine relief in Africa, I cringed as one performer after another spoke of Africa: "Oh, those poor people, but isn't this awesome and aren't we wonderful?" Africa was again the Dark Continent, its people, poor and helpless and voiceless—except that now, politicians and rock stars were shouldering the white man's burden. The causes of poverty, the systemic imperatives of colonialism, capitalism, imperialism, the struggles of liberation movements, all fell away in this mock heroic, mindless myopia. On one occasion, when I was lecturing and spoke about poverty in Africa, one student exclaimed, "What? Even after Live Aid?"

Addressing this syndrome, I presented a paper at a development studies conference a few months later titled "Speaking of the South: Northern Voices and Southern Realities." I started with a brilliant article in *Granta* by Kenyan writer Binyavanga Wainaina titled "How to Write About Africa: Some Tips: Sunsets and Starvation Are Good." He went on to detail all the caricatures of non-African writing about Africa. I followed it in the same style with how well-meaning Irish people spoke of Africa: "Start with Nelson Mandela and how he was a colossus, who saw what needed to be done and made it happen. Don't complicate things with sociohistorical forces. Don't mention the layers of negotiators and role played by others, especially if they were whites or communists, or even worse, both. Let the mass movement fade into the shadows. Don't dwell on neoliberal economic policies that Mandela insisted were not negotiable and how he was fêted by the rich, famous, and powerful on the world stage. Don't raise questions about how heroes of the liberation movement have become multimillionaires. Don't wonder why nothing will turn the masses against Winnie Mandela or Jacob Zuma. Let people know that you have seen how people live in the townships, but remark on how resilient they are and how they know that change will take time. Don't go on about shack fires, evictions, electricity cut-offs, the bucket system, and all of the protests about these issues. We know that housing is still a problem, but sure aren't Niall Mellon and the lads sorting it out? The AIDS statistics are alarming. Thabo Mbeki shouldn't go surfing on the Internet at night. Make sure to mention Bob and Bono and Live Aid. Great Irish angle here: our guys telling world leaders what to do. Sure, where would Africa be without them? Still a lot to be done, of course, but wasn't it great?" Looking to find another way, I asked: When so many voices from the North of the world strike so many discordant notes when speaking of the South, how is it possible to find a voice that is strong, significant, and truthful, yet not neocolonial and arrogant? I reflected on the problems of writing about Africa from Europe, the issues involved in forging meaningful, reasonable terms of engagement. I was sensitive to the voices of those who had already accused me of overstepping the boundaries.

The time was coming to write up the results of my research, which was interrupted by many other tasks. I had another sabbatical coming up in 2007, when I would spend a semester in South Africa and then write. When I returned in 2007, I moved through my ever-expanding network of colleagues and comrades, and probed their lives and observations, but I also spent a lot of time alone reading newspapers and novels as well as academic journals, watching television news and drama, listening to talk radio and reflecting on it all, as I usually did. Some statistics from the SA *Sunday Times*: 48 percent employed, 57 percent had flush toilets, 1.3 million lived in shacks, 1.7 million in huts, 3 percent had university degrees, 75 percent felt unsafe. There were widespread power cuts, much of the discussion concerned getting electricity generation fixed for the 2010 World Cup. Another big story on the news was that HIV/AIDS was now spreading faster among the more educated and affluent sections of SA society.

There was controversy about whose names should be inscribed in the new Freedom Park. Should those who fought and died in SA defense forces during the apartheid era be included? Some really strong views enunciated on that one. There were also a lot of voices coming in on the public battle of the songs "De La Rey" versus "uMshini Wami." The first song harked back to the Anglo-Boer War and became a rallying call for far-right Afrikaners and international neo-Nazis, although the singer-songwriter Bok Van Blerk distanced himself from them and said his song described De La Rey, who was a fighter against colonialism and imperialism. The other song, "Bring Me My Machine Gun," was Jacob Zuma's anthem, sung by Zuma himself and by crowds in stadiums and outside courts. Zuma was a contender for president of both the ANC and South Africa, despite being charged with corruption and rape. There was yet another war of words between the ANC and SACP, with Jeremy Cronin accusing the ANC of suppressing certain views and wanting to marginalize or exclude communists.

I watched the opening of parliament on television. The fashionistas were declaring kaftans and turbans out, with a more tailored look in. Mbeki's State of the Nation speech was predictable enough, with no questioning of the set agenda, no new departures. There was a new television drama, *90 Plein Street*, set in parliament. The main character was a female ANC-MP with two children, whose ex-husband was chief whip. Lots of potential there, but the script was a bit tame. There was conflict, but it was basically about extending the time a bill was in committee, versus moving legislation on, tension between doing important work and having a career, versus raising children, problems of having a working relationship with an ex. To have bite, it would have to deal with ideological tensions within the ANC, but I wondered if it would go there. This time, I had a television in my room, so I turned it on at six every morning and switched between channels for breakfast television. In the evenings, there was so much television drama. There were slots where there were three indigenous soapies on simultaneously, on different channels for five days a week. There was an excellent miniseries called *Emthunzini we Ntaba* ("His Story—Mountain Shadow") in isiXhosa with English subtitles. It was about a group of boys about to undergo Xhosa initiation and their various attitudes toward it, including the fear of death. The controversies surrounding the ceremony were intensified when news came of the death of eight real-life initiates in the Transkei, splitting the village into camps of those who supported the old ways and those who rejected them. It showed one boy caught between a traditional father and schoolteacher mother. Would he please his father and risk mutilation or death, or please his mother and forever be regarded as a boy in the eyes of his people? There was uproar among Africanist traditionalists, and SABC took it off the air under pressure.

I went to the cinema with Brian Bunting to see *Catch a Fire* written by Shawn Slovo. The plot revolved around a guy who worked in a power plant who joined the struggle and blew up the plant. Brian took exception to scenes in training camps where MK recruits were singing "Kill the Boers," at odds with ANC policy of non-racialism. Later, I went to the Baxter Theatre with Norman Levy and two epidemiologists from South Africa but at Columbia University for many years. *Truth in Translation* was a play about the interpreters during the Truth and Reconciliation Committee and the psychological impact of their having to speak the words of both perpetrators and victims in the first person. The script, singing, and music were excellent. As usual, I accepted invitations to book launches. One was on memories of Cape Town, which was unusual in that it featured a theatrical group who acted out people's memories to mime and music as well as speeches.

At breakfast, the new AAH warden Chuma Himonga was circulating and introduced herself to me. She said that she heard that I gave the first ever presentation in the AAH lecture series in 2001 and asked if I would be willing to present in this year's series. I said that I would and outlined my current research to her. The first in the new series was being given by Eric Brost, the US ambassador to South Africa on US-SA relations. Brost, who put a sophisticated, African-American face on US foreign policy during the Bush administration, had a way of seeming to answer challenging questions from the floor without really answering them. I spoke to him afterward and asked him why he did not put his talents to worthier use than defending the indefensible. He took a my-country-right-or-wrong line. The second in the series was my presentation on "Universities, Social Movements and Market Forces," where there was deeper engagement and livelier discussion.

I made my usual rounds on the upper campus, paying a courtesy call to the philosophy department. The head of department, David Benatar, was as welcoming as ever, but there was still no meeting of minds. He was an analytic philosopher who did not engage with the questions I did. His attitude was that philosophy-is-philosophy-is-philosophy (my paraphrase), but it shouldn't be watered down to make it relevant to Africans. I asked whether he thought that it was important to engage in the debate about Eurocentrism and African philosophy. He said no, basically arguing that what was called African philosophy was premodern. But shouldn't the debate be taken on, I asked. No, he said; it just raised racial tensions. We discussed Mamdani at UCT and Makgoba at Wits, two controversies where issues of Africanization of curriculum were in play. I asked him about transformation and he said that he didn't know what it meant. He did agree with me about the commercialization agenda and thought that it was very worrying for philosophy. I passed by a lecture hall where anther philosopher was giving a lecture on philosophy of mind and wondered what the listening students were thinking. In the UCT campus paper, there was an article on a student awarded a "Mandela Rhodes" scholarship from the Mandela Rhodes Foundation, who said that people who won this award should have "a little bit of Mandela and a little bit of Rhodes"!

I had a meeting with the new dean of humanities, a Marxist, Paula Ensor. I raised questions about transformation in the intellectual sense and explained my research agenda. She said that she usually dealt with things several levels down, but entered into the discussion as I posed it quite willingly. She said that there were many inspired teachers and much good research in the faculty, but not so much within an overall intellectual framework. Still a Marxist, she was sometimes aghast at the conservatism of students. Listening to my sense of how things were going globally, she thought they were perhaps protected by their distance from metropolitan centers. I met another professor in the faculty labeled as an A-rated researcher, who considered himself a Marxist, but, incomprehensibly to me, felt no pull to be active beyond the university.

My friend Andrew Nash was back from the US and based at UCT now, teaching political theory. He filled me in on the latest philosophy conference at Stellenbosch, various people at UCT, his take on university trends and procedures, imperatives to publish, performance-related pay, the UCT rate-for-the-job reports, and the mentality of students. I had to laugh when he described an exam paper where a student wrote that, for Lenin, the vanguard party was top of the pops, whereas for Gramsci, hegemony was the name of the game. He said he was looking, perhaps in vain, for some sense of a collective project at UCT, but it was eluding him. On a smaller scale, though, I thought he was part of something at UCT that I did not have at DCU. Even the elusive discourse of transformation offered an aspiration that was missing in my university. He invited me to a seminar on contemporary capitalism that he organized, leading with a reading from Perry Anderson.

There followed a stimulating discussion among academics in sociology and politics.

Another day, there was a session on SACP strategy in the sociology seminar room. It started with presentations from Andrew Nash and Mazibuko Jara. Andrew argued that it was important to engage with the SACP, which was the largest political formation on the left in SA, which was coming to see the need for left allies. Another UCT prof said that he found the whole discussion amazing, because he was not accustomed to being able to discuss the SACP without being denounced by those inside the party for being critical, or being dismissed by those outside it for engaging with it in the first place. Andrew outlined the key points of a recent SACP document, which put forward a strong critique of the parasitic character of Black economic empowerment, allowing an elite to enrich themselves at the expense of the masses, and argued that the state was still contested terrain. It saw the balance of forces as being against socialism at present, but still open to possibilities. Mazibuko added that 1994 had led to a strengthening of SA capital, while masses of people were rotting in informal settlements and rural areas. He thought that the document was ideologically weak, that there was a need for a more structural critique and a serious left project, whether it involved staying in the ANC or challenging it from outside. Ed Wethli thought the ANC was long past being a vehicle for transition to socialism. Jeff Rudin said that there was a disjuncture between the two parts of the document, almost certainly written by Jeremy Cronin, a robust critique followed by a limp remedy. Sociologist and activist Jonathan Grossman said that there was a sense of the immunity of capital, which never had to answer to the Truth and Reconciliation Commission. The notion of the developmental state was now an excuse for lack of class struggle. Sheila Barsel said that the liberation movement had turned into Godzilla. She feared a split in the party.

Lungisile Ntsebeza was at these gatherings. We met over several lunches to talk further. He spoke of life in the Eastern Cape and suggested that he bring me there during my next time in

South Africa, so I could see for myself. He told me his son had decided to go through Xhosa initiation rites. In his work, he was addressing the role and future of chiefs. We also explored the position of Africanism and Marxism in SA universities. He asked me if I would give a presentation in the sociology department. I agreed and my topic was "Identities, Ideologies, Market Forces, and Social Sciences." After I spoke, the first two to respond came at me from opposite directions. Dave Cooper, head of department, took a somewhat crude class reductionist position, saying that academics were well paid and that was why they didn't resist. Melissa Steyn said that she was a post-Marxist, as she thought that class analysis was oppressive and didn't take due account of gender. Lungisile said he wanted to publish it in *State of the Nation*, which he was editing.

Another day I went with Andrew to the Centre for the Book in the center of Cape Town. It was to be a seminar on transformation of higher education, addressed by Naledi Pandor, SA minister of education. In the event, it was addressed by the deputy minister Enver Surty. It was not good. I had already read all the policy documents that had been strung together by some civil servant to make the speech. There were a lot of questions and comments from the floor, including from me. Each question had a spark of life, but Surty's answers flattened each one until it wilted and died. A deputy vice chancellor of UCT, the same one who chaired the lecture by the US ambassador, was equally gushing on this occasion. In closing, he proclaimed that we were all absolutely spellbound by the speech. Not so. Before and after it, I had a good conversation with Andrew on the issue of transformation, asking him what his vision of it would be. He said that there couldn't be transformation in higher education without a transformation in the whole society. Assuming that, what would universities look like then, I asked. He said that people without access to universities should have access now, and that the curriculum should deal with the experience and problems of the oppressed. He didn't think that there could be any Lysenkoist orthodoxy in any area though.

I also saw a lot of Norman Levy, whom I knew from the party branch as well as academic circles. I visited his apartment in Seapoint, where there was a sea view on one side and mountain view on the other. He was an activist, treason trialist, academic here and abroad, and was writing his memoirs. We discussed a number of memoirs we both read and the traps to be avoided. Another night we went to dinner in Bo Kaap, the Malay quarter, with Mala Singh, a philosopher now in charge of the quality assurance body in higher education, and Nasima Badsha, deputy director general of education. They spoke of their vision of transformation that inspired many who worked in the higher education sector. We also addressed the decline of philosophy departments and the limitations of analytic philosophy. On another occasion, I accompanied Norman and visiting US academics to the Wolpe Forum at UCT Law School. Helen Zille, mayor of Cape Town, argued that you could not have a consolidated democracy unless there was a realistic prospect of a change of government. Then we went to a late dinner, where we took on many questions, including whether Engels was the intellectual equal of Marx. Yes, was my line.

As on previous visits, I had many good talks with Salma Ismail. She was now on the academic senate. There was a debate about interdisciplinarity, or return to traditional disciplines. She brought me to her new house in Rondebosch, where she had moved, because her previous neighborhood was becoming "too Muslim." Although she had been raised in that tradition, it was becoming uncomfortable for her to wear shorts, and her sons were coming under pressure to go to mosque. Her academic area was development education, especially for women. She had been on a trip to Afghanistan to train women and found them so hungry for knowledge. Some told her that things had been better for women when the Soviets were there.

Over three days in Salt River, I attended a political seminar, funded by the Rosa Luxemburg Foundation (RLS), on the theme "State, Party and Popular Power." The SACP were not happy with the RLS working with other left organizations on such events, but party members still took part. Presentations on the first day ranged from Marx's 1844 manuscripts, to Germany 1918, to Brazil under Lula. Many saw parallels between the Workers Party (PT) and the ANC. The second day was more focused on South Africa. Andrew Nash gave a clear exposition of the relationship between capitalism and democracy, the formal equality that allowed material inequality to continue, and the problems of the market as a measure of value. As most of the non-ANC left, he was very skeptical of the concept of the national democratic revolution (a strategy of inter-class alliance for national liberation prior to advancing to socialism). Jeremy Cronin defended it, while agreeing with much of what Andrew had said. He outlined how the capitalist class had courted the ANC and effected the 1996 class project that imposed GEAR and demobilized the mass movement. It was "a luta discontinua." He argued for struggling through the present structures for a socialist democracy that would still need a constitution, multiparty elections, and parliament, although there should also be multiple democratic entry points. Suraya Jawoodeen, of the NEHAWU union, remarked that she assumed that she was there to provide race and gender balance, but proceeded to be quite hard hitting, arguing that the present situation was unsustainable, that the ANC in government was betraying the working class. She saw the current succession debate as between those who were enriching themselves and others not getting the same opportunities about communists unleashing police on strikers. The discussion from the floor was diffuse, but at issue was the legitimacy of working through the state.

The mood was against the position that Jeremy was arguing. Mercia Andrews, speaking from the non-ANC left, conceded that it was necessary to be critical of this tradition too. This line of march had raised its flag high with a position of socialism-or-nothing, but had failed to build an alternative path to get there. Mazibuko Jara argued against writing off the ANC-led state and for seeing the state as a contested site. He also made the point that many of the left didn't give the SACP credit for how it had grappled with Stalinism. He pointed to the serious disorganization of the left project. Others made various points, including how the ANC had nearly monopolized the international view of South Africa and its left traditions. Another session was on gender and the state. Basically, most felt that feminism had been defeated in the general demobilization of the mass movement and had been replaced by the bureaucracy of the national gender machinery within a neoliberal framework. Again, the discussion from the floor was diffuse. One odd note was an intervention from an older woman from Durban, who introduced herself as "Mrs." and gave out about women who were lazy, because they shopped in supermarkets instead of growing their own fruit and vegetables. We broke up into discussion groups after that. Fortunately, I was assigned one that was meeting in the courtyard, rather than a stuffy room. The discussion was all over the place, but with some interesting recollections of how it was in days of the United Democratic Front (UDF) during the 1980s. Then there was a diatribe from a guy called Ashraf, of the anti-eviction campaign, who drew a line between the left and the poor. Calling for less talk and more action, for example, ending the conference by burning a councillor's house down. Most didn't do that but stayed for a braai. Andrew, who was my lift home, wanted to leave. We had dinner in a Mowbray restaurant, which turned out to be a lucky escape, as many who had attended the braai came down with food poisoning during the night, one even taken to hospital. The third day was devoted to group discussion again. This time I was in a group with members of Abahlali baseMjondolo, a group bravely defending shack dwellers, who also denounced left intellectuals. I didn't know what particular grievances had incited this, but I felt that the atmosphere at this session was toxic and counterproductive.

As always, I participated in protests, whether at parliament against the World Bank or at UCT over wages. At UCT, organizers announced free toyi-toyi lessons during the strike. I ran into Jonathan Grossman, very much the activist as well as academic, and we had a good talk about the dynamics of the situation, as well as the position of the global left. Back at AAH, the warden was patrolling to see who was on strike.

I attended the AGM of the party branch. There were eighteen there at the start, but more than fifty by the end. The substantive item was a political report given by Sheila, followed by discussion. Basically, it was about the relationship between national liberation and the transition to socialism. Many of the people who turned up late and voted for officers, even some who were elected, had not been seen before by Brian, Sheila, Ed, or other stalwarts of the branch, which I found unsettling. Even though Ed was ill with pancreatitis and Brian had lymphoma and was undergoing chemotherapy, they remained active. Many of our discussions were about the succession stakes in the ANC and how the SACP was looking to Jacob Zuma as an alternative to Mbeki. Mazibuko had been expelled from the Young Communist League (YCL) over his opposition to this, expressed in an article titled "What Colour Is Our Flag: Red or JZ?" Sheila and I drove to Mazibuko's house in Muizenberg to meet him. We walked to the beachfront and had dinner at a place called the Empire Café. It was a nice dinner, despite the café's name, with interesting conversation. Mazibuko, despite his expulsion from the YCL, was still in the SACP at that point, although it was only a matter of time until that became impossible. He was also talking about doing a PhD on land reform. They asked me to be on the international board of a new magazine called *Amandla*. Those involved included both ANC and non-ANC left. Throughout this trip, I met with constant references to the Cronin interviews. One person suggested that I interview Helen Zille. The code was that an interview with me was the way to bring a person down. I laughed on one level, but it made me sad on another.

As before, I found it hard to tear myself away from South Africa. Andrew arrived to bring me to the airport at 5:30 a.m. Although arriving at 6:00 for an 8:25 flight, I had to rush to board, because the airport was grossly understaffed and there were long queues for every exit procedure. In a society with such high unemployment, this was ridiculous. As always, the adjustment to Ireland was difficult, but I got back to work at DCU and struggled to write up my research, amid other tasks.

The result was a long article, "Contradictory Transformations: Observations on the Intellectual Dynamics of South African Universities," published in a critical education studies journal. Addressing the expectations about the transformation of higher education aroused by a liberation movement coming to power, I focused on the underlying assumptions shaping academic disciplines, the debates contesting them, and the social-political-economic movements encompassing them, while probing the impact of Marxism, Africanism, postmodernism, and neoliberalism on the production of knowledge. In piecing together a picture of the present, I was constantly pushed back to the past—the past of the academy as well as the past of the society in which it was embedded—often far further back into the past than I had intended. To my surprise and sadness, I found greater intellectual ferment in the liberation movement than in the liberation.

I traced the trajectories of philosophy, psychology, sociology, literature, political economy, and history. The decolonization of history had been a powerful force in the liberation movement. The master narrative of apartheid had been overthrown and a new narrative was under construction, although it was far from agreed that there could be an agreed narrative. This was a society actively reconstructing its past in the context of every conceivable complexity of the current conjuncture. At the same time, there was a marginalization of historical consciousness. In 1994, historians thought that their time had come, only to discover that it had passed. At UNISA, enrollments in history dropped from ten thousand in 1994 to fifteen hundred in 2007. Whatever government ministers and vice chancellors declared, however sincere their intentions and struggle credentials, the nation was inserting itself into a global process where the systemic logic went in the direction of increasing commodification of knowledge and surrender to the exigencies of the market. Students did not want to detain themselves with the history from below. They wanted to leap into the future and live from above. They wanted to make money, wear designer labels, drive fast cars, and live in leafy suburbs. I concluded that South African universities were caught up in a complex field of forces where they were subject to conflicting pressures. The result was a state of contradictory transformations—one stemming from the politics of liberation and the other from the demands of the global market. Both were actively at play, but the former was struggling against the dominance of the latter.

I sent the article to various people I met in the course of my research and they came back to me with responses. The email debate list debated my article. Many of the SA academics on it found it a fresh take on things that could only be written by an outsider who noticed things that escaped locals, whereas others thought it tread familiar ground. One contested my stance on the Makgoba affair, but others came to my side. Still others said that it was too focused on UCT, or that Cronin, Asmal, and Bundy got off too lightly, because they talked left but walked right. I appreciated both the affirmation and criticism, especially in the way that the responses didn't make me feel as if I were walking on eggshells and venturing where I didn't belong. I knew how fraught many of these issues were. I was also aware of the hazards of a European writing about Africa, and knew that this set of respondents would be a tough audience, because most of them knew the material far better than I did.

Meanwhile, political tensions continued and events moved on. The left within the ANC made a concerted push for power, but all the nuanced, complex debates about alternative strategies for the ANC became subsumed into a gladiatorial combat between two patriarchal titans, Thabo Mbeki and Jacob Zuma. Zuma presented himself as a simple and earthy man of the people, in contrast to the elitist and vindictive figure of Mbeki. He became a lightning rod for disparate frustrations and ambitions, both conservative and progressive, united in a coalition of the aggrieved. The

SACP and COSATU, so long at odds with Mbeki, backed Zuma, despite charges of corruption and rape, and with little evidence of commitment to the agenda of the left. Blade Nzimande appeared constantly by Zuma's side in the arena. Hein Marais, in the excellent book *South Africa Pushed to the Limit*, which I reviewed, saw this as an indefensible shortcut to power: "It willfully chose the route of theatrical campaigning around a half-baked messianic figure over the painstaking slog of building a genuinely democratic left movement that could challenge for hegemony." Marais astutely traced the shift from the rainbow nation interlude under Mandela to the alliance of pan-Africanist romanticism imbued with neoliberal exigencies of Mbeki, to retro-patriarchal dramaturgies of the rise of Zuma.

In December 2007, at an ANC conference in Polokwane, Zuma was elected president of the ANC. In September 2008, the ANC recalled Mbeki as president of the republic and replaced him with Kgalema Motlanthe as interim president, because of the charges hanging over Zuma. After the general election of May 2009, Zuma became president of the nation. His presidency was marked by many forms of corruption, including excessive public expenditure on his homestead in Nkandla and "state capture," in which his family and associates commandeered public resources for private gain and claimed to have cabinet positions at their command. Despite populist diatribes against white monopoly capital and imperialist plots, his government implemented neoliberal economic policy. Zuma also embodied many forms of venality, including a reversion to toxic tribalism and violent masculinity. The massacre of striking mineworkers in Marikana in 2012 marked a low point of this regime.

The problem of "Zanufication" of the ANC was now taking the form of Zumafication. Even worse, it was not only the ANC but the SACP as well. Blade Nzimande, Jeremy Cronin, Rob Davies, and others became government ministers. They did not effect a shift to the left. Zuma used the left to achieve power, but dumped, marginalized, or co-opted them once in power. In the SACP, those dissenting were sidelined, vilified, even expelled, including Mazibuko Jara and Vishwas Satgar. Satgar, who was SACP provincial secretary in Gauteng, declared that the SACP under Nzimande and Cronin had committed political suicide and led the party over a cliff. COSATU was also riven with strife. Its general secretary, Zwelinzima Vavi, who had supported Zuma, recanted and, in 2010, warned: "We are heading rapidly in the direction of a full-blown predator state in which a powerful corrupt and demagogic elite of political hyenas increasingly controls the state as a vehicle of accumulation." In 2013, the National Union of Metalworkers of South Africa (NUMSA), the country's largest union, withdrew support for the ANC and SACP and called on COSATU to break from the alliance and build a new left front. It also demanded the resignation of Zuma. In 2014, NUMSA was expelled from COSATU. This expulsion was opposed by Vavi, who was also expelled. Breakaway parties formed. Congress of the People (COPE) was founded in 2008 by former Mbeki loyalists. Economic Freedom Fighters (EFF) came into being when Julius Malema and his allies were expelled from the ANC Youth League in 2013 after turning against Zuma, whom they had previously supported. Workers and Socialist Party (WASP) was formed in 2012. There were many protests and manifestations of disaffection. Zuma was booed at the Mandela funeral in 2013. Although this ferment was driven by forces within the country, Zuma lashed out against "shadowy international elements and movements" and ANC secretary general Gwede Mantashe blamed the fury at the Marikana massacre on "anarchy, driven by people who are far away," singling out Sweden and Ireland. The Irish person in the frame this time was Joe Higgins, MEP, who had attended the WASP congress.

By the time the 2014 general election came, there was considerable opposition to Zuma in many quarters. Various stalwarts of the struggle spoke out against him. Ronnie Kasrils, a leading figure in the ANC and SACP for many years and government minister under Mandela and Mbeki, launched a "Vote No" campaign, asking voters to spoil ballots or vote for parties other than the

ANC. Nevertheless, Zuma won a second term despite the drop in the ANC vote, but opposition continued. The EFF engaged in colorful theatrics in parliament, and there were many street protests demanding that Zuma go.

Through all this turmoil, communists such as Nzimande, Cronin, and Davies served in the Zuma administration and said very little about the burning issues agitating others. I especially wondered what Jeremy was thinking. When he did speak, it was often to put a slippery and sophisticated spin on a defense of the indefensible. Sometimes he came out as an attack dog on the left. No one could do it better. He did not engage in crude vilification as was unleashed against other dissenters (including against him) in the way he employed his considerable verbal skills against Irvin Jim and NUMSA, while he remained silent on Zuma and Nkandla. Against Ronnie Kasrils, he reminded him of when Kasrils was his mentor in the days of struggle and taught him that organizations are bigger than individuals. He did not defend Zuma, although he admitted Nkandla was "an unfortunate debacle." He did not try to justify his silence on many issues about which he would have spoken previously, but he did accuse Kasrils of being missing-in-action when Cronin was speaking out on the burning issues during the Mbeki presidency. This accusation was fair enough, but Kasrils was redeeming himself now, and I hoped Cronin would do the same eventually. One journalist, Palesa Morudu, speculated in 2017 when Cronin would claim to have been secretly against Zuma all along, as he sometime hinted. She called him a master craftsman, a "weasel wordsmith," with his "inimitable ability to almost say something without quite saying it, while leaving a vague stain on the consciousness." That was exactly what he did about the interviews. Even Nombonisa Gasa, who had been so defensive of Jeremy and hostile to me in 2002, tweeted in 2016: "'The Poet Lied' is a title of a poem by Odia Ofeimun. It came to mind, when I heard Jeremy Cronin on SACP & Zuma." Cronin had a remarkable capacity to twist and nuance, and it blended so easily into obfuscation and deception.

The interviews kept resurfacing over the years. After Cronin again gave a false account in an article in *Umsebenzi*, I wrote to them to ask him to stop giving a dishonest account of the publication of his interviews with me and reminded them that I had documentary proof that they were intended for publication. In 2016, Thabo Mbeki wrote a series of public letters tending to his legacy, one of which referred to Jeremy Cronin as communicating "outright falsehoods about the ANC to Dr. Sheehan." Jeremy responded that he thought the interviews were background for my academic research, that he stood by the substantive points made in the interviews but apologized only for breaching confidentiality. Then he eloquently went for the high ground. "As South Africans, we are facing major crises—searing unemployment, poverty, inequality, persisting global economic turmoil, a drought, and more. Too much public commentary and too much of the energies of those of us in politics get focused on demonising (and sometimes eulogising) personalities, on the comings and goings of game-of-thrones, palace politics, and on appealing to tweet-length attention spans." In response, I wrote to him yet again, telling him that he would be more credible defending the truthfulness of what he said in those interviews if he was also truthful about the circumstances of the interviews. I know that many people have done worse things to others and to me, but to have someone with whom I had such great rapport and respect throw me under the bus over and over again was more hurtful than much of the rest. As disappointed as I was at this and his other evasions, I didn't think his motives were venal. Even when he did things that were hard to justify, I did not think it was because of egoism, careerism, greed, or other such motives, but because he convinced himself that it was necessary to position himself to do most good.

In 2013, Nelson Mandela died and the Great Man theory of history ran rampant. His life and times were celebrated in a way that was devoid of complexity, contradiction, critique, forces of history. He was *a* (not *the*) leader of a monumental liberation movement, a movement that had not fulfilled the hopes entrusted to it. I did think Mandela was a great man, but I cringed as others worldwide gushed, blandified, or distorted his role and legacy. I suspended my normal routine to watch the funeral. Many of the speakers read their texts, full of the ever-recycling clichés, at the crowd, who were quite restless. I wasn't sorry when Zuma was booed, although there was a question of whether it was the right thing to do at Mandela's funeral. I liked the singing and toyi-toyi-ing best. I cried once. It was during a hymn called "A Plea for Africa," which I often heard sung by SACP comrades in beautiful harmonies when I was in Moscow years ago, but back then it was a secular version, with words more appropriate to a liberation movement. I wasn't impressed by all the VIP positioning. I was struck by the mixture of revolutionary and oligarchic elements and how seamless all this seemed to be for so many, as it did for Mandela himself, but not for me.

In 2015, students demanded that the statue of Cecil Rhodes on the UCT campus be removed. The Rhodes Must Fall (RMF) movement began with a student throwing feces on the statue while others toyi-toyi-ed around it. Protests, participants, demands, and occupations multiplied. Within a month, the statue was removed, but the momentum continued, raising sweeping demands for the decolonization of knowledge and supporting workers' demands on outsourcing, wages, and working conditions on campus. The ferment spread to other campuses. Although this movement had morphed into Fees Must Fall, it also encompassed demands for radical transformation and escalated into militant mobilization. Happy to see Rhodes fall and impressed by the emphasis on deep and radical decolonization, I expressed my support on social media. I was also glad to see reports of teach-ins addressing the relation of class, race, and gender. However, problematic aspects began to emerge, including exclusion and silencing of supporters based on race, disruption of educational activities, and destruction of public property, including books and progressive art. I had been struck by the series of paintings by Keresemose Richard Baholo, the first Black student to receive a master's of fine arts degree at UCT. They showed the liberation struggle as it played out at UCT over the decades: images of poor people demanding entry to the doors of knowledge, earlier students protesting at the statue of Rhodes. I saw RMF in the tradition of these radical impulses at UCT. Baholo supported RMF. I could not understand it when I saw a photo showing Baholo's paintings among those being burned. I could understand why they burned portraits of Jan Smuts and Edward, Prince of Wales, but why *these* paintings? I was also shocked to hear that Ngugi wa Thiongo, who had been calling for decolonization of the mind for decades, was treated with disrespect when he came to speak in South Africa at this time.

The Fallist Movement, as it came to be called, spilled out of the campuses and onto the streets, becoming a Zuma Must Fall movement, too. Although Zuma survived multiple votes of no confidence in parliament and in his own party, the pressure on him to resign or be recalled was building. The SACP finally took a stand against the corruption and state capture after Blade Nzimande was reshuffled out of cabinet in 2017. COSATU added their voices to the many others that called for an end to his presidency. At the ANC conference in 2017, the battle lines were drawn. The Zuma candidate for ANC president Nkosazana Dlamini-Zuma was defeated by Cyril Ramaphosa. Zuma resisted all moves to force him to resign as president of the country, including being recalled by the ANC, until he finally resigned in February 2018 and Ramaphosa became president of the country. The Zuma forces continued to plot within the ANC.

As 2018 was coming to a close, I was thinking it was time to go to South Africa again. As I was circling around dates and flights, an email unexpectedly appeared in my inbox inviting me to come to South Africa as a visiting fellow. Such serendipity! It was from the Mzala Nxumalo Centre in KwaZulu Natal. This centre was set up by Blade Nzimande, as minister for higher education to honor Mzala Nxumalo, a Marxist activist and intellectual known for his strong commitment and fierce polemics, who died at a young age and did not make it back from exile to a free South Africa. I said yes and we planned an itinerary for February through March 2019. I looked forward to feeling the pulse of South Africa at this conjuncture, making new contacts and reconnecting with old ones. I also, I had to admit, wanted to escape the cold and rainy North for the warm and sunny South. Although my higher intellectual aims were fulfilled, the weather didn't work out so well. I arrived in the rain and left in the rain and got caught in the rain many days in between. In fact, it rained every day of my first five days in Joburg. This time was also a period of heavy load-shedding, so there were constant power cuts, due to long-term corruption and mismanagement of the power generation system. Nevertheless, there was much to compensate for that, and I was happy to be there.

I was met at the airport by Olusegun Morakinyo, a Nigerian working in South Africa, whose PhD I part-supervised. He drove me around different areas of the city, talking about each of them, as well as discussing SA politics and universities. We arrived at Thulani Lodge in Melville, where I was staying. It was quite basic, but I really liked it. There was lots of African art around and a pool, too. Derek Buchler, the COO of the centre, came to discuss my itinerary, and we met again later for dinner to have a more wide-ranging talk about the operation and ambitions of the centre. The next day, I attended a meeting at COSATU House, between the Chris Hani Institute and the Mzala Nxumalo Centre, about how I could best be of use to them. They spoke about their work in worker education and asked me if I could give a seminar that would address worker education, universities, identity politics versus class analysis, grand narratives, and the state of Marxism today. A tall order, but I agreed to do it. We agreed on a title, "Is Marxism relevant to our struggles today?" On other days, Olusegun, an expert on transformational thinking about museums, took me around to various museums. We went to the Apartheid Museum, the Workers Museum, and Constitution Hill and had a thoughtful dialogue about the history and interpretations of history on display. I took issue with the hagiographical treatment of Mandela and the Great Man theory of history underlying much of it.

My main event was to give the Mzala Nxumalo Memorial Lecture at University of Johannesburg (UJ). I worried about how many would come, with lashing rain and heavy security at the gates and a clashing event at Wits involving many people I knew, but the attendance was good, perhaps two hundred or more. It was officially sponsored by the university, and there were well-subsidized receptions with food and drink before and after the lecture. I was graciously received by the vice chancellor, deputy vice chancellors, deans, and various administrative and academic staff. I met the family of Mzala Nxumalo. It was a very efficient operation with a big screen and high-res projector for my image-heavy PowerPoint, which looked quite well. Tshilidzi Marwala, the vice chancellor, spoke before me, supposedly to introduce me, but went on about the fourth industrial revolution, the need to produce more engineers, the age of the current Chinese leaders, plus a misinterpretation of quantum physics, which he claimed disproved scientific determinism, which was the basis of Marxism, thereby disproving Marxism. Naturally, I took issue. My topic was "Class, race, gender, and the production of knowledge," where I addressed these questions such as: How do class, race, and gender impact the production of knowledge? Is it enough to include those who have been excluded? Or has knowledge itself been tainted by the exclusions of class, race, gender, and colonial conquest? How to proceed with such realizations? How do we decolonize our minds and our universities? Should we repudiate existing knowledge and start again at zero? Or should we return to the indigenous knowledge of our ancestors? Or should we engage in a radical and critical transformation? How has Rhodes Must Fall dramatized these dilemmas? What does Marxism have to offer in working through these issues?

The lecture was highly polemical. After that, the respondent, Sabelo Ndlolvu-Gatsheni, gave what was more a lecture of his own about decoloniality, but it was thoughtful and complementary to my lecture. After that, there was a question-and-answer session, where activists in Fees Must Fall were the most challenging. One asked, "What should we burn?" in response to my criticism of the burning of books and progressive art on SA campuses. The closing remarks were to be from Blade Nzimande, now a government minister again, but he sent a message saying he was tied up in parliament in Cape Town. After that, I mingled and spoke to many people. A dean said that my lecture blew her away. Stephanie Allais, professor of education at Wits, emailed me to say, "Absolute fire!"

In between times, I wandered around the city a bit, more so than during my previous time in Joburg. After lunch at Market Square, I passed time in Mary Fitzgerald Square, where I had just missed a COSATU rally, but there were still remnants of it, with stalls selling colorful union and political regalia—dresses, jackets, hats, overalls, bags—and groups waiting for their lifts back to their townships. Walking around Melville, I was approached by a young woman of eighteen, whom I first took to be a boy of twelve or so, who asked to recite her poem to me. It was about growing up in Alexandria township and I was quite moved by it. She then asked me to buy her food. I went into the shop with her and she bought bread, milk, peanut butter, and beans. In the evenings, I met various colleagues over dinner—Sam Ashman of UJ on one night and Patrick Bond of Wits on another. The streets were in total darkness and I had to feel my way to my residence. When I arrived at my room, I could light a candle.

After a week in Joburg, I went to Durban (or eThekwini). In the area where I was staying, the power was out when I arrived in the afternoon, until 5:25 the next morning. The next day, Derek and I went for a walk around the city, mostly by the seafront. It was a warm, sunny Sunday, and there was a great atmosphere with many people from all sections of society having a day out. We had lunch in a restaurant with live sharks in a tank that took up a whole wall. On Monday morning, I arrived at the Mzala Centre in Pietermaritzburg, where I spent most weekdays. Derek introduced me around and then set me up in an office. In mid-morning on the first day, I attended a staff meeting. The agenda was mostly reports of various activities during the past week, including my arrival and lecture, and future strategy and funding. On other mornings, I conducted seminars on such topics as Marxism as research methodology in humanities, and social sciences and Marxism as epistemology and philosophy of science. There was a good level of participation. Various people, mostly postgrads, came into the office where I was working to chat about their research projects. I spoke longest to Sandra Hlungwani, who worked for NUMSA and was now doing a PhD in media studies. She also filled me in on NUMSA, SAFTU, and SRWP, confirming much of what I suspected had been happening on those fronts. One researcher asked me to look at a research proposal that was based on a traditionalist-postmodernist conceptualization of indigenous knowledge systems. I wasn't convinced and argued about truth criteria, but found it frustrating to come up constantly against a lack of critical scrutiny of traditional beliefs and rituals prevalent in Africa, as well as actual affirmations of African magic, even among left-leaning intellectuals. Another researcher was also training to be a *sangoma*.

One afternoon there was an unscheduled staff meeting. Derek announced that Percy Ngonyama, a senior researcher at the centre, had died, suddenly and unexpectedly, at the age of 42. Everyone was shocked. He had been ill recently and even in hospital over the weekend, but nobody knew how serious it was. The mood was sombre. The following day, the centre was closed. Instead, we went to the Ngonyama home in Pinetown. We heard more details of his final days, but there were long silences. On the following Saturday, we were supposed to have gone to a YCL commemoration of Mzala in rural KwaZulu Natal, but it was cancelled, because a YCL leader had been recently assassinated and that was the day of his funeral. It also turned out to be the day of Percy's funeral. The ceremony, in a sweltering sports hall, lasted three hours. It fused traditional Zulu culture with evangelical Christianity. The problem was that the person who died was a Marxist and an atheist. There were moments when his left intellectual and political commitments were acknowledged, but the funeral became swamped by all the religion. There was more singing than speaking—quite beautiful and fascinating singing—and some dancing, too. My favorite moment was when a reggae song was played and people danced around the coffin. A participant told me that normally there would be more singing and dancing from the mass of participants, but that was restrained on this occasion, because of the disparity between the words and rituals and the dead person's beliefs. After the service, we went to the cemetery, where the singing continued while the coffin was lowered and the grave was filled. Then we went to the Ngonyama home, where a catered lunch was served to many people in the house and garden.

Most evenings, I had time to watch television and check out the news, current affairs, and the soapies. I noticed that the term "decade of decadence" was being widely used to describe the Zuma period. One evening, I went out to dinner in Durban with Mala Singh and we had a good catch-up talk, especially about the scene in higher education. I also read SA novels. *Rumours*, the latest by Mongane Wally Serote, now a professor of philosophy at UJ, was a retreat into African magic. It was also very flabby, both in literary style and intellectual position. Its protagonist, a former MK commander, had lost his way in the new South Africa, his job and marriage falling apart, drinking too much and ending up homeless. He was saved by returning to ancient rituals, communing with ancestors, and reading bones. All characters spoke with the same preachy, sentimental voice. Novels I liked better were *London Cape Town Joburg* by Zukiswa Wanner, *New Times* by Rehana Rossouw, and *The List* by Barry Gilder. I also read the detective novels of Deon Meyer.

After ten days in Durban, I was back in Joburg, where I gave a lecture at COSATU House, sponsored by the Chris Hani Institute and Mzala Nxumalo Centre, on the relevance of Marxism at this conjuncture. The respondent was Alex Mashilo, SACP spokeman, who impressed me. The discussion from the floor was intelligent, challenging, and passionate. I went out to dinner that evening with Mazibuko Jara, Vishwas Satgar, Michelle Williams, and her mother. Michelle's mother was talking about US politics, her German origins, and how awful the GDR was, so we didn't really click, but it was polite. I was keen to talk to the others about what happened with their expulsions from the SACP, the Democratic Left Front, the United Front, and such matters, which we got to, eventually. They were also very involved with practical issues, such as rural education and food security. Also during this stint in the city, Ebrahim Harvey came to interview me for a book he was writing about class, race, and gender under the ANC, although what resulted was more of a conversation than an interview.

Then it was Cape Town for my final ten days. It was great to be back, although Brookland House, the guesthouse booked by the centre's travel agent, was highly problematic. I was here to lecture on the decolonization of knowledge but was booked into an aggressively colonial residence that seemed to be trying to re-create English aristocratic life in Africa. A portrait of Churchill was the first thing I saw when I walked in the door. Everywhere I looked, there was something offensive: many monarchist crests, books on the British Army, a biography of Margaret Thatcher, a framed certificate proclaiming the owner "Lord of the Manor," huge heads of dead animals on walls. At breakfast, I spoke to a young US surgeon who wasn't bothered by the decor at all and assumed I didn't like it because I was Irish. He was doing study-work at a local hospital, and told me there were many infectious diseases, many of them HIV-related, rarely seen in the United States.

On my last two weekends, I spent Saturdays with Andrew Nash, walking and talking by the sea, one week on the Atlantic Ocean side; the next on the Indian Ocean side. Andrew was very negative about the atmosphere at UCT and universities generally, especially the lack of respect for undergraduate teaching, Blade's time as minister of higher education, and the state of the nation. The second week, he filled me in with additional background on the people and issues I had encountered during the week. We zeroed in on how Rhodes Must Fall played out at UCT, and ended with the bleak state of the planet, which was preoccupying him. Salma Ismail also told me a lot about Rhodes Must Fall at UCT when she invited me to her home for dinner. She was involved in the Black academic caucus and, for many years, had worked to pressure UCT for more radical transformation. She spoke sadly of the contempt expressed for previous generations of struggle, of the bullying, exclusion, and destruction in the tactics of RMF. She noted that many RMF activists were from elite, Model-C schools, and their Black pain stories were mostly about having white teachers. On the plus side, they came down hard on the philosophy department. Lungisile Ntsebeza, now director of the Centre for African Studies, also spoke to me of the atmosphere at UCT during the RMF years, and the blind spots of the protesters. We had a dense and convivial conversation about the history of Africa Studies at UCT, the agenda of academic decolonization, Lungisile's research plans and mine, and much more. On the UCT campus, I was so happy to see the empty plinth where Rhodes had fallen. I was also pleased to see a building named after Neville Alexander, who impressed me so much during my first time at UCT, and Jameson Hall, now renamed Sara Baartman Hall.

My main duties in Cape Town were to give a lecture and a seminar cosponsored by the Alternative Information and Development Centre and the Mzala Nxumalo Centre in the AIDC premises in Observatory. My lecture on class, race, gender, and knowledge was chaired by Wahbie Long, who taught psychology at UCT. Jeff Rudin had asked me to address the negative moralism of race and gender, and what should be a Marxist response to that, while warning me to expect a hostile reaction if I challenged any shibboleths. The Rhodes Must Fall people where there and vocal, and there were sparks flying during my interactions with them, but I felt they were responding less to my actual arguments and more to their caricature of "white Marxism." One articulated an Africanist critique of Marxism, which was extremely convoluted and hard to follow. I argued that that I was glad to see Rhodes fall, and thought the current ferment about decoloniality was progressive, and thought Marxists should engage with it. One RMF activist who had been involved in burning those paintings said she wasn't going to explain why they did it. I later discovered that both of her parents were Marxists, ones I knew, and I had been in her home when she was a child. One young guy stood up and said he wasn't very educated, but he thought that Marxism was cool. Another day, I led a seminar on the current relevance of Marxism. It was well attended and many people spoke. I also had an enjoyable evening over dinner with AIDC people, including my old friends Ed Wethli and Jeff Rudin. I was impressed by a young guy named Dominic Brown, who was striking in his knowledge of international Marxism.

I didn't attend any party meetings on this trip to South Africa, but I did spend an evening with Sheila Barsel, which gave me a good chance to catch up with her and with the party. She was aging and had mobility issues, but still had a strong sense of purpose, much of it centered on the SACP, being on its central committee and politburo. After dinner, we sat on the steps of the UCT upper campus overlooking a panoramic vista of Cape Town by night and reviewed all that had happened since we last met. She maintained that the party had admitted its mistakes with respect to Zuma. I wondered if that was soon enough and had gone far enough. I noted that the party expelled comrades like Mazibuko and Vishwas, who were right on the Zuma period. We went through the fate of various comrades from the branch. We mourned Brian Bunting, who had died. We were shocked that Mfundo died in a botched hijacking. We regretted that Lucky Montana had been corrupted during his time as railway chief executive. We were glad that Sikelela, Manasseh, and Lucian were working productively in the public sector and trade unions. Rob and Jeremy were standing down from government and parliament after the May election. I told her that I had been debating with myself about whether to contact Jeremy and she urged me to do so. I was sorry to hear that neither the Jack Simons branch nor the Fred Carneson branch were functioning. Nevertheless, the party had 335,000 members, but it was mostly confined to townships.

I wrote to Jeremy, telling him that I still felt angry and betrayed by him, that I was sad that the great rapport between us was broken, and that I wasn't sure if it could be repaired, but I was in Cape Town for the next few days and wondered if we could meet. I received a conciliatory email from him, saying that he had hoped to come to my lecture, but got tied up in parliament and would be out of town for much of the time I had left, so it didn't look possible to meet, but hoped we could get past the fallout from the interviews and resume relations, and added that he remained puzzled by my hurt, because he never blamed me. I explained, once again, that I knew he didn't blame me, but spoke in such a way that others blamed me. I expressed my persisting respect for his intelligence and commitment and told him I was glad he was stepping down from parliament and government and intended to write. He sent me a paper on the bicentenary of *Capital* as an indicator of the sort of thing he wanted to do. I read it while watching parliament on television and seeing him there.

Again, I watched as much television as time allowed, as a way to explore the terrain. Watching Ramaphosa handling question time in parliament, I was struck by how much more sophisticated he was than Zuma. On Sunday morning, I was watching a (white) preacher going on about the virtue of wealth and how the success of rich people glorified God. I also took time to walk around Cape Town to remap it for myself, reflecting on how much decolonization was still to be done. The Rhodes statue in Company Gardens had still not fallen. Queen Victoria was still standing outside parliament, despite so many Marxists inside parliament during these years. Then there was the awful symbolism and reality of the Mandela Rhodes Place, the "iconic" five-star hotel where you could stay for R3,050 a night. Outside the hotel, I encountered a demonstration of farmworkers. Then I went into the Slave Lodge, a Cape Town museum, for a very informative but disturbing run-through of the history of slavery in the Cape. I returned to the SA Museum, where I wanted to look again at those controversial exhibits and discovered that they had been removed due to ongoing tensions over racial representations. I went to the National Gallery, where I liked a few paintings and other works, but found a lot of the work to be empty bluff. At the end of that day, I ate at a Kurdish restaurant called Mesopotamia and sat watching Greenmarket Square traders pack up their wares. I was sorry when it was time to go. On the long flights home, I read *Rebels and Rage: A Reflection on Fees Must Fall* by Adam Habib, vice chancellor at Wits, who argued that he was justified in calling in police to deal with protesters.

I regretted that I couldn't stay for the Marxism conference in Durban, organized by the Mzala Centre, but I watched as much of it as I could via livestream from home. Unfortunately, that was the centre's last act before funding ran out, furniture put into storage, salaries terminated, and all work reverted to a voluntary basis.

I had come so far, geographically and ideologically, from the world of my origins, to be able to walk some of my days under African skies. Some expected that I would come back with stories about stunning landscapes, adventurous safaris, and primitive tribes. I tried to convey a sense of Africa as cities, universities, television and talk radio, parliaments, and political protests. For all its difficulties and disappointments, this was a better version of Africa, and I am glad I chose it.

CHAPTER 6

No Surrender

"RETIREMENT" IS NOT THE RIGHT word to characterize these years. From 2009, I was active politically, wrote books, reviewed papers, spoke at conferences, and traveled the world. Even the term "active retirement" usually refers to playing cards or golf, and not such activities as getting caught up in an uprising in one country and occupying a television station in another. I survived gunfire and burning buildings, an economic crisis, and a global pandemic. I struggled to make sense of unexpected events. I marked some political victories, but many more defeats. Navigating the zeitgeist was as challenging as ever.

In my final year as a full-time academic, there were constant demands, treating me as if I were essential until I was suddenly expendable. I declined to take holidays to sort out my files, to ensure my modules continued, to plan for a time without me. I endured Sam's constant scolding, reminding me of how hard the trade union movement struggled for workers' holiday entitlements. I knew he had a point, but I could never reduce working in a public university to commodified labor. I never tuned out from the job in the evenings or on weekends and I didn't do so when my salary stopped on the last day of September in 2009. October 1 was not much different from many of my previous days. Although it began a major transition, it wasn't retirement in any way except for my salary being replaced by a pension. I went into DCU every day. I continued to supervise PhDs. I advised those taking over teaching my modules. I supplied references. I wrote articles and attended conferences. I gave many interviews to students, journalists, bloggers, and podcasters. I continued living as an academic. However, I did stop teaching, except for occasional lectures, and I found it hard to let go of that. I was glad to be free from marking and meetings. Above all, I had time to write that I didn't have while doing all that teaching, meeting, and marking.

My retirement was marked by two events at DCU. The first was organized by the School of Communications. It began as a seminar where colleagues addressed my academic work in history of ideas, science studies, and media studies, followed by tributes from my PhD students. Finally, there were testimonials from abroad from such figures as ecologist Richard Levins of Harvard and historian Loren Graham of MIT. I especially liked a point made by Levins: "Unlike liberals, who repeat ad nauseam that things are not black or white but shades of gray, Helena sees the world as a rich and colorful kaleidoscope and does not use complexity to dodge judgment." There was also a university event marking my retirement as well as that of several colleagues in other areas. Most declined to speak, but I chose to speak, focusing on how DCU had evolved, valuing the multi-disciplinarity and practicality, while regretting the loss of philosophical and historical dimensions. I was appointed emeritus professor.

I established my new routine. I arose at 5:00 a.m., walked to the university at 8:00, had a swim, worked in my new office until lunch at 12:00, went home in the afternoon, where I read for a while and then wrote. My new office was a shared one with various visiting researchers and part-time lecturers. Over the years, I found most of these visitors fine, but initially I had to deal with an officemate from hell. I attended many DCU events—academic seminars, visiting lectures, and staff socials. I participated in various groups: an

African studies group, a philosophy reading group, a retired staff book club. I served on a committee to commission a history of DCU. I kept up with academic gossip. One of the first big stories was a scandal involving one of our external examiners, who was exposed as claiming to have a PhD when he didn't.

Before I settled into my new routine, I went to the US where I took up a month-long fellowship at Boston University and then spent a further two weeks in Philadelphia. It was an opportunity to get focused on writing my book *Navigating the Zeitgeist*, particularly my first chapter about the US in the 1950s. I hadn't been to the US in the autumn for many years, and the season was as attractive as I remembered. Even into November, the weather was balmy enough to read outside and I had many reflective walks on the Boston Common and along the Charles River. Not that it was all happy and scenic. The view from my apartment in Allston was of dumpster diving.

I packed a lot into my time in this intellectually stimulating environment. Some of the events that I attended at BU were a panel discussion on the Obama presidency, a debate about US policy in Afghanistan, a series of lectures on American popular culture, a conference on the "future of the book," a conference on journalism and history, a symposium on Darwinism, a lecture on scientific experiment, drama and the origins of the novel, a lecture series on narrative and autobiography, a preview of the television series *The People Speak*. On the Obama presidency, the panel focused less on Obama the man than on how his presidency intersected with the contradictory mentalities of the nation. The most critical was Howard Zinn. A student asked what he would have Obama do. Zinn replied that he should announce withdrawal of US troops from Iraq, Afghanistan, and a hundred other bases around the world, and use the trillions of dollars saved to provide free public health care. For a start. He emphasized that no president was a savior and it would take a strong grassroots movement to make the Obama presidency what it could be. The debate on US policy in Afghanistan was very liberal on both sides, making it atypical of US debate outside of high-end universities. After the debate, student journalists were swarming, looking for reaction interviews. I no sooner finished giving one interview than I had another one. The event on the television series, based on Howard Zinn's *People's History of the USA,* took place in a full hall with clips from the series and a panel including Howard Zinn. During the questions from the floor, students once again asked what they should do. Chris Martin answered well, telling them not to expect some master answer from a sage, but to think about what they care about, what they could do about it, and then to do something about it every day, "like exercise." A student said that his generation wanted change, but didn't want to do anything about it, at least not anything that couldn't be done on Facebook.

The lecture series on US popular culture was right on my agenda, especially one on rethinking the 1950s, given by a very young academic, Brooke Blower of the history department. She argued that Americans were reimagining themselves in the suburbs, that a new national culture was being forged, that there was a need for rules and advice for everything, that there was anguish underneath the surface of conformity. She used examples from magazines, films, books, and television. The conference on journalism and history focused on problems of historiography: on alternative logics in organizing a narrative, on different kinds of evidence, on what to do about lacuna in the historical record. The conference on the future of the book began with the principal of Cushing Academy, which had removed paper books from their library and replaced them with computers and ebooks. He took a stack of big books from his bag, placed them on the podium, took the Kindle out of his pocket, saying that it held one thousand books, instantly downloaded the complete works of Aristotle, and then shoved the books on to the floor in dramatic contempt. The room was full of librarians who were horrified. I agreed with a lot of his points about adopting new technologies, but didn't like his showy manner or this act of disrespect for paper books. A formal reply was given by Christopher Ricks. I also agreed with many of his points, but didn't like his haughty manner, which included a gratuitously condescending remark about the Irish. I found the whole thing interesting, but thought it was too narrowly focused on paper-versus-electronic books. The larger forces threatening the future of books—the shortening attention span, fragmentation of research, fast-track careerism—got scarce attention.

The symposium on Darwinism was in the Boston Colloquium in the Philosophy of Science series, which I had attended many years ago. David Depew of the University of Iowa spoke about shifts in conceptual framing of Darwinism, challenging geocentric and individualist interpretations of evolution and the use of Darwinism as a bully pulpit by such as Richard Dawkins, celebrity biologist and atheist. There was a return of the repressed and a new tendency to see organisms as integrated ecological flows rather than points on statistical arrays. Lynn Margulis, well known for her development of the concept of symbiosis in evolutionary biology, continued along such lines, arguing that evolution was about the whole biosphere and took place by symbiogenesis. She spoke of inheritance of acquired genomes. I was getting a grip on what was meant by Neo-Lamarckism, a revival of belief in inheritance of acquired characteristics. She opposed the fragmentation of knowledge in universities. Another day, I went to a lecture on scientific experiment, drama, and the origins of the novel by Michael McKeon of Rutgers. I had noted a building named after Irwin Silber, so I was interested to hear McKeon's negative remarks about the "dark years of the Silber era" at BU. He argued that scientific experiment and empiricist epistemology made possible a theory of literature as a distinctive form of empirical knowledge. On another day, a lecture by Joshua Landy of Stanford was on narrative form and the meaning of a life. It was a topic of great interest to me, but the lecture was unsatisfactory, because Landy saw the meaning of a life as basically individualist and aesthetic without seeing personality or aesthetic criteria as grounded in sociohistorical experience. Another lecture on this terrain was by philosopher Peter Goldie who spoke on narrative thinking, emotion, and autobiographical memory. He introduced the idea of dramatic irony in constructing autobiography, opening the gap between the author as me-now as narrator and the me-then as character in the story, dealing with the difference epistemically, evaluatively, emotionally.

With many universities in the Boston-Cambridge area, there was so much going on that I always had many options. Even looking at the websites of Harvard and BU, scrolling through faculty research interests and courses taught, I noted the vast areas of knowledge covered. There was an attempt to encompass the whole, thus justifying being called "universities." So many institutions called universities these days were organized around market-oriented niche areas and did not feel like real universities. I went into the Harvard bookshop, where there was a whole section devoted to books by Harvard faculty. It wasn't even an exhaustive collection. At DCU, in contrast, it was a struggle to have books (as opposed to research grants and journal articles) respected. During the next decade, DCU's campus bookshop closed.

In the philosophy department at BU, I met Tian Yu Cao, who told me his story. Although he was a Marxist, he had trouble with the Communist Party of China from early days when he wasn't allowed to go to university, because his father was supposedly a bourgeois, because he was a herbal medicine salesman and joined a trade union connected with the nationalists. Then, with a twist of policy, Tian was admitted to university and argued openly for a critical-versus-dogmatic interpretation of Marxism and ended up in prison. One thing after another held him back in his studies until he managed to get to Cambridge University and then to Harvard. His wife had an academic position at the London School of Economics and lived in the Engels house in Primrose Hill. There was an exhibition of post-communist art in Boston, while I was at BU, which was underwhelming. The only paintings that I actually liked were ones from before 1990. The rest were just paint on canvas, which left me cold.

This time in Boston also gave me the opportunity to catch up with colleagues I met in connection with my work in the past, especially in science studies. It was good to meet again with Robert Cohen, John Stachel, and Loren Graham, all emeritus professors now. When we met in his Harvard office, Loren told me it was the happiest time of his life. Richard Levins had not retired. Among my interactions with him was a visit to his class on human ecology at Harvard. We met several times in a café in the early morning, where we arrived in the dark and spoke many hours beyond sunrise. We discussed politics (on all major continents), universities, theories, families, etc. It would be hard to say what we didn't discuss. He believed, as I did, that the truth is the whole. We also met at a dinner party organized by Ahba Sur of MIT, which allowed me to meet with other Marxist scientists, including Richard Lewontin.

One person there was an expert in health care and gave a lucid critique of Obamacare from the left. This was a hot issue at the time, but unfortunately much of the opposition to it was coming from the right. On television news, I saw a demonstration against Obamacare, where the attitude was, "I'll take care of mine and you take care of yours." In other news on the health front, there was an epidemic of H1N1 (swine flu). Looking back on it after COVID-19, it is striking that no public health measures were put in place. There were large gatherings with no social distancing or face coverings, no daily news of numbers of cases or reports of deaths. I was in crowded public transport and lecture halls. I contracted it. I felt wretched, then better, then wretched again, over and over, which took me out of circulation for ten days, which was so hard when there was so much happening. As always, I watched a lot of television to feel the pulse of the nation, but found it so shallow, trivial, myopic, bitty. On Sunday mornings, there were mad preachers ranting about how the evil of Russia and other "rogue states" was foretold in the Bible.

While in America, I kept up with events in Ireland, especially a rising tide of protest at the national political response to global economic crisis. There was much controversy on social media about a one-day national public service strike, which provoked snide accusations about teachers wanting to use the day for shopping.

I was proud of my son, now a teacher, who answered ably. On the day of the strike, I planned to attend a conference at BU. I checked my watch on my way out the door, to discover that it was 4:00 a.m. I had mistaken a phone alert from my union about the strike for my wake-up alarm.

The train from Boston to Philadelphia brought back a flood of memories, with so many stops connected to events of my past. In Philadelphia, I met with friends and family. As always, I had a catch-up with my ex-husband, Jack Malinowski. For the first time in decades, I was with family for Thanksgiving. It was usually all my brothers and sisters, except me, but this year it was all except my brother Joe, possibly because of me. We had our differences, but we had recently come to a final parting of ways. On Facebook, he had posted a poll on whether the phrase "under God" should be eliminated from the Pledge of Allegiance. Not content with voting no, he wrote that, according to another poll, only 2.3 percent of US citizens were professed atheists, therefore they should crawl under a rock and die. I wrote back: "How many of your great majority have given one moment's thought to the arguments and evidence regarding the existence of a God? How many in your republic have any respect for those who have? What is the relation between such aggressive disrespect and the failure to face the question?" First, my comment disappeared and then he "unfriended" and blocked me. Admittedly, our relationship was already fraught. He had become a full colonel in the Marines. There was a battle of ideas and struggle for power in the world and we were on opposite sides. At one stage, he had a gun to his head in Iraq, but somehow got out of it, and credited our mother in heaven with saving him, as this occurred on the anniversary of her death. He sent an email to our brothers and sisters who were believers, citing Jeremiah 29:11, "For I know the plans I have for you," and believed it relevant to those unbelievers "who shared the same womb." My sister Theresa believed this citation related to a prophecy that some guy in a bar made that she would be the vessel for bringing me back to religion. When at her apartment, I answered her phone and Joe hung up on me. My sisters asked me to come to mass with them "for old time's sake." I declined. When they were dropping me off at the train, I spotted a huge mural honoring Paul Robeson. We doubled back and I explained who he was as I photographed it. Although we were born of the same parents, we lived in different worlds.

I settled into this new stage of my life in Dublin. My way of life was healthy, pleasant, and productive. My writing was focused and flowing. I was happy, but it was not the happiness of youth. There was a sense of possibilities closing down, a relative lack of adventure, surprise, romance. However, there was a sense of fulfillment, of looking at a body of work accomplished while I was still in a position to develop it further without anxiety and insecurity about finances, time, position.

I responded to many requests to do media interviews. The topics were varied: the future of universities, the history of Irish television, the relation of science and religion, a new biography of Engels, gender stereotyping, how atheists celebrate Christmas, a debate on "Will the centre hold or are things shifting to the left and/or right?" I believed that it was important to use such opportunities to make important points to a wider audience, but sometimes I was sorry I bothered. When I looked at the final result of a "filmic essay" for which I was interviewed, it was badly focused and edited, full of pseudo-profundity about land, myth, religion, modernity. Another time, it seemed to be a good idea to go on a late-night current affairs show to debate whether there was an alternative to capitalism, but it was a total bear pit, where well-known right-wing figures Declan Ganley and Constantin Gurdgiev constantly interrupted and insulted my fellow Marxist Kieran Allen and myself. Vincent Browne, the television host, found all the shouting amusing and let it rip, instead of attempting to get it focused. It was rule of the rudest, generating much heat but little light. Vincent Browne could be good at times, but often darted down blind alleys and missed core points. I had the good sense to decline to go on air for a "wrap party" for the tv drama *Love/Hate*, as it was premised on loving the show, whereas I was hating it, because it groveled in gritty details of gangland violence, devoid of sociohistorical context, devoid of any implicit or explicit psychological, cultural, or political analysis. As the mobile phone came into increasing use for media interviews, I took calls from all sorts of places, whether a street in Croatia, a beach in Corfu, a television station in Athens, or between connecting flights in London or Paris.

Social media, especially Facebook and Twitter, became increasingly knitted into the texture of my life. My experiences of these media were overwhelmingly positive and continuous with the life I lived on other terrain. While there was considerable continuity between most people's Facebook personae and the lives they lived, there was sometimes stunning dissonance. One person whose life was falling apart, even to the point of an attempted suicide, appeared to be happy and flirty, and to spend much time playing online mafia wars and zombie wars. Another, a failed academic, who lived off whomever he could seduce, made grossly exaggerated claims about publications, prizes, and globe-trotting successes. I also had many arguments. For example, when I supported protesters on the streets of Athens, one response was that the Greek people should grow up and stop living beyond their means. I asked how teachers earning €900 a month were living beyond their means. Another time, I got into a Twitter storm, which spread to Facebook, with John Crown, doctor and senator, who used the occasion of the death of Eric Hobsbawm to air his opinion that being a Marxist historian was like being a creationist palaeontologist. When challenged, he doubled down, calling Marx a crackpot, pseudoscientist, and believer in predestination. An academic psychologist unfollowed John Crown, saying that he was bringing the Seanad and academia into disrepute. The Royal Irish Academy retweeted Crown and later apologized.

Social media provided a forum for those who did not get invited on mainstream media to interact with those who did. It was also a forum for those of us who did to discuss topics not discussed on mainstream media, such as the opacity of the discourse when it came to class. Sometimes the public discourse across all media seemed lost in a la-la-land of shallow sentimentality, especially in the Disneyworld of celebrity visits, where the elite continued to party at our expense. The uncritical obsequiousness surrounding the visit of the British queen to Ireland in 2011 was smothering. During the receiving line at Dublin Castle, our own elite were bowing and curtseying. Seamus Heaney, who once wrote, "Be advised my passport's green. No glass of ours was ever raised to toast the Queen," sat at the top table and toasted the Queen. I let off steam on social media, reminding my fellow citizens that it was a time of intensified redistribution from below to above and asking them to get off their knees. One former student of mine reminded me it was not Paris 1968. Interesting, I replied, that a sixty-some-thing leftist intellectual was so passé and an eighty-something monarch was now so cutting-edge. DCU catering hosted a "royal tea party" on the occasion of her grandson's wedding. What sort of republic is this? I often asked.

Then there was the Obama visit, another occasion for mind-less and obsequious commentary. The big rally at College Green was a big "Yes we can" thing about belief in ourselves. Yes we can do *what*? No mention of Wall Street or Afghanistan or Iraq. Even from a low point of expectation, I found the Obama presidency disappointing. He was handsome, smart, and sophisticated, which made him in some respects worse than his predecessor, because he knew better than what he did. At least his autobiography, *Dreams of My Father*, made me think so. When Pope Francis arrived in 2018, it was more low-key and much of the discourse was about how Ireland changed since the last papal visit, what the Church would do about clerical sex abuse, and how faith should be respected as an individual choice. While a few gushed for Ireland, they were marginal. Politicians politely shook the Pope's hand and did not genuflect or kiss his ring as they had in the past. Crowds on streets in Dublin City Center were estimated to be twenty thou-sand, much less than the projected one hundred thousand. When he passed my house, very few came out. Those who did (and I did) did so more out of curiosity about celebrity spectacle than religious fervor.

My reading habits during this time shifted away from academic texts, especially ones I had to examine, to novels, blogs, tweets, and links from social media updates. I was reading more things that people wrote because they had something to say, not because they wanted degrees or promotions. Of course, I was constantly dragged back to such academic texts, with requests to examine theses, review articles, book proposals, and books. I responded to an email from a colleague about signing a pledge to refuse to peer-review articles not available in open access journals. I did not see why we should give our labor freely for journals that that did not pay authors or reviewers, while extracting a price that many readers and even some authors or university libraries could not afford to pay. That should have been an easy battle for academics to win, but not enough were willing to take the time or minimal risk of taking on this industry, thriving on a parasitic commodification of knowledge.

I attended many conferences and seminars and engaged in many debates, sometimes from the podium and other times from the floor. At a conference on the US crime drama *The Wire*, I was struck by how people could talk about class without actually talking about class. There were two papers on the white male working class that were almost totally focused on race, ethnicity, and gender but not class. The avoidance of class in contemporary academic discourse and in the wider culture was a big theme for me. At another event, specifically on culture and class, I defended an ideological analysis of culture against hollow aestheticism and bourgeois individualism.

At a conference on reinventing the university, many of the speeches simply recycled the standard clichés about competitive advantage, knowledge economy, stakeholders, diversity, and inclusion, etc.—the single transferable speech on higher education. At the final discussion, I called attention to the domination of the conference by a certain ideological position and the use of public funds to do that without a dissenting point of view being represented. I attended another conference, which dealt with more substantive issues, airing a critique of neoliberal hegemony, but diffusely, so no strategy to counter it emerged. Another event organized at DCU by SIPTU, our union, focused on the dissenting position and the need to defend the public university from the onslaught of commercialization. Everyone who spoke agreed, but only because those who accepted the dominant position, either actively or passively, stayed away. I made the point that, while much could be done within the university, neither the source nor the solution of the university's problems were within the university.

DCU's chief operating officer was there, although he didn't speak. I spoke to him afterward, in a space between an aggressive Bank of Ireland presence recruiting clients and an Islamic display attacking evolution. About the latter, I asked him if he thought there was any line that could not be crossed, if there was anything that would be intellectually and/or morally below the line to be appropriate for a university to display. He asked "Who decides?"— which was a good question, because it opened the bigger question of whether there were any common epistemological and ethical criteria for making such decisions anymore. Another day, there was a stand where passersby were invited to "See how you look in a hijab." I noted this on Facebook, including my reaction, which was NO. There were more than fifty comments, some of them nasty. One commented: "Islamophobia = racism." It sometimes seemed as if Islamophilia = anti-racism. I dissented. One suggested that I try it. I remembered that I once was a veiled woman and now recoiled from it as a symbol of patriarchy, human or divine. On still another day, there was a stall recruiting contestants for the Rose of Tralee beauty contest.

Every year, I took in the fair of university societies to see what was on offer, increasingly approaching the event as an anthropologist, studying some strange subculture. One year I passed from a sign asking, "Do you know Jesus?" to come upon two guys in combat gear with toy machine guns and other guys threw frisbees.

There were invitations to go golfing, kayaking, caving, running, weight-lifting. There were lots of free sweets, pens, and condoms. No red flags. Various political parties had stands. One guy asked me to join Young Fine Gael. I said that I wasn't young and anyway I'd rather be dead than do so. "Would you join Fianna Fail then?" a girl asked me. A wave of nostalgia for the campus of the 1960s rushed over me. Another year, as I passed the Young Fine Gael stand, I asked, "Why would anyone join Young Fine Gael?" When he couldn't find words, I pushed on: "Is it because it's a party of power and you want to get on in the world and you don't mind being a puppet of plutocrats?" He said that he didn't see it like that, but was unable to articulate just how he did see it. I stopped after a few sentences, as it felt as if I were punching a balloon.

Brian MacCraith was named new president of DCU in 2010. I took up the invitation to attend his inauguration and happily joined the academic procession in my doctoral robe. I expected there to be various nuances and absences in the speeches that I would contest, although only in my own head. However, I could not let pass the presence of prayer in the ceremony, especially since all previous ceremonies at DCU had been secular. Moreover, the assembled were expected to give a prescribed response, "Blessed be God forever," assuming the hegemony of a theistic view of the universe. It was ecumenical and based on the inference that the voices of the combined religions somehow encompassed the worldviews of us all. I went directly to my office and wrote an all-staff email, protesting that this was not the case, because there were significant numbers of staff and students who were not religious believers. There were lots of responses both on- and off-list. Most, but not all, agreeing. The prayer controversy became the talk of the campus and found its way into the mass media, following a story in the *Sunday Independent*. The president did not respond in email or in public but called a meeting with those who expressed dissent on the prayer. He claimed it was meant to be inclusive, although it turned out to be exclusive. He agreed that it was inappropriate, especially the prescribed response, and assured us that the university was a secular institution and it would not happen again.

The discussion ranged more widely, too, dealing with how DCU could be a more intellectually vibrant institution. He called me into his office again a few months later to discuss the situation of retired academics and how it could be improved, and asked if I would be willing to participate in working groups, pro bono. I would. The most demanding of these tasks was to serve on a committee to commission a history of DCU for its fortieth anniversary. I have found DCU to be a very good place for retired academics, although the use of the email system to deal with controversy was closed down, with some of the pressure to do so coming from below, from staff who wanted to know only about such matters as funding opportunities or power outages, since all the seconds it took to delete email controversies could otherwise go into teaching and research excellence.

I got quite upset by what seemed a constant dumbing down of academe. Under financial pressure, there was drastic pruning of degrees. Modules dealing with broader historical, sociological, philosophical, political, economic context, including my history of ideas, were axed, yet one on puppetry was added. Thesis and language requirements were scrapped and five-credit modules were bumped up to ten credits. One day I was stopped by students doing a vox pop for a video class assignment, who asked, "What is the most important lesson you have learned from life?" Off the top of my head, I said, "The importance of worldview." They looked surprised and said, "That's the most intellectual answer we have got." I asked about the rest. "Mostly about drink," they replied. This is a university, isn't it? I thought to myself, walking away. At the start of a new academic year, the Department of Higher Education tweeted its well wishes to students beginning higher education with a quote from Theodore Roosevelt: "A man who has never gone to school may steal from a freight car, but if he has a university education, he may steal the whole railroad." Disgraceful, although revealing. Universities devoted much attention to branding themselves with all the buzzwords about individuality, opportunity, networking, diversity and inclusion, entrepreneurship, achievement, excellence: everything except knowledge. Another day I was in a department store and noticed a corner with the word "Philosophy" in neon lights. Such is capitalism: banish philosophy from universities and use the hollowed-out word to sell skin-care products. I thought it was bad enough when bookstore sections on philosophy were filled with new-age lifestyle guides.

Sometimes, I felt like a dinosaur on the verge of extinction. However, I intended roaming the Earth and roaring for a while longer. Despite my constant critique, I was still very attached to the university in general and DCU in particular, and I felt grateful that I still had a place in it. As I donned my red robe for the graduation of my last PhD, Sheamus Sweeney, a big rite of passage for him and for me—I reflected on how important it was to be in mainstream institutions, especially ones such as universities and media, and felt proud at being able to function without either being closed out or blending in uncritically. I spent a lot of time talking with younger colleagues about academic sense and nonsense, about how some people knew the difference and some had not a clue. I felt very proud of another of my PhD students, Declan Fahy, who went off to American University for five years and came back to DCU, embodying sound intellectual and moral values and a strong commitment to both teaching and research.

At a meeting of a research center to which I nominally belonged but from which I felt increasingly alienated, I found myself moving into my anthropological mode in relating to the now-dominant model of research: funding calls, composing proposals made to fit the call, finding international partners, executing work packages, employing methodologies of content analyses, audience surveys, focus groups, receiving feeble results, clumpy reports, after much effort expended in arriving at the dead-end of gray literature that nobody reads. The drive to bring in external funding kept ramping up and I watched mediocrities who mastered the maneuvering rise. Although these academics did not conceptualize the proposals or do the research or write up the results, they were supposedly the principal investigators, and got promoted accordingly. Of course, they did little or no teaching, using research funding to buy it out. They swanned around on high salaries and public prestige while subcontracting all the actual work to academic underlaborers, in a grotesquely parasitic web of relationships. At a discussion of academic strategy, a new lecturer was all about branding, about discerning what those in power wanted "us" to be, and how to show them that was what "we" were. He sounded like a character from *Mad Men*. Although he didn't do any of the jobs that I did, he was hired because I retired. It occurred to me that universities would soon be populated only by those who remembered them no other way. During this period, there was a meeting at the Gresham Hotel of concerned academics, who issued a call for emphasis on critical thinking and social responsibility and opposition to grotesque commercialization. Speakers spanned a wide spectrum, from leftists like me to Fine Gael ex-taoiseach Garret Fitzgerald.

Several times I exploded at visiting speakers. For example, at a big international mass communications conference at DCU, a speaker lazily remarked that Irish people did not protest. This was at a time when there were more and more protests (and I sometimes felt run ragged, keeping up with them all), and I resented being discursively obliterated. My own presentation at this conference was called "The Compliant and the Defiant: Dominant v dissident narratives of the crisis in Ireland and Greece." I spoke as much (or more) as an activist than an academic without apology or veneer of detachment. At another international conference at DCU, this one on Eastern European studies, I listened to a colleague give a paper on Hungarian refugees in 1956, without the slightest hint that she was one of them—or even Hungarian. Most participants were Eastern European academics who came across as quite detached from their subject matter, however much it had inevitably impacted their lives. My own presentation was on the International Lenin School, a thread woven through all the twists and turns of the communist movement from 1926 to 1991, which was quite a fascinating and world-historically significant story. It went down surprisingly well, given my expectation that the audience might be hostile to my point of view. I did present quite factually, but I also disclosed my relation to the material and reflections on it. At the social, people spoke in a far more engaged way. As always, there was a big difference between the formal and informal discourse at conferences. Some told me of their surprise at the way I spoke at the conference, although approvingly in some cases. Through it all, I took in much detail about the post-communist world, much of it making me want to weep. Still, there were some young, intelligent, critical intellectuals looking askance at it.

At another seminar on another occasion in another university, when I was speaking about the underlying motivation that certain academics had for choosing their research areas, one guy responded cynically that he did history for money and not for passion and that was the difference between professionals and amateurs. More academics than ever were in it for salary, promotion, and prestige, and cared little about their subjects or students. Others cared, but too chaotically, because they had not taken the trouble to lay foundations. They knew too little and had not organized what they knew into a coherent view. As a result, they were flailing about and sowing confusion and chaos in their teaching and publications.

Across various disciplines, the intellectual level deteriorated. When I attended media studies events, it seemed as if the first decades of cultural and media studies had never happened. There was once a solid presence of those who, like me, analyzed culture by excavating underlying worldviews. At that time I thought bias in news analysis was a crude concept. Even that seemed sophisticated now, with the field dominated by far cruder concepts like "fake news" and "bad actors." At various events involving both journalists and media academics, there was an image predominating of mainstream journalists as bastions of rationality and virtue, up against a world of fake news and bad actors and irrational masses whose voices were getting more and more traction through social media, which, of course, must be policed. It never occurred to them that there was any problem with the worldview underlying mainstream media itself. Journalists never clarified the epistemological and ethical criteria involved in designating Trump and Putin as bad actors but not Biden and Zelensky. If I were to use such crude categories, I would designate them all bad actors. However, that would not get to the core of what was at stake. The basic problem was the absence of analysis of the deeper historical forces structuring the flow of facts and events.

Capitalism as the pulsing and problematic process shaping the whole dynamic was invisible to them. There was a striking lack of systemic analysis. Much research was based on a philistine positivism (a positivism blissfully unaware of the epistemological problems grappled with by serious positivists), crude conceptualization, unexamined epistemological blind spots, and liberal moral conceits. In media studies, this meant a revival of a naïve notion of objectivity and moral panic over disinformation, powered by a lot of funding, much of it public, being thrown at fact-checking projects, where social scientists and computer scientists united in opportunistic schemes that came up with banal results that did not challenge power but did reinforce unarticulated liberal conceits and blind spots.

University websites and events showcased announcements of funding and prizes and claims of excellence for mediocre or bad work. Much academic work skated on the surface of phenomena in a way that was not grounded in a serious philosophical framework or basic political economy. Most of it was implicitly either positivist or postmodernist but without awareness of foundational theory or debates. The pathology of postmodernism survived even when it was not named. I hated its unmoored claims of subversion, especially when accompanied by ignorant claims of superiority to Marxism. Postmodernism never had the explanatory power of Marxism, which predated it as critique. Although Marxists, such as Fredric Jameson, saw it clearly as the cultural logic of late capitalism, others were infected by it, and it undermined the intellectual life of the left. In academe, much of the deconstructionist "transgression" was individualist performance and narcissistic wordplay that did nothing to challenge neoliberalism in academe or anywhere else. It eroded rationality and morality and demanded nothing in the way of actual political commitment. I followed the publicity surrounding the Ronell-Reitman affair at NYU as symptomatic of this pathology. It was ostensibly about sexual harassment, with the unusual twist of it involving a victimizer female and victimized male, but it opened a window on the overcharged atmosphere in US graduate schools and raised many issues of gender and power as well, in a world where convoluted and meaningless texts were regarded as brilliance and professors exercised baronial power over students. I had many occasions to see doctoral theses and published texts containing sentences I had to read over and over, yet still could make no sense of them. At this stage of my life, I decided that the problem was not me. For several years, someone I didn't know in another country tortured me with their PhD thesis, paragraph by paragraph in a series of emails, perhaps hundreds of them. At first, I said something polite, but without really engaging. When I could no longer do that, they still kept coming. A sample: "Dear Professor, my claim is to show that the realism is the desert of reality that is to say materialist dialectic can be read as the de-substantialized reality. . . ." I didn't want to be unhelpful or rude, but I just did not know what to say.

There was right-wing backlash, especially on US campuses, against what conservatives called "grievance studies" and "cancel culture." However uncomfortable it made me, I sometimes had to agree with their critique when I saw relatively privileged people indulging or inventing micro-grievances, at the expense of attention to the macro-grievances of the really oppressed. This made me especially sad, because I was part of that generation that fought hard for what was now being caricatured as "grievance studies." It was a great revolution in the history of knowledge to achieve a place in universities for history from below, for gender studies, race studies, ethnic studies. However, I could see that some of what was produced was awful nonsense. I agreed with those who wanted to defend the cognitive capacity of science against epistemological anti-realism, irrationalism, mysticism, conventionalism, especially against anything-goes postmodernism. I also agreed with those who insisted on a strong sociohistorical account of science against a reassertion of scientism. However, there was a big difference between a left critique and right reaction. As always, Marxism could shed a clear light on terrain muddied by postmodernism.

Otherwise, there was too little debate on university campuses and even less protest. When Hillary Clinton spoke at DCU, the US Secret Service took over campus, determining where staff and students were allowed to go. When, in 2018, Clinton was awarded an honorary doctorate at Trinity College Dublin (TCD), there was at least a protest, although it was swamped by cloying coverage of herself with Mary Robinson, gushing over what wonderful feminist role models they were. I sensed a new mood in 2022, when I was invited to the TCD Philosophical Society (the Phil), where Engels once spoke, to debate the motion that private property be abolished. When I accepted, I thought I might be going into the lion's den, but, as I argued that what had been built by social labor should be socially owned, I felt a wave of assent in the packed chamber. When the vote was taken, the motion was affirmed, both in the TCD audience and on polls on Twitter and Instagram. Earlier that day, students across Irish third-level institutions walked out of classes in protest against the cost-of-living crisis. They did not believe that their future labor would bring them the share of social wealth it merited.

I never knew where or when my ex-students would pop up. One morning, I was walking sedately along to DCU, listening to Joan Baez on my iPod, when I was stopped by two uniformed gardai. One of them said that they had information that I was in possession of illegal drugs and they would have to search me. I was too stunned to speak. Then he started laughing and introduced himself as a former student of mine, one I remembered well. We had a catch-up conversation about the turns of his career and the joys of community policing.

There were still pockets of academe in Ireland and abroad, where an alternative vision of academe could express itself. I had an invitation from the Higher Education Academy in Britain to speak about how Marxist historiography of philosophy shaped my teaching of history of ideas. This event took place at the Peoples History Museum in Manchester, which was a great venue. I reread Engels's *The Condition of the Working Class in England* while there. At University College London, I delivered a polemical paper against a range of positions in science studies from a Marxist perspective, which was surprisingly well received, considering how many who attended embodied those positions. Tian Yu Cao from BU was there, too. The next day, I met him again, along with his wife, Lin Chun. It was good to have contacts with a Marxist analysis of China. I was curious about China and hoped that the emails I received indicating my work was known there would eventuate in an invitation that would give me a chance to explore the country, but somehow it didn't happen. While on my way to the Trojka restaurant on Regents Park Road, we passed numbers 41 and 122, both houses where Engels once lived. We were joined by Marian Kozak, mother of Edward and David Miliband, both government ministers at the time, who would soon run against each other for Labour Party leader. Ed, considered to the left of David, won, although he was still way to the right of his parents. I saw him on television speaking against a backdrop of "One Nation Labour." What did that mean? All classes living happily ever after under plutocratic rule? I couldn't bear the blandness and blindness of wealthy people approving of austerity for others but not for themselves.

As to the Labour Party in Ireland, I had drifted out of it, while Sam remained active in it. In 2010, the year he turned eighty, they honored him with a lifetime achievement award at the annual conference in Galway. It was the first time I attended the conference in some years. I was interested in meeting the younger left, who had introduced a resolution to make "Red Flag" the party's anthem, and sang the song at the close of conference. There were a number of other events marking Sam's eightieth birthday, including one organized by the Dublin Council of Trade Unions in the Mansion House. A biography of him, *Sam Nolan: A Long March on the Left*, written by Brian Kenny of the Irish Labour History Society, was published in 2011.

The political temperature was heating up. Ireland went from being the much-admired Celtic Tiger to a vassal of a Troika program. People were shocked to have the IMF arrive along with the EC and ECB to take charge of our public finances. In response to the global financial crisis, the Fianna Fail-Green Party government issued a blanket bank guarantee and paid the losses of private investors at the expense of public funds for health, education, and welfare. Public service pay and pensions were cut. Early retirement was incentivized and recruitment was embargoed. The minimum wage was reduced. Taxes were raised and new charges were introduced, while services were cut. People were furious. Numbers on marches and protests were rising, although not on the scale we were seeing in Greece, where the crisis was even more severe and resistance was stronger. I spent much of my time on the streets, at demonstrations large and small, many of them in the cold and dark. The smallest thing set me off about the whole system. One time, I couldn't get internet access and was left hanging on a helpline for forty-five minutes of recorded messages and awful music, until I finally got an agent, to whom I ranted about the political economy of telecommunications: privatization, parasitic profit-taking, asset-stripping, lack of investment in infrastructure.

Globally, the public sector was being decimated, while cordoning off what served the immediate imperatives of the market and class interests of the global plutocracy. It seemed that all that was public—health, culture, knowledge, space—was under attack. Universities were being starved of resources, and what resources were allocated were diverted from broad knowledge and systemic scrutiny into shallow and short-term commercial goals. On a day when there was a big exit from the public service in Ireland due to an incentivized early retirement scheme, I wondered why we suddenly needed fewer doctors, nurses, teachers, social workers, scientific researchers, financial investigators. It wasn't even just about making cuts in public spending to pay private debts. It was a part of a global agenda to downsize the public sector, to further the domination of the state by market forces. I asked a higher civil servant, whose job it was to raise money to keep the state afloat, how he was going to do that. "I have no idea," he said. "Nobody does." There were days of coordinated action, even general strikes, organized by European trade unions. There was resistance to new taxes and charges. A new household tax in Ireland resulted in mass civil disobedience, as hundreds of thousands refused to pay it. The victory, however, lasted only until the state later deducted the tax from our salaries and pensions, and fined us. However, there was still a big gap between protest and resistance and an alternative. In 2011, when stock markets were plunging for days, some leftists were rejoicing about the end of capitalism. The end of capitalism would be great, I thought, but what would replace it? It wasn't as if socialism was there on offer, in terms of balance of forces, even if I wished it were.

It was a time of mass disaffection with capitalism. One person said to me, "I'm no communist, but capitalism isn't working," to which I replied, "Why not be a communist, then?" There was intense discussion in these years of how a transition from capitalism to socialism might happen. There was a *Look Left* forum in 2013 where US sociologist Erik Olin Wright contrasted three broad strategic visions characterizing the history of anticapitalist social and political struggles: a ruptural vision of transcending capitalism through a fairly abrupt seizure of power, creating a disjuncture in the fundamental institutions and social structures of a society; an interstitial vision of building emancipatory alternatives inside the existing society in whatever spaces possible; and a symbiotic vision of using the existing state as a way of solving problems in the functioning of capitalism so as to also expand the scope of popular power. He argued for seeing these visions as complementary, not mutually exclusive. There were sparks flying, particularly from unreconstructed rupturalists, primarily from the Workers Party (WP) and the Socialist Workers Party (SWP). As for myself, I agreed with Wright, having moved away from a rupturalist approach and tried to work out for myself some new synthesis of these three traditions of the left, in all of which I had participated. My primary problem with the strategy sketched out by Wright was that so much weight was put on building coopera- tives, which was a genuine way of building a positive alternative, but left no way of expropriating the expropriators. So much of the world had been stolen from us and we needed to find a way to take it back, and to radically redistribute wealth. I kept coming back to the question: How to do that in these times? We had many debates about reform, revolution, and everything in between.

At this stage, the Labour Party and the Irish Congress of Trade Unions (ICTU) were part of the opposition. The ICTU supported a European trade union day of protest and later held a massive march of over one hundred thousand from Wood Quay to the GPO, in the snow and freezing cold. Sam was struggling with mobility and barely made it, with a walking stick in one hand and clinging on to me with the other. At the GPO, singers Christy Moore and Frances Black were applauded, while trade union leaders David Begg and Jack O'Connor were booed. I did not agree with booing them in the streets, but I became increasingly critical of the trade union leadership during the crisis, especially after Labour went into government. Sometimes, they were like deer in the headlights as the crisis intensified. Other times, they were like well-fed cats, sleeping in a cozy corner while apocalypse threatened.

There was a general election in February 2011. The Labour Party was polling well, but constantly distanced itself from left forces, which were gaining strength. My local member of parliament (Teachta Dála or TD), Rosin Shortall, made me furious when, on a television panel, she referred to forces to the left of the LP as a "ragbag" and stressed stability. Joan Burton, another Labour TD, gave a car crash of a performance on another show, where she was arrogant, boastful, petulant, and petty, concentrating her venom on Joe Higgins, the candidate to her political left. I finally and formally resigned from the Labour Party, since I wasn't even voting for them. The government was massively defeated. Many cabinet ministers lost their seats. Fianna Fail was decimated and the Greens won not a single seat. The Labour Party did well, went into government with Fine Gael, and pursued the same policies as the previous government they criticized so sharply in opposition. Sinn Fein and the left became the opposition. It was a better parliament, but not a better government. After that, the LP was on the other side in the protests, and the official trade union movement was harder to mobilize. We were no longer protesting with them but against them. I felt so sad looking at Labour TDs, most of whom I knew and once considered to be comrades. I asked how those who had once been in the Workers Party or Labour Left could end up where they were now. I didn't mean only the particular measures they supported, but their failure to address whose class interests they served. I asked one TD how he could be so pliant to the will of the global plutocracy. He replied that I was only on the streets making trouble and advocating completely unrealistic solutions. I didn't think the party fit its name anymore. We needed a party to stand for labor against capital, and the LP was not it. They spoke of the nation as if it were classless. I was asked to speak at an event in Kells on the question, "Can the left unite?" I argued that, though we did not all have to be in the same party and agree on everything, we could be more open and cooperative and aim for common effort as far as possible. The next speaker argued the opposite, dismissing all forces to the left of the Labour Party.

There was also a presidential election in 2011 and Michael D. Higgins was the LP candidate. Going from one protest to another, I passed the Mansion House after the selection conference nominating him and stopped to talk to him. He launched into a tirade against Slavoj Žižek. I couldn't have agreed more. I signed a letter of academics supporting Higgins and voted for him, but was too busy with my other political activities to campaign for him. I overheard a conversation on the bus where one woman asked another how she intended to vote and she said she didn't know. The first woman proceeded to go through the seven candidates, emphasizing the most salacious details of each. The second one then decided: "I think I'll go for the terrorist. As long as he doesn't terrorize my own country, I don't mind." Michael D won. A Trump-like independent came second and the Sinn Fein candidate, the so-called terrorist, Martin McGuiness, came third. Fine Gael got a derisory vote and Fianna Fail, which had dominated the presidency until then, did not even field a candidate.

Meanwhile, the Arab Spring had burst forth. Masses came onto the streets in Tunisia, then Egypt, then Libya and spread from there. Before it began, I had received an invitation out of the blue, full of flattering comments about my international reputation, to give a lecture in Libya. I hesitated, but then accepted. I didn't know much about Libya, but had cheered the Green Revolution of 1969 as part of a wave of national liberation movements sweeping the world during those years. Gaddafi had seemed to be a revolutionary leader of a movement that overthrew a monarchy, set out to forge a form of Arab socialism, and stood among the anti-imperialist forces in the world. Jamahiriya, the Libyan form of government, was supposed to be government by the masses, a direct democracy that was superior to representative democracy, although I had doubts about how democratic it was in practice. Over the years, Gaddafi seemed more and more eccentric, and Libya was implicated in activities, such as the Lockerbie bombing, which seemed both bewildering and indefensible. I had a lot of ambivalence about Libya. Although I had some sympathy with its declaration to be anti-capitalist and anti-imperialist, I also had qualms about its dynastic cult of the leader and Islam as a state religion, Gaddafi having declared himself "King of kings of Africa" and "Imam of the imans." When my son considered taking a job teaching at the International School of Martyrs in Tripoli, I hoped he wouldn't go. I did not think that accepting this invitation for me to speak meant supporting the regime. After all, I had lectured elsewhere, while opposing governments in power. I noted that the

Department of Foreign Affairs advised Irish citizens visiting Libya that there were severe penalties for criticism of the country, its leader, or religion. Refraining from criticism was not my modus operandi anywhere, but, when it came to current politics there, I planned to do more listening than talking. I assumed that Libya was different from Tunisia and Egypt, because it had better distribution of wealth, as well as greater wealth to distribute. I wrote a paper on the philosophy of history titled "Is History a Coherent Story?" which was translated into Arabic. My lecture was an argument against grand narratives imposed from above (therefore implicitly opposed to Islam as a state religion) and for grand narratives forged from below.

As the date for my departure on February 18 drew near, I wondered if I was flying into a firestorm. Although fearful, I was determined not to be cowardly and felt I should honor my commitment. February 17 was announced as a "day of rage" in Libya, but already on February 15, there was an uprising in Benghazi. The flight from Amsterdam to Tripoli was relatively empty. Disembarkation was delayed. After finally leaving the plane, my passage through passport control was protracted, stressful, and confusing, involving demands for money but not euros, until some official arrived, gave orders, and handed me over to a driver. Along the road, the driver kept talking on his phone or pointing to the many portraits of Gaddafi in various exotic outfits and heroic poses, saying that Gaddafi built Libya. He left me at the Four Points Hotel, which was in the middle of a building site, and not in walking distance of anywhere I might want to go. I was pleased to have television, mobile phone, and internet connectivity, at least initially. On the BBC, reports stressed opposition to the regime among exiles and crowds in Benghazi, while Jamahiriya state TV ran footage of pro-regime demos in Tripoli, showing lots of young men waving green flags, holding up portraits of Gaddafi, and chanting slogans. My host, Dr. Jamal Elzway, a political scientist of the Jamahiri Thought Academy, arrived to welcome me. In discussing the protests, he assured me that they were confined

to Libya's east, which was more tribal, and would not happen in
Tripoli, which was more cosmopolitan. The international news was
reporting protests spreading westward, with security forces firing
at demonstrators and the death toll rising, destruction in Tobruk
of a monument to *The Green Book*, a book setting out Gaddafi's
political philosophy, and areas in the control of the opposition.
There were no international news teams in the country. Instead,
media were relying on exile reports from outside and amateur
video and phone interviews from inside. State television showed
pro-regime demonstrations in a collective frenzy. They also ran
historical footage of Arabs at war with colonial powers and mon-
tages of the glories of Gaddafi at various stages in Libyan history.

The next day was cool, cloudy, and windy. Dust from the
desert was everywhere. I had breakfast at a table overlooking the
Mediterranean, which was looking very rough, much like the politics. Jamal arrived with his friend Osama Mehar. We drove along
the coast, seeing many new high-rise buildings, and then to the
old town with narrow streets and crumbling facades, where there
were shops, homes, restaurants, mosques. People on the street,
male and female, were wearing both modern and traditional attire.
Most women had their heads covered. While walking around, we
had intense political discussions. The dominant topic, recurring
again and again, was the current protests. Both Jamal and Osama
were quite concerned about them, but opposed to the protesters, contending that their grievances could be dealt with in other
ways. I specifically asked about police shooting at peaceful protesters. They denied this, saying that security forces were defending
themselves, and institutions were under attack—an arsenal had
been raided. The protesters were just imitating Tunisia and Egypt
and it would blow over, they kept saying. When I asked about the
strength of Islam and whether there were any atheists or agnos-
tics, Jamal said that there are very few. I asked if there were any
Marxists. One, he said. Marxists were free to function and have
their views, but not to try to convince others. When I asked about
television, specifically about current affairs where issues could be

debated publicly, Jamal said that he had hosted such a program for a time. I probed further, querying whether there could be a program now, where supporters and critics of the protests could debate. No. On the topic of unmarried mothers: they were illegal and could be sent to prison. If an unwed mother named a man, he was compelled to marry her.

When we arrived at Green Square in downtown Tripoli, there was a march going past; people were waving green flags and carrying portraits of Gaddafi. We talked about Libya's system of government. Neither capitalist nor socialist, but left and anti-imperialist. All Libyans over eighteen were members of the People's Congress. There were local committees that discussed the needs of their areas to forward these to the People's Congress. The distribution of wealth was through state ownership of big industries, but there was also much private ownership of small businesses. I wondered if some people wanted to take a capitalist road and integrate fully into the global system. Yes, a few, even Gaddafi's son, Saif al Islam, but the majority didn't want that. We drove out to a satellite campus of the university, where Osama collected his daughter. I asked her what she thought of the protests and she said that she didn't want to talk about it. We arrived back in the old city and had lunch in a traditional restaurant. Then it was back to the hotel, where I saw the same contrast between national and international news. There were reports on the internet of protesters now in control of more areas where the old monarchist flag was flying. In the evening, I heard noise outside and went out on the balcony. There was a cavalcade of cars honking horns, people shouting slogans and waving green flags. I fell asleep watching a carnivalesque pro-government rally on Green Square on television, with lots of singing and dancing, which seemed quite obscene, considering the bodies piling up to the east.

When I woke up the next morning, I had no internet access and the satellite signal was intermittent. On state television, an angry Black woman in a green-sequined veil was waving a *Green Book*, ranting for Allah and Gaddafi. While waiting for Jamal to pick me up, I spoke to someone working in the hotel. He told me he studied philosophy at university. When I asked why the lack of internet access, he replied, "You know why." We discussed cutting off international media and internet access as means of dealing with protests. He advised me not to talk so freely with others as I did with him. Then Jamal and Osama came. They said that the lack of internet access was just an everyday technical issue. They took me to a restaurant in the old town and we had tea afterward on the roof overlooking the sea. The arrangements for my lecture were becoming vague, because a number of the professors involved were on a crisis committee, advising the government on how to deal with the crisis. In the evening, I went for a walk alone in the local area. The atmosphere seemed eerie, but I only later realized how dangerous it was. State television spoke of protesters destroying peace and security by robbing banks, destroying files, breaking into police stations, and accused Arabs from other countries of fomenting the protests. Then there were scenes of more green-flag waving demos and music featuring tonight's crowd at Green Square. I fell asleep to the sound of gunfire, both from the media soundtrack and live, near my hotel.

The next day, the international news was reporting that the opposition were in control of Benghazi and that the fighting had spread to Tripoli. Buildings in Tripoli were on fire. There had been a massacre on Green Square last night and snipers were preventing retrieval of bodies. Saif al-Islam was saying that this crisis would lead to civil war, but they would fight to the last bullet. He blamed Libyan exiles, Arab foreigners, trade unions, and Islamic organizations. The BBC were predicting the fall of the regime, with uncertainty about how long it would take, but certainty that it would be bloody. When I went down to breakfast, it was clear that many staff and guests had departed, taking with them food and other supplies. Lots of people were in the lobby, checking out. Groups of building workers outside were feverishly talking. I could see huge plumes of black smoke out the window. There were helicopters flying low overhead. Internet access briefly returned and I updated on social media. After that, I was inundated with media requests. Then came a call from reception saying that the hotel was being evacuated. I threw my things together and took a taxi to Hotel Corinthia, where all foreigners were herded (at €245+ a night). After multiple efforts, I finally got through to Jamal around midnight. He sounded odd, but said all will be okay. I didn't think so. I got no sleep.

The following day, it was clear that my hosts had abandoned me. The hotel seemed to be winding down and running out of supplies. Then I heard that all commercial flights were canceled. I spoke to others in the hotel who had been elsewhere in the country and told of shooting, looting, roadblocks everywhere. Some had been to the airport, trying to get flights to anywhere, but the airport was packed and chaotic and there were no flights. Airline offices and foreign consulates had closed. Some people I met outlined possible scenarios more frightening than anything I had yet imagined. It was not only a matter of regime-versus-rebels, but marauders moving into the breach. I was feeling very stressed and depressed. I had no idea about how to get out of the country. I thought I might die there. I got a call from the Department of Foreign Affairs, telling me that, although an Irish flight was departing for Malta, the plane hadn't got permission to land in Libya. They told me to make my way to the airport in the morning. That gave me a fragile thread of hope, but I spent the night sleepless and terrified, hearing constant gunfire and looking out on burning buildings. Communications were unreliable, but the landline in the hotel still worked, so I was able to phone home and give media interviews.

Once I left the hotel, I was incommunicado. I had asked the hotel to call a taxi to bring me to the airport, but they put me in an ordinary car. I was terrified on that trip. With the country moving toward breakdown of law and order, and reports of looting and hijacking, I was afraid of being robbed and abandoned or kidnapped for ransom. As it happened, the driver only overcharged me. It was hard to get into the airport, as there were a lot of cars converging and massive numbers of people queuing to get into it.

Along the approach road, there was an apocalyptic encampment of migrant workers in the rain. I latched on to a group that seemed to be succeeding in getting into the airport. Once there, it was airport hell. There seemed tens of thousands of people, mostly Arabs, people who lived and worked there, with all the possessions they could carry, including televisions and radiators. There seemed no one I could ask for help. I was nearing despair when a young Thai woman approached me and asked about my situation. When I said I came from Ireland, she showed where there was a group of Irish people, mainly teachers, along with others of various nationalities, awaiting evacuation. I spent twenty-two hours in their company. They told me terrible stories of everyday life here: a boy expelled from school for possessing an article about February 17; a nineteen-year-old nephew shot dead when he went into Green Square to celebrate rumors of Gaddafi's departure; a son shot while going to buy bread; a father and son who were uploading news of protests to the internet disappearing; Tunisians crossing the border by land having their phones, cameras, computers, money taken by Libyan security; roadblocks; burnt-out police stations; destroyed petrol stations; ransacked offices; hijackings; murders. One woman told me that they had buried seventeen of their neighbors on Monday and twenty on Tuesday. Still, they hoped to return to their jobs and homes here.

In the airport, conditions deteriorated. One guy was nearly crushed to death. Another discovered his laptop gone. One woman had reached the end of her endurance and started screaming. Airport staff profiteered on distress, including charging massive sums for access to a filthy lavatory. There was waste and filth everywhere. In the evening, a baton charge and tear gas. There were shots fired. However, through it all, there was also great civility, consideration, and conversation. I learned more about Libya on this day than on all previous days together. In these hours, I saw another face of the regime and heard the voices of its victims. The gap between the theory of direct democracy and the practice of coercive autocracy was stunning. Waiting for our Irish evacuation was like waiting for Godot. We made contact with civil servants from the British Foreign Office and got ourselves on the list for the British evacuation. Then, in the evening, we were told that the Irish plane had finally arrived, but would take no luggage. I abandoned my suitcase, while some stayed for the British flight rather than leave their belongings. We got on a bus and went round and round the tarmac for forty-five minutes, unable to find the plane. It had come and gone without us on it. From what I could piece together, based on a conversation I overheard between a British pilot and civil servant, the airport staff kept renegotiating extortionate fees, and I suspected the Irish rescue people didn't grasp the rules of the game. The British Foreign Office people looked after us in a most competent and generous way.

At 5:45 a.m. on February 24, we finally took off from Tripoli and arrived in Gatwick a few hours later. Upon arrival, there was a reception area set up for us, where we were debriefed and offered food, drink, and counseling. There was a media scrum in the exit area, but many did not want to speak to journalists because they were media-shy or wanted to return to Libya and didn't want to fall out of favor with whoever ended up in power. One reporter asked me, "What was it like?" I said, "Libya is descending into hell." This was picked up by the wire services and appeared in newspapers all over the world. I gave my mobile number in response to one request and then every news service in the world seemed to have it. My mobile kept ringing. I booked a flight to Dublin for €350 and was delighted to be home. On adrenaline overdrive, I gave media interviews nonstop for many hours by phone. I wasn't up to going into television or radio studios, so I had to decline those requests. I talked to RTE, BBC, CBC, NPR, CNN, and many more, before finally collapsing in exhaustion. I gave more interviews through the next few days. So many people contacted me and expressed concern. DCU sent flowers. The president gave me a big hug and welcomed me back. The Irish Department of Foreign Affairs did not contact or debrief me, and I hoped my life was never in their hands again. Shortly after, there was a change of Irish government.

The new foreign minister, Eamon Gilmore, was someone I had known for many years and I told him that. These were among the worst days of my life.

I kept up with news from Libya, now caught up in a full-scale civil war, exacerbated by NATO intervention. So much death, destruction, displacement. I was not sorry to see the regime fall, nor did I mourn the death of Gaddafi, but I could see that much of value was lost as the country succumbed to chaotic and brutal rule of rival militias. Author Richard Seymour, in his blog "Lenin's Tomb," articulated my own attitude: "No tears for Gaddafi. No cheers for NATO." Despite this, I was attacked, on the one hand, as if I supported the regime and defended totalitarianism and, on the other, as if I opposed it and was an agent of imperialism. The nastiest attacks were anonymous. I hated this anonymous dimension of social media that allowed cover for the cowardly to slander with impunity. Another postscript from this episode was a communiqué from the son of my Libyan host who had abandoned me, claiming that Jamal and Osama were never really supporters of the regime, despite all their apologetics to me to the contrary.

The ferment spread from North Africa to Europe to America. Anti-austerity Indignados occupied the squares of Spain in the spring of 2011, and by autumn the Occupy movement surged all over the world. In a thousand cities across every major continent, there were round-the-clock encampments, assemblies, concerts, conversations, lectures, direct actions, and marches, where many people, some of whom had never protested before, defiantly declared, "We are the 99 percent," and expressed their rage at the one percent who ran the world and expropriated its wealth. The start of Occupy Wall Street in the United States that September was a key moment in setting other occupations in motion.

In Dublin, we set up Occupy Dame Street (ODS) in early October. I was there on the street for several hours every day, and dealing with it on my computer during many of the other hours. At assemblies, there were new rituals, including a "mic check," where crowds repeated words spoken by one person, which generated a call-and-response rhythm rippling through the crowd, who expressed their agreement, using "jazz hands." I spoke on the first day and again at the rally after our first big march, and it was bracing to hear my words repeated back to me by so many other voices. All sorts of people came forward at assemblies to tell their stories and explain why they were angry and weren't going to take it anymore.

In the first days, the atmosphere was open, fresh, unified, and hopeful, and there was a sense of strong bonds being forged. The unity did not last. There was an aggressive tendency to define the movement as nonpolitical, as neither right nor left. There was a "no politics" mantra and people were told they were welcome as individuals, but had to leave their politics at the door. I argued against this, asserting the need for a conception of politics that was broader and deeper than party politics. I also noted that we were outdoors and had no door. There was a tendency that was explicitly hostile to left political parties and trade unions, countered by a grouping holding the opposite view, while still others simply didn't understand these debates. I tried to explain and educate patiently, but often exploded with anger and frustration. I tried not to be an old know-it-all, who had been-there-done-that, but so many things being said and done did remind me of so much that *had* been said and done in the past, and I did find myself saying so. At the same time, I knew that this historical conjuncture was unique. I felt that I had something specific to offer as a voice connecting past and present, as someone who could tell this story within the framework of a longer story.

Ultimately, four main demands emerged: (1) an end to IMF/ECB control of the Irish economy; (2) repudiation of private bank debt that had been socialized; (3) national control over our oil and gas reserves; and (4) participatory democracy. While this movement was about occupations and demands, I warned against believing that this occupation, in itself, would lead to the achievement of these demands, and argued that we needed to build a movement to engage in a complex, protracted, and difficult struggle to unravel the structures of political and economic power that made it possible for the 1 percent to rule at the expense of the 99 percent.

I devoted much of my time to Occupy University, which organized two to three lectures a day on the street. Many talks were about the global financial system: hedge schools versus hedge funds. We also concentrated on previous social movements, as well as branching out to ideology and culture. There were also workshops on practical matters: writing, media, music, direct action. Those attending were of different ages, genders, races, occupations, and, most importantly, different educational levels. Professors and doctoral students mixed with people who had left school at an early age. Most speakers—academics, journalists, politicians, poets, bloggers, trade union officials, alternative media practitioners—pitched their talks well to encompass this diversity. Sometimes discussions stayed reasonably well focused and sometimes they went all over the place. There were conspiracy theorists and currency crazies and fluoride fanatics, who used the discussion of anyone else's talk as a platform to give their own talks. Mostly, there was a sincere sharing of knowledge and earnest interaction, pursued with a purity of purpose all too absent in academe. While some engaged in a critique of capitalism, others were just against corporate greed, while still others wanted a return to barter and early Irish Brehon law. The most controversial speaker, in the sense of whether he should be allowed to speak at all, was Eamon Ryan, leader of the Green Party and minister in the outgoing government, which had inflicted on us most of what ODS was there to protest. He had lost his seat in Dail Eireann, along with most of the cabinet, and proposed to speak to us now on energy with no politics. I chaired the session and made it clear that this was open season on politics. The ensuing discussion veered from people losing their tempers at his very presence and walking away, to engaging him in ideological debate, to others being seemingly honored by his presence, trying to impress him. In two months, we organized seventy-eight talks and workshops.

Some who lived at the encampment, the "campers," never

attended the talks and even resented them. From day two, there was tension between camp and movement. Those who had to balance participation with work, children, and other responsibilities often felt marginalized by those who were free to camp 24/7, who had a disproportionate voice in defining the movement and deciding what would be said and done. The theory was that the occupations would be exercises in prefigurative politics, in giving and receiving food, shelter, culture, knowledge, and labor, all liberated from the circuitry of commodification. The practice was less lofty. Most campers became obsessed with the camp and conveyed an inflated image of themselves as the core of the project, even referring to themselves as "heroes of the revolution." From their point of view, they were outside in the cold, the rain, and the dark, vulnerable to the drunks, drug addicts, thieves, and crazies on the city streets, while others were asleep in their warm beds. They stayed up all night on security duty, while others arrived from home after a good night's sleep, seeking interesting company and intellectual conversation. Money, laptops, mobile phones were stolen. Inappropriate sexual conduct had to be addressed. Knives were pulled. People got on each other's nerves. As with most occupations, the people who were homeless before the encampment came and found a higher standard of food, shelter, security, and community than was their norm. At the same time, people often became homeless because of problems that a political encampment was not equipped to cope with, let alone solve. I respected the campers who chose to stay there in difficult material conditions, especially those who got on with it and remembered the political purpose of it, but I found it hard to take the attitude of some campers, who guilt-tripped the others and questioned their right, as non-campers, to have a say. At one assembly I asked: "Do you want to build a camp or do you want to build a movement?"

The ongoing tensions about trade unions and political parties, specifically parties of the left, became more vociferous. The most insistent declared over and over that left parties and trade unions had failed, despite their utter ignorance of the history of the left and labor movements. It was as if 2011 was Year Zero. One young woman, in response to a lecture on trade unions given by an activist of many years, said that the unions and parties should disband and come occupy, because this was the reality now. They did not have the vocabulary of vanguardism, but they had the mentality on overdrive. I was not part of any entrist project to recruit new people to existing left parties and presented myself as old left looking for a new way. An invitation from the Dublin Council of Trade Unions to participate in its prebudget march triggered a number of acrimonious assemblies. Although there was much support for this, and many activists did participate, some campers blocked it. Some days, a more positive mood prevailed, such as the day of a big march, when Billy Bragg sang at Dame Street, powerfully bridging the gap between the old and the new. He sang a few songs about banks and plutocrats, catching the mood of this new movement, and then articulated the need to get support from organized labor and to honor the struggles of the past. He then sang "Power in a Union" and the "Internationale." By this time, there was much evidence of a healthy and progressive relationship between the Occupy Movement in the United States and organized labor. They sang "Solidarity Forever" and actually enacted many forms of concrete solidarity, from giving material assistance to marching together, to blockading ports. Many occupations even had special working groups to reach out to organized labor. Many speakers at ODS assemblies invoked this, but to no avail. The blockers wanted to keep their project pure. They did not need the left or the unions, they had "the people," a mystified entity that was constantly invoked against anyone who criticized.

There was also a generational dimension. I noticed that a number of my new left contemporaries in the US were writing about this movement as "them," analyzing what "they" were doing, thinking, saying. They supported the movement, visited the occupations, spoke at the teach-ins. They marched. But they saw Occupy as essentially the movement of another generation, whereas I saw it as a multigenerational movement. However, sometimes I felt as if

I had wandered into a crèche and I was supposed to pretend to be one of the kids. I needed to be patient with those having their first experience of activism, while cautioning against nonsense that made it easy to dismiss this as a movement of those too inexperienced in the ways of the world to know how futile such efforts were. Actually, most of the young people with whom I worked, in this crucible of practice, learned a lot in a very short time. They, too, were critical of the lack of historical consciousness and were keen to enhance their own knowledge of history, especially the history of the left. Their political judgment was sometimes more astute than some older participants. However, there were mentalities that were not reducible to generational patterns. Both old and young experienced exhilaration, exhaustion, disappointment, and revival on the rollercoaster ride of this autumn. There was a general need to take stock as winter came and numbers declined.

These tensions resulted in a number of serious participants walking away. I stayed, but with more difficulty and less enthusiasm, feeling that something with great potential was unraveling. We watched while so many encampments in the US were evicted. I took particular notice of those in New York City's Wall Street and in Philadelphia. Without dramatic scenes of police charging in with truncheons and pepper spray, we in Dublin began to feel a loss of our encampment, too. It was less dramatic but, in its way, more difficult. The camp-versus-movement dynamic became increasingly unhealthy. The movement virtually disappeared, leaving only a camp, more and more preoccupied with its own existence and lashing out at those who disappeared, even though they were the ones who had driven so many people away. By December, I came less often and found fewer and fewer people there. Early in 2012, I met with more upbeat activists to discuss how to bring the positive energies unleashed by Occupy into a new phase that would focus on organizing, not camping, receptive to other groups, such as trade unions. Projects such as Anglo Not Our Debt and Unlock NAMA (National Asset Management Agency) provided new focus. In January, we demonstrated against payment of unsecured bonds in a three-day carnival of resistance. We occupied a NAMA building on Great Strand Street in order to hold an economics seminar, although we were evicted by the gardai in mid-afternoon. There was a new rhythm now, a slower, steadier rhythm, more aligned to the ordinary rhythm of life. Occupy University continued with a series of lectures on radical movements in Irish history, televised on Dublin Community TV, that I chaired. By the time the gardai came to clear the camp, five months after it began, it had become an embarrassment to most of us who were there at the beginning. The evictees continued to do direct actions under the name of ODS, which became more and more ridiculous.

The truth was that the wave was crashing, here and every-where. In the US many activities continued through the spring of 2012 under the Occupy banner, but the energy had gone out of it. Globally, this was a genuine grassroots manifestation that had unleashed a tide of powerful resistance to global structures of power. It brought new focus, new energy, new fluidity into the convergence of forces confronting a powerful plutocracy, but it failed to find a sustainable form. The problems it set out to con-front had not been solved, so the most constructive activists moved on to other projects. In Ireland, among those I knew who were new to activism, one became a trade union official and another an editor of a left magazine. The most destructive continued to wreak havoc in ever-decreasing spaces, while most disappeared without trace. For a period, there was a rise, then fall, of small lumpen groups, constantly forming and fragmenting, generating momen-tary middle-aged male messiahs competing with each other, full of inspirational quotes and self-romanticizing behavior and street stunts and stances aimed at provoking the left and trade unions. On one occasion, they came to an ICTU march demanding to head the march, one asserting his right as a "sovereign man of Eire to walk this land." They were there more to protest the left and the trade union movement than the government and the troika. After a year, I attended an event to mark the anniversary of ODS, trying to emphasize the positive: the resistance it embodied, the hope it engendered, the bonds of solidarity it forged instead of the negative: the desultory course it took, the divisions it sowed, and the bitterness it left in its wake.

A chapter I wrote about the Occupy movement appeared in a book titled *Politics, Participation & Power,* which was launched in City Hall. I went in, looked around, drank wine, and mingled with various academics before the speeches started. The main speech was given by Emily O'Reilly, Ireland's Ombudsman and Information Commissioner. I tend not to expect much of launch speeches, as most are badly strung together bluffs about a book that a very important person hasn't really read. This one was structured, reflective, and provocative, addressing the crisis in our society, the participation and protest in response to it, and the lack of a shared narrative about how to proceed from it. O'Reilly singled out my chapter and quoted from it extensively, which had me blushing, as well as feeling surprised that my words had such traction in this milieu, especially since she had read out a passage about the discordance I felt on moving from the ODS assembly to a reception at the Mansion House.

Although the Occupy form was unsustainable, resistance to the global system sought more sustainable forms, including radical challenges within the electoral arena. In Greece, there were two general elections in 2012. In between them, it looked as if the radical-left coalition Syriza would win, and in 2015 they did win. In Spain, Podemos ("We can") gathered the energy of the Indignados into an electoral form and became the second-largest party in Spain. The rallying cry in Europe was "Syriza, Podemos, venceremos." Other left parties and coalitions surged. In Ireland, too, left parties and independents secured more seats in the national parliament and local councils. In the hierarchy of hopes for left governments in Europe, it was Syriza, Podemos, and then Sinn Fein. In Spain and Portugal, Podemos and Bloco de Esquerda went into governments in coalition with social democratic parties. In Britain, Jeremy Corbyn won a tightly contested battle for leadership of the Labour Party in 2015, setting left energies soaring. In the US, Bernie Sanders galvanized considerable enthusiasm and support in the 2016 presidential election. In Latin America, the "pink tide" of left governments surged, ebbed, and began to surge again. To one extent or another, many of these victories led to deeper defeats. While there were widespread critiques of capitalism and waves of resistance, the system itself, although deeply damaged, had the power to withstand it.

These were years of so many protests. Some days I felt acute protest fatigue. What made it worse was that we protested over and over and over, but people still asked why Irish people didn't protest. It made me rage. It was hard enough to keep going when we saw the masters of the universe get their way, no matter what we said or did. Then, on top of that, our voices were discursively obliterated in the dominant narrative that repeatedly, lazily, and dishonestly insisted that Irish people didn't protest. It was true that there weren't enough of us, even in this time of rising numbers and increased activity, but at least we didn't watch the world being stolen from us and let it go uncontested.

No one said that the Greek people didn't protest. I became quite caught up in the struggle in Greece, seeing it as the cutting edge of the global crisis, as well as a possible alternative to it. Here, I thought, was the best and worst of humanity, in high-energy collision with each other. From 2012 on, I went to Greece often and interacted with Greeks of many points of view, but mostly the Greek left. I supported Syriza and got to know many of its activists, including those who went into parliament and became government ministers. I sometimes spoke to Greeks on the streets or in offices, but often over food and wine in homes or tavernas. I participated in their protests, even joining their occupation of a television station one day in 2013, after the government announced its shutdown of public broadcasting at midnight. I supported the alternative broadcasting network that continued for two years. On the second day of the occupation, I appeared on alternative television and, during the next two summers, I was on radio in Zakynthos. I was involved in efforts to build international support for Syriza and, in 2014, organized the visit of party leader Alexis Tsipras to Ireland. When Syriza won the election of January 2015, I was elated. I informed myself of their every move, gave lectures and interviews on Syriza, updated about it on social media, and brainstormed with others on our Greek Solidarity Committee to build support as the new government was put under extreme pressure by international institutions, particularly the EU. Even apart from our efforts, there was massive support for the Greek government in Ireland, and hundreds of Greek flags appeared on the streets at all our own anti-austerity protests during those months.

It was a David and Goliath struggle, except that Goliath won. After a referendum resulting in strong support for the government's resistance to EU demands to pay debts by privatizing public property, cutting wages, pensions, and public services even further, and other expropriating measures, Alexis Tsipras agreed to a deal even more severe than what the electorate had rejected. Syriza activists, including government ministers and members of parliament, either defended or denounced the agreement, and the Syriza I knew was in tatters. I sided with those who renounced it and was with them protesting outside parliament when we were teargassed by the government that we had so recently and ardently supported. Much of the party's national and international support dissipated. Syriza went from being a horizon of hope to a vortex of despair. It was yet another lesson in the power of the global system to crush our fragile efforts to build an alternative.

I divided my experience of Greece into two periods: before and after July 2015. During the first period, there was a constant decline in material conditions, but there was also resistance and hope. In the second period, the material conditions continued to decline, but there was only weak resistance and little hope. Even those who were still politically engaged, after so many had disengaged, were leading flattened lives with diminished horizons. Even during the days of the July 2015 crisis, there was shock, anger, energy to decide what to do, but as time went on, that energy dwindled and the despair deepened.

Although many outside Greece moved on, I stayed with the story and wrote my way through the whole tragedy, including what happened in the aftermath of this denouement, because I have always been interested in what happened when the international media were gone, and because I had built relationships there that I did not want to let go. Although it wasn't part of my plan for this period, I ended up writing a whole book about it. In *The Syriza Wave*, I told the story of how the momentum of this movement surged and crashed, as I surged and crashed with it. While I was at it, I traveled widely in Greece, saw many stunning places, walked among ancient ruins, swam in the sea at sunrise, met wonderful people, amazed sometimes that this was still possible amid the devastation being visited upon the country. Tourists still came and went, taking narcissistic selfies against the backdrop of ancient ruins, with no apparent thought about those ancient societies or the contemporary society unraveling around them. I could still see the beauty, but it was bittersweet, because I could also see the erosion of living standards, the evaporation of hope, the scattering of forces, the onset of depression, the abyss of despair. Because I have written an entire book about this, I am only summarizing all this briefly here.

Because I was freer to travel than I ever was before, I did so quite often, sometimes in response to political and academic invitations, and other times just to see places I had somehow never been, such as Barcelona, Lisbon, Faro, Rome, Florence, Naples, Pompeii, Sicily. For a time after Libya, I was wary of invitations coming out of the blue, but I was glad I overcame it and accepted an invitation to go to Mexico to give a series of lectures at the National Autonomous University of Mexico (UNAM) in Mexico City. For a month before I left, in autumn 2014, in addition to preparing my lectures, I gave myself a crash course in Mexican history and politics. I arrived during the Day of the Dead. Wherever I went, there were themed commemorations: one in front of the Palacio de Belles Artes was devoted to the assassinated and disappeared; another in Zócalo, the main square of Mexico City, focused on dead Latin American writers; others in academic departments remembered colleagues who died. I inquired about a colleague I had met at international conferences and learned that he had been murdered. My hotel was near the university, overlooking the 1968 Olympic Village and the mountains and volcanos surrounding the city.

My host was Julio Muñoz Rubio, evolutionary biologist, university professor, and left activist, who showed me around the city and university, while we talked about almost everything under the sun in perfect weather. I saw many murals of Diego Rivera, David Siqueras, and José Clemente Orozco. I had always admired them from afar, but it was fabulous to see the originals and also so much of their work I didn't know. I was especially moved by Rivera's world-historical history of Mexico series in the National Palace. There were more impressive murals on the campus of UNAM, which was like a city in itself. I was especially struck by the mosaic mural forming the entire exterior of the Central Library by Juan O'Gorman, depicting the history of culture. I responded strongly to the sense of the scope and depth of knowledge here, visually evident in all the world-historical murals, but also in other ways that manifested an approach to knowledge that was bigger than the stripped-down, market-oriented institutes that called themselves universities. The sheer scope of UNAM was staggering: the amount of space, the number of students and staff, the range of degrees and research programs, plus the museums, concert halls, radio and tv stations, libraries, archives, publications, and much more. I found the audiences for my lectures, both professors and students, to be intellectually sophisticated and politically engaged.

This was a time of turmoil in the schools and universities. There were assemblies on campus to decide about whether to go on strike in response to the missing forty-three students from Ayotzinapa, a rural teachers college, who had, in late 2014, disappeared on their way to Mexico City to commemorate the 1968 Tlatelolcpo massacre of protesters. As some of my lectures were canceled due to this strike, I took part in some of the protests. There was a massive march from the Paseo de la Reforma to Zócalo. There were people of all ages and jobs, but the crowd was overwhelmingly young, mostly students, all demanding answers to questions about the fate of the missing students. The effect was colorful, creative, noisy, and energetic, with elements of street theater. I especially liked the big stage, where huge puppets of "Lady Iguala" (María de los Ángeles Pineda, who, with her husband, José Luis Abarca, mayor of the town of Iguala, was linked to drug cartels and the disappearance of the students) and a cast of other evil characters. When some provocateurs began breaking windows, mainstream marchers turned on them and the science students chanted, "¡Banditos!" There was more destruction of public property, such as the wrecking of a tram station near the university, the burning of Iguala's town hall, and the storming of the National Palace door by black-bloc protesters.

Other days, I visited various museums. The National Anthropological Museum was especially impressive. It took me through a sweeping story, from the country's primordial times to the present, from a historical materialist point of view. My colleague informed me that Marxist anthropologists and artists were crucial in the shaping of this project. The artifacts and reproductions were strikingly and coherently presented with a great sense of space and thought. Another day, we went to Templo Mayor, the archaeological site of a massive Aztec structure. What dominated my attention was the fact that human sacrifice had been central to the rituals conducted there. This reality somehow resonated with other events of the day, especially a press conference at which the Mexican government announced that the missing students were dead. Death was a constant theme running through my visit, not only natural deaths, but violent murders, past and present. The murals I saw everywhere were full of slaughter. In the museum, on the site of the Inquisition, there were life-sized reconstructions of trials and torture. The facial expressions on the statues, of both victims and victimizers, were striking and haunting. I also visited the house in Coyoacan where Leon Trotsky lived his last days before he was assassinated. The interiors were smaller and darker than I imagined. I was very moved when I stood in the room where the murder happened. Although I was never a Trotskyist, I always felt that Trotskyism was a branch of the same movement and this was a dark moment in the history of that movement. Trotsky's murder was a terrorist act, indefensible by any norms, especially by communist ones. I couldn't help thinking of all the remarks about "Trots" and ice picks, which were too frequent in the culture of communist parties in years past. I found them objectionable and obnoxious then and even more so looking back now. I was glad that the atmosphere between these different traditions on the left had improved considerably in our time, in Ireland as elsewhere. I also went to Frida Kahlo's house nearby where Trotsky had lived when he first came to Mexico. It was bigger, brighter, posher. It was now a Frida Kahlo museum. I had never taken to Kahlo as an artist, finding her work too narcissistic, too lacking the outward-reaching perspective of Rivera. Mexico lingered in my thoughts, especially in the days just after I left when it was still in international news. Only days after my departure, police entered UNAM campus and fired at protesting students.

As well as discovering new places in the world, I returned to old places, although I felt poignantly the passing of time, the ruptures of history, and the absence of those who were once so present, especially when in the spaces of countries that had disappeared since I first came to them: the GDR, Yugoslavia, and Czechoslovakia. So many of those who defined these places for me had died. At least, when I went to Berlin every few years, I could still visit Herbert Hörz, but when I went to Prague, everyone I had known was gone. I walked the streets imagining the conversations I would have had with them and mourned for them and for the trashing of their lives and dreams. I came in 2014 for a meeting of the left think tank Transform, but took extra days to roam and reflect. I was struck by how many palaces and churches there were. Although the monarchies and aristocracies were gone, and although the Czech Republic was one of the least religious countries in the world, the visual impact of the city was dominated by tributes to monarchs and saints. Why? Where were the monuments to the people who built it all? I knew statues of Lenin and Gottwald had been toppled, but what about tributes to labor? In one park by Charles Bridge, I saw a statue of a mounted monarch with others who fulfilled other functions in society at levels below. I liked that, though perhaps not in the way it was intended. I went on a political tour of Prague, organized for those attending the Transform meeting, involving a counternarrative to the dominant narrative of the city. We stopped, for example, at the memorial to Jan Palach, a student whose self-immolation in 1968 in protest against the Soviet occupation, memorialized as a victim of communism, a symbol of resistance to communism. Our tour director, Miroslav, who had been a student leader in the 1960s and had organized Palach's funeral march, declared that Palach was not an anticommunist. He was, in fact, for communism, but against the Soviet occupation. The next day, at a seminar on the left in post-socialist countries, I spoke about the need for a counternarrative of the socialist years.

Another day in Prague, I went to the Communist Party's *Halo Noviny* press festival. In contrast, I made myself go to the Museum of Communism, which was appropriately over a McDonald's and next to a casino. The museum's artifacts were interesting: photos, statues, banners, posters, film, etc., but they were not well displayed. Instead, they were dumped together in too small a space and treated with contempt. The narrative was unremittingly hostile. It turned out that the place was privately owned by two Americans and one Czech. I asked the person working there how these things were acquired. They could not tell me. It was all wrong. These things belonged to the state and party. There should be a proper museum of communism in Prague, I thought, but it should be publicly owned and give scope to alternative interpretations. It was the contestation history that should have dominated. I have seen museums, especially in South Africa, giving scope to conflicting interpretations of facts and artifacts. I left this one in a rage, after writing an angry entry in the visitors book. Berlin, too, had quite a few museums slandering the communist past. Much better was Berlin's Topography of Terrors, charting the rise of Nazism, which was good in analyzing the forces and motives of the many people involved as victims and victimizers, as well as passive enablers, instead of it being only about Hitler and Jews.

On a visit to Vienna for another conference, one on Austro-Marxism, I went on the trail of Red Vienna. The Red Vienna Museum was set in Karl-Marx-Hof, an impressive public housing scheme erected during the time of Red Vienna, from 1918 to 1934. It was exactly what I needed to satisfy my curiosity about what everyday life was like in Red Vienna. There was massive construction of public housing, clinics, crèches, libraries, baths, parks, theaters, schools, sports facilities, communal kitchens, and laundries for the working class. It was great seeing the photos, posters, and other artifacts and hearing the songs. The film footage was vivid and stirring, especially the scenes from the massive and magnificent May Day celebrations in the 1920s. Utopian but real, until the fascists crushed it. I also had two swims in Amalienbad, an art deco monument of working-class public physical culture from that era. It was a world away from Hofburg, where images of palaces, aristocracy, and high culture prevailed. Ironically, my hosts booked speakers into a hotel called Altwienerhof, which, despite being a three-star hotel in a red-light district, was full of pseudo-aristocratic décor, with portraits of the Habsburgs on the wall, promising a luxury it decidedly didn't deliver.

On a visit to Belem in Portugal, I found contrasting narratives at play at the Monument to the Discoveries, the point of departure for exploration of the "New World." I thought of what I had learned in school about these voyages being about navigation, new frontiers, and spreading the faith, and how I had later come to see them as about conquest and acquisition. The monument, with sculpted exterior and exhibition rooms inside, was erected in 1960 and raised questions for me about Portugal's conception of these expeditions, when Portugal was a fascist state. On the outside was a mural that fascinated me with its blend of monarchism, colonialism, and fascism conflated with postmodernism. The statement of the artist confirmed this throw-it-all-in-together view of history. I walked along the Tagus River into the sunset, thinking about the difference between eclecticism and synthesis. With António Salazar's fascist state long ago broken in 1974, I went to the Monument to the Carnation Revolution. Even knowing how phallic so many monuments are, this obelisk was the most phallic one I have ever seen, appropriate only if you assume that all revolutions are gigantic male orgasms. I wondered if Portugal's current left government might erect a better monument to this event. While I was there, I was interested in speaking with Portuguese activists about how the social democratic government was ruling with support from communists and radical leftists. I had the best contacts with the latter in Bloco de Esquerda. As always, I observed guidebook tourists interested only in castles and churches and restaurants. They didn't seem to care about the present government or everyday life in Alfama. One American guy even told me that it wasn't worth knowing who won elections here, because the country was only the size of one US city. He thought it was only right that the whole world followed every detail of US elections, about which he used the lesser-of-two-evils argument to justify voting for Trump in 2016.

On a trip to Rome with my daughter and granddaughter, we rambled through the Colosseum, up the Palatine Hill, down to the Roman Forum, trying to imagine ancient life there. I stopped and listened to an American guide singing the praises of the Romans, who "believed in themselves" enough to conquer the world, bringing the most advanced technology to lands that were grateful to be conquered by them. I wanted to barge in and argue with him, but I didn't. Instead, I photographed an arch and tweeted, "Great Rome is full of triumphal arches. Who erected them?" from Brecht's magnificent poem "Questions From a Worker Who Reads," a manifesto of history from below. When I was in London for a Historical Materialism conference and took a walk through the British Museum, I was again reciting this poem to myself, although I wanted to shout it: "Who built Thebes of the seven gates? In the books, you will read the names of kings. Did kings haul up the lumps of rock?" At every corner I turned, I asked how these things came to be here and how were they still here. When I exited the museum, I came upon the Trade Union Congress with a large statue celebrating workers and union solidarity. Here, at least, the role of labor came into focus.

Issues about how the past was memorialized arose not only abroad but also at home. Ireland embarked on a decade of centenaries when there were many public events commemorating the turbulent and transformative years between 1912 and 1923. One of the first big events was the commemoration of the Dublin 1913 lockout organized by the government and trade union movement. I felt somewhat ambivalent about the way the event unfolded. Various people were in a VIP enclosure on O'Connell Street while the rabble, including me, were kept too far from it all, in over-the-top security arrangements. More important, I resented the sanitization of this naked historic struggle between capital and labor, and the current hypocrisy of Eamonn Gilmore, leader of the Labour Party, along with David Begg, general secretary of the ICTU, to the fore of the event, in spite of their dubious role in the class struggle of today. At the same time, it was significant that the state marked this event with overt sympathies so clearly on the side of labor. Too easy, though, to celebrate class struggle in the past while quashing it in the present. There were wreath-laying and readings from *Strumpet City*, James Plunkett's great novel set in 1913, and street theater with 1913 reenactments. My son Cathal was among those in period costume. There was Jimmy Kelly singing "Dublin City 1913" as he stood by the statue of socialist and trade union leader James Larkin, which has occupied a central place in the city since 1976.

On May Day, there was more a commemoration from below, thanks to the steady organizing efforts of those stalwarts of the trade union movement, the Dublin Council of Trade Unions, combined with the cultural creativity of the Spectacle of Defiance and Hope community group, the energy and intelligence of the new youth bloc, plus the presence of many trade unionists and left activists. The theme was 1913: Unfinished Business, connecting that great struggle for trade union recognition with the struggles of today. There were banners from the past, as well as contemporary ones; people wore 1913 attire with long dresses and brimmed hats, along with jeans and macs of today. Many songs and speeches juxtaposed past and present. Much had changed over the decades, but there was still a formidable struggle to be waged, in some ways a far more complex and difficult one. Another day, marching through a cemetery to the sound of a single piper, we went to the grave of Alicia Brady, a young worker who was shot during the lockout. The oration was given by Jack O'Connor, who castigated those of us who failed to support the Labour Party in government in coalition with Fine Gael. O'Connor called for left unity, by which he meant rallying to his position. The best speech was by feminist Therese Caherty, who spoke of the struggle of women workers over the decades as a "fight for the right to fight." Then came a woman's voice from the edge of the crowd. It was a dramatic reconstruction of Alicia Brady on the day she died, right up to the moment she was shot. Before leaving, I sought out Jack O'Connor, to tell him what I thought of his speech, which resulted in quite a sharp exchange of views. I told him that I regarded him as a comrade and didn't approve of those who heckled him on the street, but I thought he had made a bad speech at the grave and had generally failed to give the leadership that the trade union needed. A year later in the same cemetery, this time at the grave of James Larkin, O'Connor gave a speech emphasizing class struggle, without attacking those of us who believed that class struggle meant opposing the Labour Party. It was difficult on these occasions, mixing with those I once regarded as comrades, who were trying to have it both ways, pretending (even to themselves) that they hadn't crossed over to the other side.

The two events dominating 2016 in Ireland were the centenary of the 1916 Easter Rising and the general election. Both revealed a nation in the throes of radically redefining itself, with widespread disagreement on that redefinition. The Rising centenary brought forth official and unofficial commemorations, television dramas and documentaries, social history seminars, school pageants, newspaper features, and much more. It was not only celebration but contestation, bringing to the surface some of the seething contradictions of our national life. Some denounced the original Rising as violent and unjustified. Without any sense of irony, they were generally the ones who believed that bloodshed in the service of the Crown on the battlefields of the world war was justified, but not the bloodshed on the streets of our city in the name of a republic. Others felt proud that Ireland struck the first blow against the mighty British empire, and that we are today citizens of a republic and not subjects of a monarch.

The state played a balancing act, but displayed much sympathy for the first position. A commemorative wall was erected in Glasnevin Cemetery, inscribed with the names of all who died in the Rising and subsequent struggles from 1916 to 1923; not only those who fought for the republic, but also those who fought for the British Empire, along with civilians caught in the crossfire. This approach was promoted as being "mature" and "inclusive." It gave rise to bitter controversy, not only in words, but with paint and sledgehammers as well, until the cemetery announced it would cover all the names with blank panels. The official state commemoration combined appropriate elements, such as the reading of the Proclamation of the Republic and the playing of "Mise Eire" and "Amhran na bhFiann," along with the presiding presence of those who were the colonial administrators of the empire bearing down upon us, now posing as the successors of those who fought against the empire bearing down upon the people then. In the general election, when the votes were counted, it became clear that the outgoing government had lost, but it was less clear who had won. The result was all over the place, as was the nation, in a major shakeup of the electoral spectrum. Labour had the biggest down-fall, going from thirty-seven seats to seven. Significant numbers of voters turned away from the parties that had governed Ireland until now, many to the left but not in sufficient numbers for a left government. The left appropriately quoted Gramsci's observation about the old dying but the new not being born. The following year, we had high hopes of a Labour victory in the British general election. It was a good election for Labour, although not good enough for Labour to form a government with the excellent Jeremy Corbyn as prime minister.

For several years, in Ireland and in Europe, there was much commemoration of the World War of 1914–1918. So much of it was awful bombastic nonsense about men sacrificing themselves for our freedom. I remembered those who fought and died as victims of an imperialist war, people whose lives were sacrificed by forces most of them did not comprehend. I honored those who opposed the war, who were braver than those who fought in it, especially those who did so in the face of the international socialist movement being torn apart by it. I honored those who fought for the Irish Republic and October Revolution instead.

Throughout the world in 2017, there were many events, documentaries, conferences, books, and special issues of journals commemorating the October Revolution of 1917. I was happy to take part in commemorations in Ireland and Greece, because I believed that revolution to be one of the most monumental events in the history of the world, and because coming to that conclusion about it did so much to shape my own life. I spoke at seminars organized by the Irish Labour History Society, Maynooth University, and University of the Peloponnese. At these seminars, academics zeroed in on specific areas where they had done fresh research on the subject. In my case, I focused on the International Lenin School, beginning with its formation in the Comintern period, through my own time there, to the school's demise coinciding with the demise of the USSR. I also contributed to a special issue of *Monthly Review*, writing about the conferences in Eastern Europe, where party intellectuals debated the legacy of the October Revolution, even as the world was turning upside down and overturning its achievements.

Inspired by the October Revolution, there were soviets, or councils, springing up throughout Europe, taking power transformatively, if only temporarily, in Germany, Poland, Hungary and even in Ireland. There were commemorations marking these with the most elaborate program of events commemorating the Limerick Soviet, which ran Limerick during April 1919, organizing food, transport, communication, and even its own currency, during the War of Independence. The current government took little notice of these events, but chose to organize in 2020 an official state commemoration of the police forces who enforced the rule of empire during the War of Independence. Dublin City Council condemned it, as did many other individuals and organizations, while others proclaimed themselves angels of reconciliation and pronounced others immature because they were afraid of the ghosts of dead policemen. The government abandoned it. Commemorations of the treaty and Civil War of 1922–1923 were expected to be the most fraught, but turned out somewhat low-key. Attempts by the state and public broadcasters were meant to seem evenhanded here, but overall, the balance was toward the pro-treaty position of the men of property.

There were various voices, accusing those who declined to honor oppressors of wanting to erase history. The accusation constantly arose in debates about removing statues and renaming places. In Britain, when the statue of slave trader Edward Coulson was thrown into Bristol's River Avon by Black Lives Matter protesters in 2020, the accusation was the same as it had been in South Africa for Rhodes Must Fall in 2015, and for many similar protests. It was, in fact, the opposite. People actually learned much more about history from toppling statues than they ever did from standing ones. My own position on toppling statues had to do with which statues were toppled. It was a matter of which side you were on.

There were also events marking fifty years since 1968. The City of Limerick and University of Limerick organized a program of events over several months, and I spoke at the first and last of these events, speaking about my own experience of the new left and reflecting on those times, as well as addressing various issues arising from the historiography of 1968 at these events and in various publications. I also participated in US-based online events dealing with the fifty years since May Day 1971.

I kept an eye on trends within popular culture, especially for what they revealed about the zeitgeist. I was interested in the way *Capital*, a 2012 film by Costa-Gavras, focused on changes in international finance capital. It interrogated the process, but indicated that the system was so total, so inevitable, that there was no way out of it. I asked Costa-Gavras, who was present at a screening in Dublin, if this was what he intended. He replied Yes and No. Another opportunity I had to interact with a producer was with Camilla Hammerich, producer of the Danish TV series *Borgen*, at a seminar at DCU. She sketched the history of television drama in Denmark and the double vision underlying *Borgen*, which was not only an overt narrative, but also a layer of ethical and educational discussion dealing with politics, media, and the interface between public and private life. I queried the center of gravity of the narrative in centrist politics, not only as a perspective, but as valorization. She said it came from political pressure to balance between left and right. I said that I didn't think it did justice to the left. She said that was because they were defending themselves from being seen as too left.

As always, the United States produced much escapist emptiness, but also some solid reflections on the tensions within the social order. I paid acute attention to *The Wire*, which I thought was a Marxist's dream of a television series. Starting with the pursuit of a major drug operation by city cops, the drama moved outward, inward, upward, and downward to the docks, city hall, the media, and the schools. There were murders, affairs, bribes, trials, exams, elections, promotions, statistics, bylines, prizes, careers rising and falling, and much more. It bristled, even boiled over, with systemic critique. I also found *The Americans* fascinating. A world away from *I Led 3 Lives* in the 1950s, it actually positioned the audience to root for the KGB. The last series was especially riveting, as it explored the tensions between perestroika supporters and hardliners in the KGB. *Masters of Sex* was another series that would have been unthinkable in the times in which the drama was set. I also took to the HBO miniseries *Olive Kitteridge*, which was well-observed everyday life in a small Maine town, probing character and context with insight. I thought this was also true of *Mare of Easttown*, which was set in Delaware County, Pennsylvania, where I grew up and where much of my family still lives. The series effectively and movingly showed the differences between life then and now, both for better and for worse. Its texture was authentic and its characters, compelling and credible, were all too caught up in their day-to-day burdens to reflect much on what had happened to themselves or their society—but the drama made the viewer (or me, anyway) reflect on it. Ireland wasn't making as much good television drama as it had in the past, but *Prosperity* showed Ireland in the Celtic Tiger years from the perspectives of those shut out of the economic boom. When *Normal People* was airing, there was a running debate on radio and social media, which was a last-ditch battle of holy Ireland holding back the tide of modernity in a rage over the promotion of fornication. In the past, these righteous people could have driven such dramas off the airwaves, as they did with *The Spike* in 1978. I liked both the series and book by Sally Rooney but didn't love or hate it as much as those on either side of the debate did.

I continued to participate in international gatherings of left intellectuals, large and small. The big annual ones, such as Historical Materialism in London and Left Forum in New York City, were massive with dizzying choices to be made among multiple parallel sessions and packed plenaries. There were more questions than answers and an openness to a variety of positions. The atmosphere of orthodoxy and denunciation that once characterized the relations of different left factions was absent. There were people from all over the world and from different stages of the life cycle. It did me good to see newer generations of the left that would be there when my generation, already disappearing, would be finally gone. I was happy to see new publications, like *Jacobin*, come along to convey the left case with a new energy, while older ones like *Monthly Review* still carried on. While there were nuances of style and position between them, I was happy to write for both.

In some left conferences and publications, however, I encountered young intellectuals who were smart and serious, but spoke within a cloud of ideas and texts floating above the flux, where I thought that activist intellectuals should situate ourselves. Internalist history of ideas has a long academic tradition, but it seemed incongruous in a milieu devoted to historical materialism. I preferred to philosophize in a way that was more earthy, more grounded in the flow of history, more true to the wellsprings from which ideas arose and contended with each other. At the more progressive mainstream academic conferences, I found much sincere searching, but with a tendency to excess conceptualization, most of it tentative, decentered, parenthetical, plural, and fragmented, leaving me with a sense of their irresolution and ungroundedness. There was much about whiteness, maleness, westernness, but not much about class or capitalism. Even at a working-class studies conference, sessions were mostly focused on class as culture and identity, rather than on work, without much reference to capitalism, class struggle, left movements, or socialism.

While I made the most of my travels, I still spent most of my time in Ireland and focused on the tasks of building the Irish left. The United Left Alliance (ULA), running from 2010 to 2013, was a coalition of several small left parties and independents that won five seats in the 2011 general election, while being active on the streets and in numerous campaigns. It was driven by Trotskyists reaching out to those who were not part of their traditions, emphasizing areas of agreement, while still being able to debate differences. Politicians, such as Richard Boyd Barrett and Paul Murphy, were particularly effective in striking the right note on this. I attended their events, spoke on their platforms, voted for their candidates, and worked with them in many ways. I was sorry that the CPI and WP did not join the ULA, but they did sometimes cooperate with it. When the ULA dissolved, I became preoccupied with the project of building a broad left party, giving rise to Left Forum, a project to bring together unaffiliated activists with left parties to discuss how we might up our game. My own ambition for the forum was to lay the basis for a Syriza-type party. We had several large and successful state-of-the-left events over two years, some of them in global-café format. On the whole, the atmosphere was constructive, but at times there was a lot of empty posturing and nonconstructive opposition. At one event, I was afraid we would need bouncers, because of controversy over the presence of a Sinn Fein speaker and the absence of dissident republican groups on the platform. We also ran a seminar series on topical issues and a lecture series on Marxist theory. In the end, the project failed to meet its objective. Among other reasons, some key activists found it too difficult to form something new and decided to channel their energies into reviving something already there. They joined the Workers Party, which was not thriving, and revived it, to some extent, and for a short time.

Even if we could not form a broad left party, the Irish left still cooperated well in parliament and on the streets, while also sustaining a continuous exchange of ideas and strategies in conferences, periodicals, and social media. There were well-attended gatherings across a broad spectrum of the left, even the SWP's annual Marxism conference, and periodicals articulating many points of view, such as *Irish Left Review* and *Look Left*. Our ties to each other on Facebook and Twitter maintained a daily rhythm of interaction. The biggest campaign uniting us on the streets and bringing new people into activism was water charges. This took the form of mass marches (up to one hundred thousand on some occasions), refusal to pay water charges (66 percent noncompliance), blocking installation of water meters, and burning of water bills. The campaign was supported by left political parties, trade unions, community groups, and many unaffiliated households. Chants in the streets ranged from "From the rivers to the sea, Irish water will be free" to "You can stick your water meters up your ass." The ostensible sentiment was about water, but it was much more than water. After so many new taxes and charges, combined with cuts to public services, this was the last straw. There was also the problem of monetization as a prelude to privatization, which fired this battle. More broadly, it was one more front in the battle against the whole mode of governance and distribution of global wealth. In its immediate objectives, the campaign was successful. The government withdrew water charges. It was great to have such a concrete victory, even if it left so many of the larger battles still to be fought. This battle also threw up many of the problems of the Occupy movement, including hostility to the left and trade unions among some protesters, who wanted to prove that they were the most revolutionary. They used tactics like blocking bridges after big marches and making it impossible for working people—and even other protesters—to use public transport to get home. At the age of seventy, after marching and standing for hours already, I wasn't up to walking back to Ballymun.

By 2016, the whole global scene was in flux, provoking massive disaffection of people from the forces that ruled the world, but much of that disaffection was confused and inchoate, and played as much to the right as to the left. Brexit was one of many indicators of the global system unraveling. At times, I had a terrible sense of initiative passing from left to right, especially after the capitulation of Syriza, the rise of Front Nationale in France and Lega in Italy, the election of Donald Trump in the USA and Boris Johnson in Britain. Remembering Gramsci writing in the 1930s, "Now is time of monsters," I thought how much truer it was now. It was a real challenge to process the causes and consequences of the Trump presidency. It was a total freak show and a dangerous game. Although much could be explained by the pathology of the Trump psyche, it was a mistake to become too narrowly fixated on that and to avoid analyzing the wider forces in motion in terms of social psychology, popular culture, and political economy. The alt-right were moving from online irony to taking to the streets with paramilitary garb and assault rifles. It was good to see the countervailing energy gathered around Jeremy Corbyn and Bernie Sanders. Even if defeated in elections, their movements brought new people into motion and raised consciousness. Pegida (Patriotic Europeans Against the Islamisation of the Occident), an international far-right, anti-immigration movement, attempted to launch an Irish branch at a rally at Dublin's General Post Office in 2016. A counter-demonstration, outnumbering them, chased them from the streets. The foreign organizers were deported on the same day, but some counter-demonstrators, including my son, a secondary school history teacher, were charged with violent disorder.

As throughout my life on the left, I got caught up in legal trials supporting those who bore the brunt of attempts to criminalize political protest. In 2011, I attended High Court hearings when the US government sought to extradite Sean Garland of the Workers Party in a case based on an exotic plot of a global conspiracy involving North Korea and counterfeit "super dollars." I was happy to see the extradition denied and Sean given several more years of political life in freedom, during which the Workers Party experienced a small surge. In 2017, I attended many sessions of a long trial in which community activists and elected politicians, including Paul Murphy TD, were charged with false imprisonment, after a crowd of protesters surrounded a car carrying Joan Burton, tanaiste and leader of the Labour Party. Although Joan and I were once comrades and even friends, I found her increasingly difficult to respect as she rose in her political career. When she took the stand in this trial, she seemed to have no idea why she was so unpopular in working-class communities. She portrayed herself in such a way that it would seem a wonder that the community didn't raise her aloft and sing hosannas. The courtroom spectators gasped when she proclaimed herself the successor to James Connolly. On the stand, she was caught in several lies, which were revealed by video evidence rebutting her testimony. At one point, the defense lawyer asked the judge to instruct her to stop making self-serving speeches that didn't answer the questions. At another point, the lawyer asked, "Do you even remember what the question was?" Because so much of the testimony at this trial, including garda testimony, was contradicted by video evidence, the jury found the defendants not guilty, a huge relief for them and all of us supporting them.

During 2017, after the publication of my book *The Syriza Wave*, I flew to the United States, where I did a round of media interviews, book talks, and all kinds of conversations in New York, Philadelphia, Baltimore, and Washington. At one stage, I was in four cities in three days. My granddaughter Ciara was born while I was in transit. I met with *Monthly Review* comrades as well as Joanne Landy, a cofounder of Campaign for Peace and Democracy, who, in the last months of her life, helped organize my trip. I met with my relations and others who asked what people abroad thought of Trump and whether they realized there were Americans who were angry and embarrassed for the country, as well as worried about such practical matters as losing their medical coverage. My niece Molly Sheehan was running for US Congress as part of a movement pushing scientists to run for political office in response to a perceived assault on science by the Trump administration. I was there during Memorial Day and found it hard to take all the rhetoric about the military as "heroes who died for our freedom." At the (US) Left Forum, I heard much decent analysis, along with some ultra-leftist nonsense. Most outstandingly, I had many meaningful conversations with many people from various countries, but mostly Americans, the sort never seen on television, who had a lot to say that was worth hearing, as they coped with the monstrous scenario in which they found themselves. When Trump came to Ireland in 2019, we organized large numbers of people to protest, with a gigantic blimp of Trump as an angry baby with a cell phone.

In 2018 and 2019, there were massive global actions calling attention to the emergency that is climate change. It was sad to see, on the faces of so many young people, a sense of a doomed future. At the same time, it was inspiring to see them rising up and taking responsibility for the world. People of all ages began to wake up to the stark science of ecological crisis. When it came to elections, concern over green issues led to rising votes for Green parties, which was not necessarily a good thing. In Ireland, the Green Party lacked any kind of systemic analysis. In DCU, we had candidates from all parties for an election debate in 2020. At first, it wasn't much of a debate, but people asking small questions about funding for this-and-that, and all candidates answering that they would fund this-and-that. I tried to get some edge into it by challenging the Green Party slogan, "If you want green, vote green," countering that others argued, "If you want green, vote red," because you can't understand green issues without a systemic analysis of capitalism. DCU academic Roderic O'Gorman, the GP candidate who became a government minister after the election, answered without saying anything about capitalism. Andrew Montague of Labour said he was a centrist and as comfortable with the right as the left. I voted for Conor Reddy, of People Before Profit, a young Marxist scientist. In constituency after constituency, Sinn Fein topped the poll, exceeding the quota with large surpluses going left. Mainstream commentators were flailing about, trying to avoid talking about right and left. Fine Gael and Fianna Fail did not have enough votes between them to form a government, but they managed to do so with the Green Party. We felt hopeful for a left government in the future.

In Britain, there was the opposite of hope. There was an outpouring of collective grief on social media, as it became apparent that there would be a massive Tory majority and a defeat for Labour, under its most left leader ever. Of course, the 2019 election was about much more than two men, but in this case, the contrast between Boris Johnson, a vain, lazy, careless, deceitful paragon of privilege, and Jeremy Corbyn, a thoroughly decent man with the best interests of the people at heart, was stark. I tended to focus on ideas, ideologies, policies, parties, sociohistorical forces, more than personalities. However, personalities are part of the whole melange. Movements do need faces to the front to embody their ideas and values, and, yes, to lead. I had seen many left leaders in my life. I had seen many who were more eloquent and exciting than Jeremy Corbyn, but I had never seen anyone manifest such humility in the face of fame, such grace under pressure, such dignity and decency when subjected to indecency, such unwavering commitment under duress. I had never seen anyone so undeservedly being subjected to such relentless vilification, and still stay on track.

From 2018 through 2020, the eyes of the world were on the excruciatingly protracted process of the US presidential election. The array of contenders for the Democratic Party nomination produced two who were children of Marxists, neither showing any sign of it wearing off on them. Of Pete Buttigieg, there was a meme circulating: "My father used to read me Marxist texts at bedtime. My favorite character was the ruling class." Kamala Harris wasn't any more Marxist. The Sanders campaign advocating Medicare-for-all was losing ground, just as it was becoming overwhelmingly clear that Medicare was badly needed. Instead, Biden prevailed. Although he had always stood against the interests of working people and for those of oligarchy, Biden managed to convince many working people otherwise. Still, after four years of the chaos, lies, racism, violence, ignorance, narcissism, expropriation, and intensified inequality of the Trump administration, millions of Americans again voted for Trump, including members of my own family. This I saw as a symptom of a society in decline.

As glad as I was to see Trump defeated, I could not be happy at Biden's victory or welcome a return to neoliberal imperial normality, although I was glad that the new administration restored cooperation with the World Health Organization and Paris Climate Agreement. It was a contest between extreme right and center right, where a left position was not on offer. Of course, politics was more than its electoral dimension, but it highlighted the deep fissures in US society and the monumental work that the left needed to do to address such massive false consciousness, much

UNTIL WE FALL

of it heavily armed, manifesting itself in this crazed drama. Trump was not the problem and Biden was not the solution. The transition from one to the other was as fraught as it could be, with a right-wing mob storming the Capitol building and disrupting the certification of the election. The riot was shocking to behold. As someone who was once arrested at the Capitol for peaceful protest, I noted the glaring contrast between the policing of right and left protests. This was, in many ways, a clown coup, with images circulating of the "Q-Anon Shaman," sitting on the presiding seat in the Senate chamber, t-shirts on sale proclaiming civil war, three-cornered revolutionary war hats, kevlar vests, crusader crosses, Confederate flags, Trump-as-Rambo t-shirts, MAGA hats. Many Americans, outraged at this, still spoke of their nation as a beacon to the world. Did they have any idea how the rest of the world saw them? Did they remember when Yeltsin ordered the storming of the Russian parliament? The same people who deplored Trump inciting the storming of the US Congress today were cheering for Yeltsin. However, although neoliberalism might be ascendant again, I didn't think it could return to its status as normality, because there was such massive alienation and opposition to it from right, left, and confused on a global scale.

Meanwhile, normality had taken another massive hit. Whatever plans any of us had at the beginning of 2020, the year turned them upside down. At first, it was a story unfolding far away in China, one of many stories in the news, a novel coronavirus, which was met with strong state-mandated public health measures. Meanwhile, I went about my everyday life, going to the university every day, planning trips to Italy and Greece in the spring, having no idea how quickly that life and those plans would unravel— along with the lives and plans of millions of others. As the curve of new cases went down in China, they soared elsewhere, beginning with Italy, then the rest of the world, along with shocking details of a wide range of symptoms and high level of mortality. There were horrendous reports from hospitals, which were now unable to treat other conditions, including trauma and stroke, and no one over sixty-five was even being assessed. At the same time, we saw videos of people singing from their balconies, including the stirring anthems of the Italian left. Before long, COVID-19 was everywhere, where public measures were also mandated, but without the social discipline possible in China. There were quarantines, cancellations of events, closures of educational institutions, businesses, and public facilities, travel bans, and restrictions beyond anything in living memory.

The pandemic took all of us by surprise to one degree or another, but we should not have been so surprised. The science was there. Epidemiologists had been warning that such a pandemic was inevitable. Moreover, writers such as Mike Davis and Rob Wallace, who put epidemiology in a wider social-political-economic context, had been explaining to a wider public the factors creating the conditions for such a pandemic in contemporary agriculture, science, pharmacology, medicine, politics, and economics. Despite reading such authors, I was still unprepared for the pandemic's suddenness and scale. I became preoccupied with making up for that. In quarantine, as the news became all-virus-all-the-time, it was hard to concentrate on anything else. When I settled down to work, it was sometimes as if I was studying for exams in epidemiology, virology, and immunology. When I reflected, it was about my own mortality, the fragility of our species and ecosystem, the devastation that capitalism has wrought on our bodies, our societies, and our planet. I veered between the specific details of reorganizing my everyday life and pondering the world-historical meaning of unfolding events. In coming to terms with this, I had the considerable advantage of a worldview, worked out with great care over many years, while always being open to new facts, events, and ideas. I wrote articles and delivered Zoom lectures on what Marxism brought to bear on our understanding of how the pandemic came to be, what forces were in motion in dealing with it, what problems arose from that, and why conditions were still ripe for further and fiercer pandemics.

Capitalism was the dominant reality giving rise to the pandemic and driving responses to it, yet certain elements of capitalism were necessarily in suspension. We lived for a time, however partially and temporarily, in a scenario where public health and welfare overrode the imperatives of the market and enacted the priorities of socialism. In Ireland, health care was public and free, there was new funding for biomedical research and clinical resources, a ban on evictions, a rent freeze, a reduction in carbon emissions, and government supports to mitigate the effects of closures and unemployment.

Ireland was neither the best nor the worst place to be. Social mobilization did not match what was possible in China, Cuba, Vietnam, or Kerala, but there was not the laissez-faire scramble we saw on our screens playing out elsewhere, especially in the US and UK. Constant conflicts between public welfare and proprietary interests played out on many levels: the scramble for personal protective equipment, for medicines, for access to and profit from vaccines. The rich made their way to safer places with their own medical teams and intensive care units "just in case," while others faced into the frontlines every day. There was a moment of blinding clarity about who were essential workers and who made the world go round, although this did not translate into redistribution of the wealth they created. There was much applause, but few pay raises.

Compliance with public health measures was relatively good during the first wave of the pandemic, but declined in subsequent waves. Even in my limited movements in my own area, I saw many examples of vandalization of public property, streams of visitors when household visits were banned, and numerous violations of public health regulations. I got into unpleasant altercations over brazen violations. One woman said to me proudly, "We're rule-breakers." I asked her what criteria she used for deciding what rule and why: Did she engage in protests against social injustice or did she just want to do what she wanted to do? There were irate people phoning into talk shows and making such declarations as, "If my child on any given day does not want to wear a mask in school, he will not wear a mask." In many countries, including Ireland, right-wing populist crowds gathered to oppose public health measures, refusing to wear masks or socially distance, as a defense of individual liberty. They often claimed that the virus only killed older people who were going to die anyway, ignoring the considerable numbers of other deaths, particularly among health workers, who were young and fit enough to be working in intensive care. They argued that this was a "plandemic," a conspiracy to herd us all into servility, to chip us into constant surveillance and submission. In Ireland, they gathered in rowdy and rude protests, although without the full paramilitary gear with grenades and assault rifles seen in the United States.

We had to adapt our political modus operandi, and much of our activity took place online. I participated in many Zoom seminars and events, which gave a sense of continuity to our collective life. On May Day 2020, the first in decades when the left was not on the streets in Dublin, I hung a red flag out the window. A neighbor came to the door, asking if we needed any help, thinking it was a distress signal. Other neighbors were in a panic and found risk assessment difficult. One night, my sleep was disrupted by frantic shouting outside. The electricity had gone off, and someone from the apartment block next door screamed nonstop for twenty minutes, as if it were the apocalypse. By the time Sam turned ninety in September, guidelines allowed for organized outdoor events of up to fifteen people, so the Dublin Council of Trade Unions organized a very scaled-down form of the celebration that was originally planned. Members of the executive committee assembled in our garden, displayed the DCTU banner, gave speeches, sang songs, read tributes from the president of Ireland, Michael D. Higgins, general secretaries of various unions, retired union leaders, and old comrades. The general secretary of Sam's union presented him with a scroll honoring his contribution to the trade union movement. Louise O'Reilly TD noted his birthday on the floor of Dail Eireann.

I had never spent so much time in my back garden or local

park. I met my friends for walk-and-talk rendezvous in the area. I rarely moved beyond one kilometer from home, yet I felt as if I was inhabiting the world when I realized how in touch I was with what was happening, not only in the way of global news, but also in terms of what so many people were thinking and feeling, through both mainstream and social media. It made me think about how different quarantine must have been during epidemics of the past, how isolated from knowledge and contact vast populations were. For an entire year, I never even set foot in Dublin city center. When I went for an eye test, I found lots of closed shops, cinemas, and hotels, and fewer cars and people than usual. So much of my life in the city center had been about demonstrating against this or that—against US wars, against Irish government cuts to public services, whatever—sometimes miserable in the cold winds and lashing rain, but happy and warm in the comradely bonds we forged in common cause. The year 2020 was the first year since 1965 that I did not protest in the streets. After my eye test, I took a long walk along the River Liffey, thinking of how much had been done to improve the space along the river. Much of the work had been to accommodate the financial services industry, which colonized the docklands, but it was good that we, whom they preyed upon, got to enjoy these public spaces, too. I never ceased to marvel at the juxtaposition of the Famine Memorial with the International Financial Services Centre, monuments to exploiter and exploited. Sitting on the boardwalk, listening to two homeless guys talking about hostels, prisons, robbing shops, police harassment, I observed drug-dealing that was not only open but loud, sloppy (high on the stuff themselves), and exhibitionist.

Considering the stress and suffering the pandemic inflicted upon so many, I did not feel I had such a hard time of it. Unlike most people I knew, I did not contract COVID. My daily routine changed drastically when the university closed down, and even more drastically when the government decreed that those over seventy were not to leave home for any reason. Although I thought I could take this in stride, with reading and writing to occupy me, I often woke in the night, my heart racing, pain in my chest, gasping for breath, and feeling out of control. One night, I passed out and fell. The public health service came to my rescue and, after many years of symptoms, which had intensified during this period, I finally got a diagnosis of cardiac arrhythmia and had two cardiac ablations. Although always rigorous about diet and exercise, I stepped it up and felt quite healthy, even fit, otherwise. I did four workouts a day and engaged in intermittent fasting. I took up gardening and grew much of what I ate. The same week as my first ablation, I also had my first vaccination. Ours was a centralized public system, where we were prioritized by age. I was sent to a DCU hall, where I had seen so many of my students graduate. I felt proud of our public health and education system, without forgetting past and future battles over the neoliberalization of our universities and two-tier health care. Meanwhile, Sam, now in his nineties, became increasingly frail and sometimes difficult to manage. His daughter and her family came to the rescue and took over his care.

Millions of people died from COVID-19, including several I knew. The death to hit me hardest was that of Leo Panitch. We had met in Yugoslavia and again in many parts of the world, over several decades. He was always striving to analyze the current conjuncture, bringing Marxist analysis to bear on whatever new issues arose, including the pandemic. It was hard to believe the virus struck him down. I also knew quite a few people who died of other causes during periods of quarantine, so could not attend their funerals. I attended some services via livestreaming. At another, most of us marched from the house to the crematorium, but remained outside while the ceremony took place inside. Globally, there were sad stories of those who died alone and those who lived on, thinking about them dying alone.

There was a flurry of media discussion and academic writing about the pandemic as it was happening. Much of the conversation was sound, but some of it was utter nonsense. Self-styled sages predicted that all would change utterly. Others discoursed about pathogenic bodies in new epistemological and existential modalities in the epidemiological imaginary. Too much of the discussion failed to ground itself by focusing on the pulsing, ever-changing, but still resilient system structuring it all. Listening to the voices the mainstream media chose to articulate the meaning of this time, there emerged a hegemonic story for the privileged talking heads that went something like this: What "we" learned when "everything stopped" was "to live in the moment," "to go back to nature," and "to realize that family was what mattered."

However, I thought, everything did not stop for health workers, manufacturing workers, supermarket workers, lorry drivers, waste collectors, and so many others who supplied the privileged with everything they needed or wanted in their comfortable lockdowns. Their "living in the moment" was the source of a myopia that led to many problems stemming from a failure to search out causes and consequences. As to "nature," it was not only the morning birdsong, blooming flowers, calm seas, and clean air. Nature was also storms, fires, and floods. Nature was the virus. Nature was us. Family was not all that mattered. Yes, it was lovely to see our children and grandchildren during winter holidays, and sad for those who couldn't do so, but we were tied to each other in so many other ways. What I already knew, but more fully realized during this time, was that you cannot understand anything, including the pandemic, without an analysis of the global system giving rise to it and structuring the possibilities for dealing with it. The media covered the same ground over and over and substituted lazy and class-ridden clichés for systemic analysis. Never did media pundits probe the capitalist nature of global agribusiness, the state channeling public funding for medical research and vaccine development through Big Pharma, the trajectory of the pandemic in Cuba, Vietnam, and Kerala, the vaccine inequity constantly being called out by the World Health Organization.

My questions about this period, which I tried to address in Zoom talks, articles, and social media posts, were: What has the pandemic revealed about ourselves? About our society? About capitalism? About socialism? How has our experience of it been shaped by class? By nation? By race? By gender? What shifts took place in the role of the state vis-à-vis the market, under pressure of the pandemic? What role did science play in this crisis? Why did some anti-science currents wither while others thrived? How did the pandemic highlight the best and worst of our species? What were the sources of social cohesion and compliance and the countervailing forces of discord and dislocation? How did television, radio, and internet mediate the experience of the crisis? What images and sounds of this global trauma will linger longest? How did the left deal with the pandemic? What is being revealed by the pattern of exit from lockdown? What has changed as a result of this crisis? What should change?

When restrictions were lifted, before the pandemic was over, the media was full of the new freedom to shop, to worship, and to go to hairdressers. All through the pandemic, with different levels of restrictions, there was constant pushback making mental health arguments about the necessity of such activities as having beauty treatments and going to nightclubs. At all stages of the pandemic, other events and issues broke through and demanded attention, not always as much as they deserved. Black Lives Matter resurfaced and some statues of slave owners fell. Afghanistan fell to the Taliban as desperate people clung to US military planes taking off without them. There were reports on climate breakdown, conferences called to address it, marches calling for climate justice, but only limited measures taken, falling far below what was necessary to prevent global disaster. Media interest surged during the UN Climate Change Conference (COP), but then dropped when COP26 ended, as if the problem had somehow been solved. Same with COP27. Crisis tumbled upon crisis.

When war broke out in Ukraine, I opposed the Russian invasion, but did not support the Ukrainian government, as it gathered massive international support in the US, UK, and EU based on a false narrative of Ukraine as an innocent, democratic nation, which did nothing to provoke such hostility. Mainstream media gave no voice to those alienated from post-2014 Ukraine, those whose parties were banned and traditions disrespected, those who lived under siege in Donbas, as Minsk accords were repeatedly violated. The left was severely divided between those who saw the conflict as a war of national liberation demanding support, even to the point of going to fight or sending weapons, and those of us who saw it in larger geopolitical terms, as a proxy war fermented by the US, especially in the aftermath of the Euromaidan coup of 2014. It was hard not to see this war as part of the continuingly tragic fallout from the dissolution of the USSR and other socialist states in Eastern Europe. In Ireland, the state and mainstream media went all out to support the US-EU-NATO narrative on Ukraine. Those of us who used the limited influence of our social media accounts to query this narrative or pose a counter-narrative faced menacing hostility. One anonymous tweeter demanded that I be stripped of my public service pension, based on the pattern of my tweets and retweets about Ukraine.

US hegemony had been slipping since the war in Vietnam, and many subsequent wars, including this one, were fought to restore it. The New World Order was far from orderly. It was increasingly disorderly. A system exhibiting multiple symptoms of decadence was, nevertheless, still dominant. The forces of the left, although displaying brilliant analyses of various disorders and of the system itself, spoke in voices not heard by those who needed to hear them, while sometimes being in organizational disarray. I long to see the left coming from the margins to be heard by the 99 percent, in whose interests we speak.

As I conclude, I think of the people I knew, many of them appearing in these pages, who have given so much to this effort, who have died during the years covered here. It is one of the most difficult aspects of old age to deal with the reality that so many of those who have shared our lives have gone forever, although they have left their trace in our memories and their work. I am thinking now of Adam Scaff, Marx Wartofsky, Ulrich Roseberg, Richard Levins, Richard Lewontin, Stephen Cohen, Tom Hayden, Rennie Davis,

Dave Dellinger, Todd Gitlin, Paul Sweezy, Harry Magdoff, Ed Herman, John Raines, Brian and Sonia Bunting, Manolis Glezos, Thanasis Anapolitanos, Leo Panitch, Mike Davis, Ellen Wood, Sean Garland, Joe Deasy, Tom Redmond, Jimmy and Edwina Stewart, Kevin McMahon, Terrence McDonough, John Molyneux, and so many more. I also miss the voices of those who sang out the truth of the world, such as Pete Seeger, Mikis Theodorakis, and Alistair Hulett, while still feeling their energy as I dance to their music under the moon and stars. Even before the pandemic, I could not attend the funerals of many who were important to me, because we lived in distant parts of the world. In Ireland, I could, and noted the changes in the rituals over the decades. There were fewer of those utterly alienating ones, where atheist communists were seen on their way in off-the-shelf masses. Most were honest rituals that told the truth of their lives and ended in rousing renditions of the "Internationale" or "Red Flag." On those occasions, it was good to see red flags flying in the streets of Dublin or, even better, amid all those Union Jacks in Belfast. Otherwise, social media and sometimes Zoom events became the platforms for our commemorations. When Tom Hayden died in 2016, one person wrote, "Our collective story is nearing its end," and many of us felt a strong sense of our whole generation passing from the world.

With a strong sense of my time running out, I long to see the left rise again on a significant scale and turn the tide. I no longer dream of melodramatic insurrections, but I do hope for a chain of events setting the world on a path leading from capitalism to socialism. Each of us must bring what clarity and energy we have to that task, until we fall. Others will take it up until they, too, fall.

The world we face is dark and provokes despair. Only the presence of the left lights it up and offers hope.

Acknowledgments

It is hard to know where to begin and end to acknowledge others in an autobiography, because it is not only about the book but the life set out in it. Generally, I am relying on the text itself to acknowledge the role played by others.

Yet, when proofreading the index, it struck me that names appear of people who were peripheral to my life but nevertheless named in relation to specific events, whereas others, so much a part of my ongoing life are not named. There are so many places where I use plural nouns and pronouns, especially "we," without naming others, especially in the case of colleagues or comrades. For example, one person who was both was Marnie Holborow, my co-conspirator in organizing anti-war and anti-neoliberal critiques of the university, whom I knew from the streets as well as the corridors of DCU. Although DCU was never the leftist hotbed we did our best to make it, it has gone even more quiet on such fronts since she and I "retired." Nevertheless, I still go in every day and keep myself informed of what is happening in universities in general and DCU in particular. I thank Debbie Ging, Eugenia Siapera, Declan Fahy, and Mark O'Brien for the steady stream of conversation and being among my best informants.

I thank DCU for giving me space to be, to teach, to swim, to interact on so many levels in so many ways, often in sharp critique (which continues in this book), always giving me a hearing, even if I did not always get my way.

There are so many others who contributed to my life during these years still submerged in plural nouns and pronouns that I cannot name them all, but I hope they will see their contributions acknowledged within these pluralities in the text.

There are always those, other than the named author, who work away unnamed in the production of a book and other publications. I acknowledge not only the specific work but the collegial and comradely spirt of those who make *Monthly Review* and Monthly Review Press happen: Martin Paddio, Michael Yates, John Bellamy Foster, John Mage, Susie Day, Rebecca Manski, Sarah Kramer, Camilla Valle, Erin Clermont.

At the same time, writing a book can be a very lonely business at times. There is a big gap between the acts of writing and reading. It is natural to wonder who will read it and what they will think. I am grateful to all who have written to me about my past publications. Often, they tell me, not only of their responses to my ideas and experiences, but also their own. I hope that will be the case with this book too. My e-mail is helena.sheehan@dcu.ie.

Finally, I thank the international left for the community of enquiry and endeavor that is unrivaled in intelligence and purposefulness, giving each of us strength we could never have alone.

Index